RETHINKING LEGITIMACY

This book presents a new perspective on the debate around legitimacy, politics and constitutional law in Supreme Courts.

Moving away from the troubling perception that Supreme Courts are trampling on the wrong side of the law/politics divide, it accepts and defends the critical claim that constitutional law is intrinsically and inescapably politics: in style, substance and outcome.

It explains what is involved in that claim and recommends a more nuanced and compelling account than it is caricatured to be. The book proceeds to demonstrate how the legal and judicial process can proceed if the law-is-politics critique is taken seriously. Insisting that it cannot be business as usual, the author offers a series of constructive proposals about how constitutional law and judicial decision-making can continue in anything like their present format and style.

Recognising that a more radical approach could be taken to the way in which democracy might be re-organised, the book runs with the idea that it is possible to incorporate and accommodate the law-is-politics argument within a governmental system of constitutional democracy that resembles closely what now occurs. In that sense, the book is both critical and constructive as well as principled and pragmatic.

Rethinking Legitimacy

Courts, Constitutions and Politics

Allan C Hutchinson

·HART·

OXFORD · LONDON · NEW YORK · NEW DELHI · SYDNEY

HART PUBLISHING

Bloomsbury Publishing Plc

Kemp House, Chawley Park, Cumnor Hill, Oxford, OX2 9PH, UK

1385 Broadway, New York, NY 10018, USA

Bloomsbury Publishing Ireland Limited, 29 Earlsfort Terrace, Dublin 2, D02 AY28, Ireland

HART PUBLISHING, the Hart/Stag logo, BLOOMSBURY and the Diana logo are
trademarks of Bloomsbury Publishing Plc

First published in Great Britain 2025

A catalogue record for this book is available from the British Library.

A catalogue record for this book is available from the Library of Congress.

Library of Congress Control Number: 2025932640

ISBN: HB: 978-1-50998-532-6
       ePDF: 978-1-50998-534-0
       ePub: 978-1-50998-533-3

Typeset by Compuscript Ltd, Shannon

For product safety related questions contact productsafety@bloomsbury.com

To find out more about our authors and books visit www.hartpublishing.co.uk.
Here you will find extracts, author information, details of forthcoming events
and the option to sign up for our newsletters.

A2J[9]

PREFACE

This book is a continuation of themes that I have pursued throughout my academic (and jurisprudential) career – the critical claim that 'law is politics'. I have sought to pursue that idea across the board. In particular, I have been at pains to demonstrate how law, lawyering and legal theory are best understand by grasping the full import of the law-is-politics approach. This can be a powerful and destabilising set of ideas and interventions.

However, this book takes a slightly different line in pursuing that critical project. Until now, I have generally stopped short of asking and answering how the legal and judicial process can proceed if the law-is-politics critique is taken seriously. Apart from insisting that it cannot be business-as-usual, I have not made any constructive proposals about how constitutional law and judicial decision-making can continue in anything other than their present format and style. Although I have presented in earlier work some radical suggestions about how democracy might reorganise itself to respond to this critique, I have not considered or pursued the idea that it might be possible to incorporate and accommodate the law-is-politics argument within a governmental system of constitutional democracy that bears resemblance to something like what occurs in the United States and Canada. At some risk to my intellectual and political integrity, I am now following through on that possibility and seeking to see how it might work out.

As always, I am grateful to many people in bringing the ideas in this book to fruition. In particular, my conversations with Ross Rudolph have been pivotal; he both suggested that I try this approach and made many recommendations about how I might (and might not) go about re-thinking legitimacy. He has been a wonderful, erudite and supportive friend who, while not agreeing with all of my ideas, has impressed on me the worth of the project. Also, I am grateful to a host of colleagues and commentators, both positive and negative, who, over the years, have had a much larger impact on my thinking that I might have admitted and they might have expected. Thank you to them all. Also, the sterling work of Amelia Cox is much appreciated in finalising the manuscript. Finally, I have borrowed small parts of the book from some of my earlier published essays in the Harvard Law Review Forum, Santa Clara Law Review, Nottingham Law Journal and Osgoode Hall Law Journal.

November 2024

CONTENTS

Preface... *vii*

1. **Looking for Legitimacy: An Introduction** 1
   Courts at Risk..2
   Politics and Power...6
   Moving Forward 9
   Conclusion..10

2. **Finding Legitimacy: Democracy, Politics and Courts** 12
   Looking for Legitimacy...13
   Political Legitimacy 16
   Curial Legitimacy 21
   Conclusion..24

3. **By Way of Apology: Constitutional Law and Theory**................................26
   From One War to Another 27
   A Proper Herbert 31
   In a Bickel 35
   Getting Political 38
   Conclusion..42

4. **In Search of Principles: From Origins to Equilibrium** 43
   A Raft of Theories 44
   A Principled Failure..48
   Lost in Neutral 52
   Originalist Sin 55
   The Modern Move 58
   Conclusion..63

5. **The Good, the Bad and the Ugly: A Constitutional Reckoning** 64
   The *Dobbs* Debacle 65
   A Legitimate Problem of Principles 68
   Breaking Bad 73
   Turning Ugly 76
   Conclusion..81

6. **The Politics of Law: A Clearer and Deeper Dive** 82
    Law's Politics 83
    Principles, Philosophy and Politics 87
    Walking the Line..91
    Into the Constitutional Haze...93
    Visions of Federal Order...96
    Conclusion...99

7. **Rethinking Legitimacy: A Jurisprudential View** 100
    The Politics of Law's Politics 101
    Constitutional Authority 105
    Beyond Candour...109
    Toward a New Legitimacy 112
    Conclusion...117

8. **Rethinking Legitimacy: A Judicial View** 119
    An Open Court 120
    A Public Stance 123
    On Abortion 125
    Beyond Pollution 127
    Conclusion...130

9. **Rethinking Legitimacy: A Political View** 131
    Making a Fresh Start 132
    Constitutional Territory...134
    An Expressive Function 138
    Take it to the Limits...140
    A Political Reckoning..143
    Conclusion...146

10. **Rethinking Legitimacy: A Democratic View**.. 147
    Democracy and Majorities 148
    A Different Dilemma...152
    Off Centre 156
    Balances and Challenges..160
    Making Progress...164
    Conclusion...168

11. **The Justices' New Clothes: A Cautionary Tale** 170

Index *177*

1

Looking for Legitimacy:
An Introduction

'Will this institution survive the stench that this creates in the public perception that the Constitution and its reading are just political acts? I don't see how it is possible.' Spoken in December 2021, the institution in question was the Supreme Court of the United States and 'this' was the possible overruling of *Roe v Wade* by that Court. As we now know, that 1973 ruling on a constitutionally protected right to an abortion was overturned in *Dobbs*. But, most significantly, the speaker was not any old critic. It was none other than Sonya Sotomayor, a Justice of the same Supreme Court. She went on to state that 'if people actually believe that it's all political, how will we survive? How will the court survive?'[1] In no uncertain manner, Justice Sotomayor put squarely and bluntly in play a central challenge in modern constitutional law that has threatened to undermine and unravel present arrangements – what makes the Supreme Court a legitimate and authoritative decider of constitutional questions in a democracy?

The traditional answer that still holds centre stage today is that, to earn its status as the final and legitimate interpreter of the Constitution, the Court must function as a forum of law, not another theatre of politics. By this, it is meant that the core of the judges' work must be something separate from politics; judges must be legal professionals, not political operatives. There are, of course, different and competing accounts of how this is possible and whether it is achievable. But the connecting thread is that, as unelected and unrepresentative government officials who exercise very significant power over the polity, judges must earn and ensure their legitimacy by demonstrating that they put aside their own political leanings and follow the objective dictates of constitutional law. It is in this way, so it is argued, that courts can maintain a proper level and style of performance that will garner the approval of citizens, even if (and especially if) their decisions are regarded as unpopular and not agreed with by many citizens. This is no small order. As Justice Sotomayor's impassioned queries make clear, if the Supreme Court fails to live up to this challenge, then the legitimacy and perhaps the very survival of the Court will be at risk. And, as she also graphically suggests, recent rulings have made that daunting possibility into a very real existential threat.

---

[1] Peter Coy, 'The Politicization of the Supreme Court Is Eroding Its Legitimacy' (*New York Times*, 27 June 2022) www.nytimes.com/2022/06/27/opinion/dobbs-supreme-court-legitimacy.html.

In this book, I want to re-focus the whole debate around legitimacy, politics and constitutional law in Supreme Courts. Rather than constantly fighting the perception that Supreme Courts are trampling on the wrong side of the law/politics divide, I will build on the criticisms that constitutional law is simply politics, nothing more and nothing less. My ambition is to demonstrate that, as a matter of both jurisprudential thought and practical politics, democracy can be served by a recognition and acceptance that Supreme Courts' decisions are intrinsically and inescapably political in style, substance and outcomes. In pursuing this line of critical inquiry, while I will give considerable time and space to the goings-on in the American Supreme Court, I will not restrict my analysis and critique to them. In particular, I will also look at how the Supreme Court of Canada deals with these issues and challenges as both a way to legitimate itself and to stave off the kind of criticisms that Justice Sotomayor offers. Although less in-your-face than American judges, this challenge – explaining and defending the performance of judges as democratically legitimate – remains as telling and as debilitating for their Canadian counterparts, albeit in a more muted and less intense way.

Courts at Risk

The nature and extent of Supreme Courts' legitimacy has always been a pivotal, yet delicate matter. This is nowhere more apparent than in constitutional law. Having neither purse nor sword to enforce its judgments, the approval of Supreme Courts' work much depends on the views of their citizens – do they have a good opinion not only of what the Courts are doing, but also how they do it? Not surprisingly, approval ratings have risen and fallen in response to particular decisions at particular times and within particular communities; there is no consistent or compelling conclusion that can be made about public support for Supreme Courts across society and throughout history. Indeed, the conflicting standing of the American Supreme Court and the Canadian Supreme Court in their respective communities is noticeable and has varied considerably; there is no one set of conclusions that can be reached or defended.

More than most countries, the United States is fixated on its Constitution. Not only is its Constitution the founding design and blueprint of the country, but constitutional doctrine is treated as the normative lodestar by which today's politics are to be illuminated, guided and criticised. For almost all Americans, the Constitution is an article of civic faith that, if understood properly and respected appropriately, will ensure the United States is and remains an enviably just and justly envied society; it will set a shining example for other polities to follow and emulate. As Lon Fuller noted without any sense of irony, 'there must be a general belief that the constitution itself is necessary, right, and good.'[2] In short, for

---

[2] Lon Fuller, 'Positivism and Fidelity to Law: A Reply to Professor Hart' (1957) 71 *Harvard Law Review* 630, 642.

Americans, the Constitution is considered the embodiment of all that is good and true about the nation, its values and its people. For a document and tradition that is now over 230 years old, this is no small challenge or achievement.

As much as this basic viewpoint is broadly shared, there is no shared understanding of what the Constitution and its developed doctrines mean or how it should be given meaning. Through *Marbury*, Chief Justice Marshall seized enormous power for the Supreme Court to be the authoritative interpreter of the Constitution; it can invalidate federal and state laws violating the Constitution.[3] Although the Court and most citizens pretend otherwise, the Constitution has been as much a site for conflicting interpretations as it is a source for the fixed resolution of such conflicts. The history of constitutional law is mixed at best. For every *Brown*, there is a *Dred Scott*;[4] for every *Goldberg*, there is a *Hobby Lobby*;[5] for every *Harper*, there is a *Citizens United*;[6] and for every *Obergefell*, there is a *Masterpiece Cakeshop*.[7] There is no single narrative of America's constitutional development that can showcase the Constitution as an unqualified social and progressive good.[8] In confronting this truth, the basic manoeuvre for many is to highlight the ups as being reflective of what the proper or true Constitution demands and to treat the downs as examples of errors or anomalies where the courts have got it wrong. Of course, there is no general agreement on what the up precedents are and what the down ones are.

Until recently, many Americans felt the Supreme Court operated generally in the people's best interests. But they also agreed that the Court often 'gets too mixed up in politics'.[9] However, in the last few years, the situation has become more fraught and urgent. At present, the Court's standing and approval rating has hit record lows; it was at 40% in September 2021, experienced a slight up-tick a year later, and then dipped back to 40%. Significantly, even though there was an across-the-board decrease in support, people's political affiliation is a major differential in the available statistics. Whereas 62% of Republicans approve of the Court's performance, only 17% of Democrats do; 41% of independents approve of the Court's work. Indeed, the Court's legitimacy appears to be at greater risk today than at any time since President Roosevelt's attack on the institution in the 1930s.

---

[3] *Marbury v Madison* (1803) 5 US (1 Cranch) 137, 178.

[4] *Brown v Board of Education of Topeka* (1954) 347 US 483 and *Dred Scott v Sandford* (1857) 60 US 393.

[5] *Goldberg v Kelly* (1970) 397 US 254 and *Burwell v Hobby Lobby Stores Inc* (2014) 573 US 682.

[6] *Moore v Harper* (1923) 600 US 1 and *Citizens United v Federal Election Commission* (2010) 558 US 310.

[7] *Obergefell v Hodges* (2015) 576 US 644 and *Masterpiece Cakeshop, Ltd v Colorado Civil Rights Commission* (2018) 138 S Ct 1719.

[8] For a strong rejection of that thesis, see Adam Cohen, *Supreme Inequality: The Supreme Court's Fifty-Year Battle for a More Unjust America* (New York, Penguin Press, 2020).

[9] 'Most Americans trust the Supreme Court, but think it is "too mixed up in politics"' (*Annenberg Public Policy Center*, 16 October 2019) www.annenbergpublicpolicycenter.org/most-americans-trust-the-supreme-court-but-think-it-is-too-mixed-up-in-politics. ('Two-thirds (68%) of those surveyed trust the Supreme Court to operate in the best interests of the American people … more than half of Americans (57%) agree with the statement that the court "gets too mixed up in politics".')

As well as recent controversial decisions made on abortion and gun rights, the politicised and bitter wrangling around recent judicial appointments to the Court have jeopardised the Court's legitimacy as a purely legal as opposed to political institution of government.[10] The idea that constitutional law is only politics dressed up in legal garb seems to be ascendant. But the deeper issue is whether this contemporary state of affairs is a temporary blip on the constitutional radar or whether it speaks to a more permanent problem that is now being more exposed and appreciated – that constitutional law is unavoidably and always political.

Canadians take a much less reverential and more prosaic approach to their Constitution. Less polarised and hostile than the American political culture generally, Canadian politics takes place in a more low-key environment. Indeed, the level of interest and publicity given to Supreme Court decisions is low, even though it does rule on a wide range of divisive political issues. As with the American situation, the Canadian Constitution has been as much a site for conflicting interpretations as it has been a source for the fixed resolution of such conflicts. The history of Canadian constitutional law is mixed at best. For every *Roncarelli*, there is a *Christie*;[11] for every *Rodriguez*, there is a *Bedford*;[12] for every *Morgentaler*, there is an *RJR-MacDonald*;[13] and for every *Patriation Reference*, there is a *Quebec Reference*.[14] Accordingly, as in the United States, there is no single narrative of Canada's constitutional development that can showcase the Constitution as an unqualified social and progressive good; opinion fluctuates and changes over whether the Supreme Court is doing both a good and legitimate job in fulfilling its constitutional responsibilities.

Mindful that the Canadian Constitution was repatriated and supplemented with a Charter of Rights as recently as 1982, Canadians seem to be much less disturbed by the idea that constitutional law might be a specialised corner of general politics. Relying on an explicitly organic approach to constitutional interpretation that accepted that the Constitution 'planted in Canada a living tree capable of growth and expansion within its natural limits',[15] it is not surprising that a political appreciation of the Supreme Court's role is more widely conceded. Indeed, opinion polls regularly find that there is a clear preference of 59% in terms of favourable performance for the Supreme Court of Canada over almost any other government institution. Further, such support is much stronger among

---

[10] See generally Michael Nelson and Patrick Tucker, 'The Stability and Durability of the US Supreme Court's Legitimacy' (2021) 83 *Journal of Politics* 771 and James Gibson, 'Losing Legitimacy: The Challenges of the Dobbs Ruling to Conventional Legitimacy Theory' (2024) 68 *American Journal of Political Science* 1041. For a more in-depth discussion, see ch 2.

[11] *Roncarelli v Duplessis* [1959] SCR 121 and *Christie v York Corporation* [1940] SCR 139.

[12] *Rodriguez v British Columbia (AG)* [1993] 3 SCR 519 and *Canada (AG) v Bedford* [2013] 3 SCR 1101.

[13] *R v Morgentaler* [1998] 1 SCR 30 and *RJR-MacDonald v Canada* [1995] 3 SCR 199.

[14] *Reference re Resolution to amend the Constitution* [1981] 1 SCR 753 and *Reference re Secession of Quebec* [1998] 2 SCR 217.

[15] *Edwards v Canada (AG)* [1930] AC 124 (JCPC) 124 (Lord Sankey).

middle- and upper-class Canadians than lower-class ones. However, the same opinion polls find that a strong majority of Canadians believe that the current system for appointing Supreme Court Justices by the Prime Minister alone, without any parliamentary oversight, is 'unacceptable'.[16] Moreover, the reaction of many politicians to having lost a case before the Supreme Court is much more muted and respectful; there is no discernible challenge to the Court's continued primacy or legitimacy in matters of constitutional interpretation.[17]

None of this speaks to whether the Canadian Supreme Court's legitimacy is based on solid and traditional jurisprudential grounds (ie, that it does not make political decisions as opposed to legal ones). Of course, it may be that the Canadian public are largely ignorant of the Court's internal workings or that the Court's more middle-of-the-road decisions and reasoning are not perceived as being overtly political and are more to their liking. Also, it may be that what is happening in the United States has the rather perverse effect of reassuring the Canadian public that its own Supreme Court is not as political or, at least, not as divisively so as the American Supreme Court. Nevertheless, whatever the explanation, Canadian judges are considered to be acting more legitimately than their American colleagues. As such, the clear upshot is that the Canadian Supreme Court can proceed with a confidence, albeit perhaps temporary and superficial, that it is business-as-usual for its judges in making decisions and giving reasons.

This contrast between the approval ratings of the Canadian and American Supreme Courts has something important and telling to suggest about the connection between politicality and legitimacy. In the United States, it is seen as essential and non-negotiable that the Supreme Court is not only seen to be not acting in a partisan and political way, but it actually follows that institutional mandate in its work and decisions. In Canada, there seems to be a greater acceptance of the fact that constitutional law will be a mix of law and politics. Of course, citizens do not think that the Court should have *carte blanche* to do as the judges please either collectively or individually, but that there will be limits in place that are respected. Without making too much of this state of affairs, I will argue that a recognition that constitutional law is politics will not in itself be the death knell for the role or legitimacy of a Supreme Court in a constitutional democracy.[18] With certain balances and checks in place, a politicised Supreme Court might well have a continuing, if more modest, place in modern North American governance schemes.

---

[16] 'Canadians have a more favourable view of their Supreme Court than Americans have of their own' (*Angus Reid Institute*, 17 August 2015) www.angusreid.org/supreme-court/.

[17] John Tasker, 'Supreme Court rules Ottawa's carbon tax is constitutional' (*Canadian Broadcasting Corporation*, 25 March 2021) www.cbc.ca/news/politics/supreme-court-federal-carbon-tax-constitutional-case-1.5962687. For example, then Alberta Premier Jason Kenney said he was 'obviously disappointed' with the Supreme Court's decision to uphold the federal government's carbon tax.

[18] See chs 7 and 8.

Politics and Power

The appropriate role for judges in polities that consider themselves democratic in structure and sensibilities is contested and controversial. The range of possible options is broad. There are some that loom large and extreme in the literary and popular imagination that hold little sway in more professional circles. One is Niccolò Machiavelli's young Prince who also functioned as a judge.[19] His advice was to be worldly and hard-headed; he should countenance all manner of actions whether cynical, sly, underhand or manipulative if the ends to be achieved advanced his agenda and consolidated his position of power. Another is François Rabelais' Judge Bridlegoose.[20] After thoroughly reading the bulky pleadings, this judicial character would use his set of dice (small ones for complicated cases and larger ones for more straightforward cases) to reach a decision. When asked to explain his method of judging by Trinquamelle, the Grand President of the Court, and why he did not throw his dice without more, he replied that formalities must be observed; throwing the dice gave him honest and healthy exercise; and because time ripens all things.

These figures were, of course, meant to be satirical exemplars of what judges should not be doing rather than what they should be doing. As such, they were put forward as ironic and critical portrayals that sought to expose and caricature the serious, if sham practices of judges. As such, they held little appeal to professional lawyers and judges. But what they did do in drawing such an unflattering image of the judge was to emphasise the kind of high-minded and earnest expectations that real judges should aspire to in their exercise of official power. For these insiders, the legitimate and assumed role of the judge was to rely and reflect upon the legal resources available and the legal arguments made. After due consideration, the judge is expected to arrive at decisions and provide reasons for that decision that were principled and made in good faith. In so doing, it is taken for granted that judges will set aside their own preferences and predilections and act in a scrupulously professional and strictly honourable manner; there would be no dices, no ruses and no similar distractions involved.

As regards modern jurisprudence, the broader debate over the nature of law and its relationship to political and moral values is heated and intense. It is perhaps at its most fiery in constitutional law, even if it touches all areas of law. Antagonists tend to divide over whether there is some professional way to read and apply legal texts, rules and principles that does more than act as a cover for relying on political partisanship or imposing loaded moral preferences. Indeed, traditional legal theory is premised on the idea that law and political morality can be effectively

---

[19] Niccolò Machiavelli, *The Prince* (first published 1532, HarperCollins, 2012).

[20] François Rabelais, *Gargantua and Pantagruel* (first published 1546, Penguin, 2006). Bridlegoose judged for over 40 years and, in that time, had decided over 4,000 judgments. In a nice twist, the over 2,000 cases appealed were all affirmed. See John Gest, 'The Trial of Judge Bridlegoose' (1924) 58 *American Law Review* 402.

and consistently kept at some distance from each other such that law does not only work exclusively as a formalised site of irreducible ideological or normative contestation; adjudication is about morality, but it is law's own morality, not that of the judge or jurist, that wins the day.[21] As such, most traditional jurists presume that there exists a solid and detectable, if elusive, basis for judicial decision-making that can act as a realistic hedge against ideological unruliness, moral preference or personal political agendas.

On its face, this traditional rendition of the judicial role has much to recommend it. This is particularly so when it is presented as the alternative to courts acting, as Herbert Wechsler put it, as a 'naked power organ' or as mimicking 'the *ad hoc* in politics'.[22] However, although now considered as ground zero by constitutionalist theorists, this jurisprudential contrast between principle and politics has done more harm than good in both law and politics. If judges are not as principled as constitutional jurists insist, then legislators need not be understood as being as crudely ideological as this dichotomy suggests. Judges and politicians are neither principled nor ideological simply by virtue of their status as politicians or judges. While the realm of politics might well (and, in present circumstances, can often more correctly) be characterised in such crude terms, there is no reason why this has to be the case. It is reasonable to think about the possibility that the world outside the courts can also be understood as a principled undertaking; reasonable opinions and reasoned argument could be as much expected in the political world as the accepted practices of raw ideological horse trading, bare-knuckle confrontations and crass power grabs.[23] So Wechsler's black-and-white depiction of modern government does justice to neither the performance of courts nor the work of governmental institutions.

Within such a frame of reference, it is not surprising that, when judges are criticised as failing to perform in a thoroughly professional and principled way, they are condemned as also being little more than Machiavellian ideologues or Rabelaisian tricksters in disguise.[24] This criticism is therefore seen to place them in an indefensible and incorrigible role that is self-evidently unacceptable. Because each is seen as a negation of the other, there is little room to recommend that judges (and politicians) might be acting in a way that is both principled and political. This dichotomised approach is an unfortunate and unnecessary understanding of both law and politics. Moreover, by accepting Wechsler's limited schema, critics of judicial decision-making have allowed themselves to be trapped within the

---

[21] See generally Allan Hutchinson, *Hart, Fuller, and Everything After: The Politics of Legal Theory* (Oxford, Hart Publishing, 2023).

[22] Herbert Wechsler, 'Toward Neutral Principles of Constitutional Law' (1959) 73 *Harvard Law Review* 1, 12, 15.

[23] For a biting contemporary critique along these lines, see Yascha Mounk, *The People vs Democracy: Why Our Freedom is in Danger and How to Save It* (Cambridge, Harvard University Press, 2018) 54–57, 80–98.

[24] See, eg, Mark Tushnet, *Red, White, and Blue: A Critical Analysis of Constitutional Law* (Cambridge, Harvard University Press, 1988).

same limited and limiting straitjacket. In short, they face an unnecessary Hobson's choice – judges can be principled, even if they occasionally fall short of such an exacting standard, or they can be 'manipulative', in that they make no attempt to be principled or honest.[25]

Instead of this, I want to propose a way of thinking about legal reasoning in constitutional law that will provide a more sophisticated and realistic framework for both appreciating and criticising its judicial performance. This involves cultivating a jurisprudential understanding that allows constitutional reasoning to be seen to straddle both the principled and the ideological as well as the professional and the partisan. Indeed, the American Supreme Court's opinions in *Dobbs* offer a timely and telling opportunity to do that.[26] This is also true of the Canadian Supreme Court's recent decision in the *Greenhouse Gas* case.[27] If the majority and minority opinions are viewed through the traditional lens of a Wechslerian approach, there is nowhere to go once it is established that they both can claim a certain legitimacy in terms of 'principled appraisal'[28] or that they both fail to meet that standard and are labelled as political. The critical jurist can only conclude that they are both exercises of raw political power and manipulation. In contrast, I want to demonstrate that they can both be better understood as professional and as political performances at the same time.

In sharp contrast to almost all other constitutional jurists and scholars,[29] I am insisting that an appreciation that constitutional law is a thoroughly political exercise as well as a professional undertaking is something that needs to be accepted or, at least, tolerated. Efforts to do otherwise will merely perpetuate the problems and allow members of Supreme Courts (as well as their juristic apologists) to pretend that they are doing constitutional law *tout court*. However, if the fact that law is always and unavoidably political is truly grasped, it become possible to recommend ways in which that understanding can be incorporated into judicial practice and juristic thought. Although there are more radical and disruptive alternatives to be explored,[30] there are reforms and changes that can be made within the broad and existing framework of present governmental arrangements that can pass constitutional muster as well as live up to the demands of a robust spirit of democratic governance. In short, as the popular legitimacy of the American Supreme

---

[25] Wechsler, above n 22 at 15. Of course, there will be occasions when the allegation of bad faith and manipulativeness might be warranted.

[26] *Dobbs v Jackson Women's Health Organization* (2022) 597 US 215. For a full discussion, see ch 5.

[27] *References re Greenhouse Gas Pollution Pricing Act* (2021) 2021 SCC 11 (*GGPPA*). For a full discussion, see ch 6.

[28] Wechsler, above n 22 at 16·

[29] See, eg, Jesse Wegman, 'The Crisis in Teaching Constitutional Law' (*New York Times*, 26 February 2024) www.nytimes.com/2024/02/26/opinion/constitutional-law-crisis-supreme-court. html. Many teachers were thoroughly discouraged and distressed, but they still clung to the belief that constitutional law and its legitimacy could still be salvaged and understood in legal as opposed to political terms.

[30] Allan Hutchinson, *Democracy and Constitutions: Putting Citizens First* (Toronto, University of Toronto Press, 2021).

Court (but not the Canadian one) is increasingly imperilled, I want to take the next obvious step and abandon entirely the idea that Supreme Courts are institutions of law, not politics – they are both.

Moving Forward

Trying to make sense out of what the judges of Supreme Courts do is, of course, an enduring preoccupation of lawyers and jurists. As much as scholars and commentators tend to delve and dive deeply into constitutional doctrine and its *problèmes du jour*, a genuine sense of being part of a shared enterprise remains elusive. This is no mere academic indulgence as the Court's work has a deep and lasting impact on many practical aspects of North American life and routines. Whether by way of grand theorising or through case-by-case criticisms, academics and commentators have sought to understand and handle the tensions between power and principle, politics and personnel, tradition and change, and much else besides. Of course, this challenge is all the more pressing and acute in times of political turbulence as today; divisiveness and antagonism are the standards of the day. In such contemporary circumstances, for good and for bad, the role and performance of Supreme Courts and its judges is being thrust even further than usual into the critical spotlight, and its fragile legitimacy is subject to even greater scrutiny.

In this book, I will develop, analyse, criticise and rethink the ideas and practice in constitutional law and judicial decision-making around democratic legitimacy. What follows is an effort to both accept that constitutional law is thoroughly political in style and substance and that, when understood as such, it can still have a place in today's constitutional democracy. This is a delicate balancing act, but one that it is necessary to attempt. This is because there is no option other than to grasp the jurisprudential nettle and recognise that constitutional law is politics. To continue to do otherwise is even more of an affront to democratic sensibilities and ambitions than operating under the present charade of pretending that, although both contemporary law and judicial decision-making might fall short of the traditional ideal of constitutional law as a distinctly legal undertaking, it is still a realisable and necessary project. Instead, I will insist that constitutional law is politics *tout court* and that this must be the ground zero of any account of constitutional law and judicial decision-making. Any fresh proposals and reforms must begin there and accept its validity.

With this as my overall guide, I will first explore how the idea and practice of legitimacy have been framed in the philosophical and theoretical literature in order to contextualise more detailed and specific jurisprudential forays into the area. Next, I will look at those leading jurisprudential efforts to explain and justify how the work of courts fits into these explanatory frameworks and whether they can provide persuasive answers to the questions around the legitimacy of courts. After that, I make a more concerted assault on the whole idea of principled reasoning as a governing and legitimating standard for legitimate decision-making in constitutional law. In the next chapter, there is a sustained fleshing out of these general ideas and criticisms in the context of the whole American episode of *Dobbs*, its jurisprudential ramifications and its popular aftermath. After that, I develop further the key idea of what is and is not meant by 'law is politics'. To do this, I will pay close attention to the recent Canadian challenges responding to climate change in the *Greenhouse Gas* case.

The next four chapters take a more constructive turn. I make some proposals and recommendations about what the jurisprudential and institutional implications are for the central critical claim that 'law is politics' for the practice and legitimacy of constitutional law and adjudication. To do this, I push through on what would be the kind of jurisprudential, judicial, institutional, political and democratic proposals that might follow. The challenge here is to be practical and pragmatic, but still remain true to the critical mind-set that undergirds the whole enterprise. As such, my proposals are intended to be suggestive more than determinative. Finally, I offer a slightly different and allegorical take on the problem of legitimacy in constitutional law. Throughout the book, the ambition is to take seriously and act upon the critical insight that law-is-politics. In so doing, I maintain that the resulting set of arrangements and alternatives can better advance and protect a wider democratic and constitutional politics than the existing commitments of judges and jurists.

Conclusion

Justice Sotomayor's dismay and even despair might be more easily dismissed if it was a lone voice that might be thought motivated by a renegade's sensibility.[31] But it is not. Two of her colleagues have also entered the fray with equally powerful concerns about the Court's troubled performance and tenuous legitimacy. Taken together, these insiders' invested views cannot be lightly dismissed. The usually understated Stephen Breyer took the *Dobbs'* majority to task because those judges 'by dint of numbers alone expunge' constitutional rights and, in the process, 'undermine[] the Court's legitimacy'.[32] For him, it was a concession that the public could no longer avoid the 'view that this institution is little different from the two political branches of the Government'.[33] In a similar vein, Justice Elena Kagan offered the opinion that 'law should not look like a form of politics where just because the composition of the court changes a whole batch of legal rules change with it'.[34] Along with Sotomayor, Breyer and Kagan offer an insider's view of the Court and its failure to maintain performative and political legitimacy.

[31] See above n 1.
[32] *Dobbs*, above n 26 at 2350.
[33] ibid.
[34] Adam Liptak, 'Hours After Trump Argument, Cautious Reflections From Justice Kagan' (*New York Times*, 12 February 2024) www.nytimes.com/2024/02/12/us/kagan-trump-colorado.html.

For mainstream supporters of constitutional law and adjudicative method as well as the viability of maintaining the belief that constitutional law is not reducible to constitutional politics or judges' own political allegiances, these are troubling statements. This is especially so because these three speakers are not only part of the Supreme Court (and, therefore, have a clear interest in preserving the Court's legitimacy), but also because the fact of them simply speaking out will add fuel to the legitimacy fires. Yet, although these comments will be understood by most to recommend that constitutional law can have an objective and meaningful existence independent of the Supreme Court's present incumbents and that it must be followed and respected as such, they can be interpreted in a very different and more positive way. In particular, Justice Kagan might be taken to mean that 'yes, we might be political, but the legitimacy of the Supreme Court will be irreparably harmed if we are seen that way.' As such, her warning is more about appearance than actuality. In this book, I intend to show that the appearance is also the reality – constitutional law deserves no legitimacy if that legitimacy depends on the Court's unconvincing claim that it is acting as an institutional forum that prioritises law as being above or beyond politics. Moreover, 'irreparable harm' will continue be done to both constitutional and constitutional politics if this crucial fact continues to be ignored, trivialised, overlooked or hidden. Instead, I insist that constitutional law is politics and that an acceptance of this can be understood to advance, not hamper, the democratic project of accountable governance.

2

Finding Legitimacy: Democracy, Politics and Courts

While travelling recently, I began chatting with a fellow passenger. He had emigrated to the United States as a young person from India over 50 years ago. He was now a citizen, had been successful in his career and lived well in Florida. When he discovered that I was a lawyer, he opened up quickly. He told me that, when he first came to the United States, he was a great admirer of the American system and culture of democratic governance. In particular, he viewed the Supreme Court as an essential partner in the government's efforts at achieving social justice. He held this view for many years. For him, there was a sound balance between the governmental branches and the political forces in play. However, he had recently become very disappointed and even disillusioned by several turns of events. In particular, he lamented the performance of the Supreme Court. It was not so much that he did not agree with or was offended by any specific decision: it was that the Court seemed to be merely indulging its own members' partisan preferences. He had always appreciated that the Court was a political institution in the broadest sense, but he now felt that its recent work was ideological and had undermined the Court's reputation and role – 'I have lost confidence in the Supreme Court and thereby the overall legitimacy of the American commitment to constitutional democracy.'

It was his choice of 'legitimacy' that struck a strong chord with me. The Supreme Court is regularly criticised by some (and often many) for the particular decisions reached; its decisions are met with a mixed chorus of approval and disapproval – correct and incorrect; good and bad; and right and wrong. This all seems par for the legal and constitutional course. But a suggestion that the Court itself and the constitutional arrangements of which it is part are somehow illegitimate takes the criticism to a whole different and higher level. It points to a level of discontent and disapproval that goes well beyond a particular instance or episode of governance; it recommends that the whole process, organisation and practice of government has become suspect and undeserving of general support and respect. Indeed, it may be that acquiescence and even obedience to its pronouncements might no longer be assured. Of course, my fellow passenger was only one voice. But it seems fair to note that he is likely far from being alone in his views. Significant sections of the populace have also come to a similar opinion.[1] This does not bode well for the present stability and future progress of constitutional democracy.

In this chapter, I intend to examine the idea of legitimacy when it is applied to the operation and opinions of Supreme Courts within a formal scheme of constitutional democracy as practised in North America. In the first part, my focus will be broad and general: I will look at how legitimacy is understood by philosophers and political theorists. The next section explores how legitimacy is understood in political terms, with especial attention being paid to what this means in large societies that are committed to some form of democracy. After that, I will concentrate on how modern courts and their constitutional rulings fit into this general appreciation of democratic legitimacy. To do this, I will introduce and rely upon the recent reaction to rulings around the *Dobbs* case and its overruling of *Roe*'s guarantees about so-called abortion rights. Throughout the chapter, the emphasis will be on gaining a more informed and critical appreciation of the demands of legitimacy as regards controversial decisions in constitutional law.

Looking for Legitimacy

Power and authority are part and parcel of any society. Whether that power is diffuse or concentrated and whether that authority is limited or total, there is a need for a certain legitimacy to be maintained in their distribution and exercise. Even when used or exercised to bring about what may be seen as bad outcomes personally or collectively, power and authority are considered to be granted under a range of limitations, restrictions and permissions. Many of those may be legal in nature, but there is also often a requirement that, if the assumption of power and the exercise of authority are to be treated as valid and supportable, they must also be acceptable to and considered appropriate by those subject to them. This notion of 'legitimacy' will be present in societies or organisations that are not only democratic or voluntary in character, but also autocratic or repressive in type. Tyrants as well as elected officials seek a degree of acceptability and justification for their power and authority in order to impose their will and decisions on others; fear and oppression usually cannot do all the work. As a seasoned commentator phrased it, 'legitimacy involves the capacity of the system to engender and maintain the belief that the existing … institutions are the most appropriate ones for the society.'[2]

Although an elusive and unstable notion that shifts and changes in different contexts and for different purposes, legitimacy can still be understood and

---

[1] See chs 1 and 9.

[2] Seymour Lipset, *Political Man: The Social Bases of Politics* (Garden City, Doubleday, 1960) 77. See also Max Weber, *The Theory of Social and Economic Organization* (Talcott Parsons tr, New York, The Free Press, 1964) 382 ('the basis of every system of authority, and correspondingly of every kind of willingness to obey, is a belief, a belief by virtue of which persons exercising authority are lent prestige').

analysed profitably in broad terms. It will be obvious that, in making any determination about legitimacy, the details of the historical and social context will be paramount. Social pressures, historical contingencies, institutional environments, organisational clusters, normative assumptions and many other contextual factors will combine to dictate what counts as legitimacy for a particular group, at a particular time, and in a particular place. Moreover, being evaluative, these judgments of legitimacy will be contested more than conceptual and will be pragmatic more than methodical.

That said, it is possible to suggest that there are three interacting components and conditions that need to be satisfied if there is to be any claim about an action or decision being treated as legitimate:[3]

- *Expectations* – what people think should be the case will be important in evaluating any action or decision. There is no standard that applies that will transcend the understandings and beliefs of those subject to power and authority; it will be adequate for there to be an alignment between what is being done and expectations about what can or should be done.

- *Assent* – whether directly or indirectly, people must exhibit a mode of confidence in the fact that power has been granted and authority exercised in a certain way. Even if the situation is simply perceived to be the least-bad alternative available, people need not go so far as providing positive consent, but they must refrain from outright disapproval.

- *Conformity* – at a minimum, there must exist a general, if not universal, phenomenon of compliance with or acceptance of acts done or decisions made. This is not at all the same thing as approval. While people might well approve or disapprove, it is not a requirement for legitimacy to exist; it is sufficient that people conform with the demands made.

Further, in reaching any conclusion about the legitimacy of the ascription of power and the exercise of authority, it will be important to distinguish between correctness and legitimacy. Although people's perception that the use of power and authority was correctly designated and exercised will contribute to more constructive evaluations of legitimacy, it is not a *sine qua non*. Indeed, the operation and force of a judgment about legitimacy becomes most telling when legitimacy is conferred upon power and authority when those affected do not think that a decision or action taken was correct or fair. As such, legitimacy is often less about the substance of decisions made or actions taken, but as much about the process or reasons for proceeding in that way. This is not to suggest that there are objectively better and worse processes in general, but that some procedures are considered

---

Interestingly, the etymology of the word 'legitimacy' derives from the Latin verb *legitimare* that means 'lawful'. Its use here is much broader and less confining than that.

[3] See generally Eric Schoon, 'Operationalizing Legitimacy' (2022) 87 *American Sociological Review* 478. See also Tom Tyler, 'Psychological Perspectives on Legitimacy and Legitimation' (2006) 57 *Annual Review of Psychology* 375.

to be more appropriate for some decisions and actions than others; schemes for the imposition of punishment might well differ from those that offer privileges or benefits.

Accordingly, the importance of legitimacy is found in the fact that people might be accepting of adverse (or what they perceive as incorrect or unjust) decisions so long as they are perceived to be within the range of legitimate actions. However, it is also worth pointing out that if an action, decision or the conferral power and authority might possess a general and initial legitimacy, its justification can be undercut or even done away with later. When an action does not live up to certain minimum levels of expectation, its legitimacy will be suspect or lost. So, while there will be a range of deviation that is considered acceptable or inevitable, an action or decision that places itself outside that range might well be labelled or condemned as illegitimate; people's expectations will be offended, assent will not be present, and conformity may well be jeopardised. As Cristina Lafont puts it, 'substantively incorrect decisions may nonetheless be legitimate,' but 'grave substantive injustices can undermine ... legitimacy.'[4] Of course, exactly when that threshold is crossed will be uncertain and context-specific as will the ensuing results in terms of popular response and reaction; decisions about the appointment of certain officials might well have a different threshold of legitimacy than those about the availability of health care.

In order to give this generalised and abstract discussion some practical bite, a more prosaic example can be used. A contested area of decision-making is law school admissions. Decisions are made on the basis of a number of factors – Law School Admission Test (LSAT) ranking; undergraduate grade-point average (GPA); personal identity and characteristics; and a personal statement. A process is put in place by individual law schools, and an overall approach to balancing each substantive factor is settled upon. Many applicants are rejected. Most, if not all, tend to accept these adverse decisions and, although disappointed and occasionally distraught and offended, move on. However, there are some who do not accept the decision; they allege that not only is the decision incorrect (eg, administrative errors, inaccurate grade calculation, conflicts of interest, etc), but that the substantive factors relied on and the process used, even if adhered to, were not legitimate. These allegations may be specious, but they also need to be taken seriously.

The general presumption is that, while far from perfect, the overall admission process has a certain degree of legitimacy – there is a loose alignment between people's expectations and the overall goals of the process; there is no widespread disapproval and people offer tacit assent to existing arrangements; and there is general conformity with and willingness to abide by decisions made. But that conferral of legitimacy is fragile. While there no doubt exist simply some sore losers, some applicants, including successful ones, have genuine and serious reservations about the whole business; they question its legitimacy. For instance,

[4] See Cristina Lafont, 'A Militant Defense of Democracy: A Few Replies to My Critics' (2021) 47 *Philosophy and Social Criticism* 69, 71.

some argue that the LSAT is culturally biased and should not be given much or any weight. Perhaps more significantly, others insist that the any reliance upon a person's identity is wrong and discriminatory; there are claims that entry to law school should be entirely individual and meritocratic. These opponents frame their concerns in terms of legitimacy – they maintain that, in modern-day society, the standards to be applied lack the requisite appropriateness to satisfy people's expectations about what is fair and just.

Of course, nothing necessarily follows from an increasing chorus of disapproval; the scheme for determining who does and does not get into law school will not collapse or change without more. However, if that gap between expectations and performance grows and dissent becomes more widespread, legitimacy will become suspect. As a result, the pressure on law schools to adjust their schemes (along both substantive and processual lines) will increase; a sense will spread that the factors relied upon and the processes deployed are lacking in legitimacy and have perhaps become illegitimate.[5] Indeed, this points up the fact that, when compared with legality, legitimacy is measured along a band or scale; it is not an on/off switch. Because a scheme is not considered entirely legitimate will not result in it being condemned as fully illegitimate; there is a broad space between legitimacy and illegitimacy whose significance, volatility and impact will depend on contextual and structural considerations. Accordingly, the legitimacy of power and authority will rarely comprise a uniform, consistent or final appraisal of an action taken or decision made.

In relying on this example of law school admissions, I am not suggesting that legitimacy will function the same way in all other situations: the details of the historical, social and organisational setting will be decisive. But law school admissions do offer an illustrative glimpse of the kind of forces and factors that will arise in discussions and judgements about legitimacy. The contested terrain of perceived injustice will overlap with legitimacy. As such, the acceptability of social arrangements and practices will not simply be about legal validity or normative correctness, but will draw upon contested and contingent views about what is fair and appropriate. When this approach is applied to matters that are more obviously political and broadly public than law school admissions, a general understanding of legitimacy will be helpful in evaluating and analysing the dynamics and standards at work.

Political Legitimacy

Political legitimacy is based upon popular assent to a system of governance and its constituent institutions. There is no need for there to be moral approval of all that

---

[5] Indeed, law schools' processes have been on the move for some time. However, in the case of so-called affirmative action initiatives, the debate has moved from legitimacy to legality. See, eg, *Students for Fair Admissions, Inc v President and Fellows of Harvard College* (2023) 600 US 181.

is done, but there must be a certain level of acceptance whether by way of consent or, at least, by an unwillingness to take collective action to challenge the existing state of affairs. Also, there must, of course, be some basic congruence between what the designated officials say and are expected to do and what they actually do; the reasonable expectations of the populace must be met to some workable degree. None of this is to suggest that the form of government in any particular society must conform with some universal standard of good governance. There have been (eg, Nazi Germany) and still are (eg, modern-day Iran) schemes of government that might be considered unjust or repressive by most measures.[6] However, they might and often do resist popular claims of illegitimacy; people are prepared to hold their noses or turn a blind eye as part of a widespread sense that the status quo does advance certain public interests, even if perversely so.[7] The test for legitimacy, therefore, is much more pragmatic than metaphysical and much more descriptive than evaluative.

A particular and important mode of political legitimacy is that which is demanded in societies that consider themselves democratic. In such cultures, more is asked than that there is a simple acquiescence in governmental power and a begrudging compliance with its operation. In regard to political legitimacy in a democratic society, the emphasis is upon the extent to which there is a popular perception that the elected government and its officials are functioning in line with accepted democratic principles and that the government can be held accountable to the popular will. Of course, what counts as 'democratic principles' will be a robust matter of political contestation, but there will exist a general popular sentiment that government should be, as close as possible to, a government of the people, by the people and for the people. As such, a scheme and practice of governance that aspires to be treated as democratic will need to meet a threshold of democratic legitimacy (ie, reasonable expectations met; moderate assent given; and general conformity available). However, societies are not so much democratic or undemocratic, but more or less democratic in their relative merits. In an important manner of speaking, the smaller the gap between the rulers and the ruled and between the powerful and the powerless, the more democratic that society will be.[8]

Of course, democratic societies come in many different shapes and sizes. Perhaps the most common form in large and diverse societies is that of 'representative

---

[6] In this sense, I resist the claims of some liberal theorists that political legitimacy is the same as moral justification. See John Rawls, *Political Liberalism* (New York, Columbia University Press, 2005) 42 and Jürgen Habermas, *Between Facts and Norms: Contributions to a Discourse Theory of Law and Democracy* (William Rehg tr, Cambridge, MIT Press, 1996). See generally Peter Fabienne, 'Political Legitimacy', *The Stanford Encyclopedia of Philosophy* (29 April 2010) https://plato.stanford.edu/archives/sum2017/entries/legitimacy/.

[7] The challenge of determining exactly why people comply with governmental directives is almost impossible to meet; citizens may comply with legal rules out of a combination of habit, fear of sanctions, or utility-maximising self-interest. See Alan Hyde, 'The Concept of Legitimation in the Sociology of Law' [1983] *Wisconsin Law Review* 379.

[8] See generally Allan Hutchinson, *Democracy and Constitutions: Putting Citizens First* (Toronto, University of Toronto Press, 2021) chs 6–7.

democracy'. Rather than allow for regular and direct involvement of citizens, such governmental schemes settle for the periodic election of representatives. There are two primary accounts of the role of such democratic representatives. One is the 'delegate' view: representatives should see themselves as conduits for the opinions and values of their constituents and defer to those norms in developing and voting for particular policies and legislative initiatives. The other is the 'trustee' view: representatives should give priority to their own considered judgement of what is best and what would advance the public good without ignoring entirely the opinions of their constituents.[9] In many contemporary democracies, there tends to be a combination of the two accounts; representatives should consult their constituents, but they need not become hostage to those views in reaching their own informed conclusions.

Importantly, there is nothing about democracy generally or representative democracy particularly that gives licence to politicians to act in the manner of political hacks or flunkies. Any serious account of democracy does not recommend that politicians can fulfil their duties in an *ad hoc*, capricious, self-serving or unprincipled manner. If they do, they will be reneging on any commitment to be serving a democratic purpose or being justified in their views and stances by democracy. As such, democracy does not give elected representatives or government officials any right or legitimacy to engage in the kind of posturing and mud-slinging that characterises some contemporary politics. Indeed, it is extremely important to emphasise that, in a society that aspires to be treated as truly democratic, its representatives and executives should act in a principled manner.[10] It is not only insufficient for them to claim any democratic privilege in acting dogmatically or arbitrarily, but it is also illegitimate. As such, being principled is not something that is markedly different from being political. In the democratic playbook, being principled is simply the preferred way to be political. While this allows for the robust exchange of divergent views, it places a politico-moral obligation on politicians to participate in a good faith discourse that eschews name-calling, ideological posturing and blatant self-interest without more. This responsibility should include a considered and principled evaluation of how the Constitution should apply to the matter in hand.[11]

Another feature of many democratic polities is that they are subject to constitutional constraints. As well as establishing the structural framework for the

---

[9] See generally Marc Bühlmann and Jan Fivaz, *Political Representation: Roles, Representatives and the Represented* (Oxford, Routledge, 2016) and Stefan Rummens, 'Staging Deliberation: The Role of Representative Institutions in the Deliberative Democratic Process' (2012) 20 *Journal of Political Philosophy* 23.

[10] This is a very significant requirement in developing my account of judicial legitimacy. While there is no easy or straightforward explanation of what 'being principled' requires, it does place serious demands and constraints on the nature of political and legal discourse. See chs 4 and 8.

[11] It has been noted that, while there is an almost obsessive concern with courts in regard to their constitutional role, little time is spent 'examining how a legislator or President should carry out her constitutional responsibilities'. Tara Grove, 'The Supreme Court's Legitimacy Dilemma' (2019) 132 *Harvard Law Review* 2240, 2275.

allocation of power and the distribution of authority, constitutions often contain various rights and protections that are intended to inhibit the extent and activities of democratic governance. Among other things, this creates an obvious tension between democracy and constitutionalism: people's beliefs and their acceptance of government action will depend on both their support for the democratic and constitutional process. Indeed, it can be argued that constitutional democracy and constitutionalism are contradictory goals.[12] Insofar as constitutions are meant to place limits on democracy, much will depend on whether there is strong constitutionalism and weak democracy or vice versa. A commitment to strong constitutionalism weakens and attenuates the influence of the democratic will. However, others maintain that constitutionalism supplements the processual benefits of democracy with the substantive advantages of constitutionalism; 'majoritarian democratic decision procedures are necessary, but not sufficient to identify legitimate outcomes.'[13]

For example, the United States has a constitution that is considered to be superior in its protection of individual rights and freedoms from the activities of the democratically elected legislature. In any conflict between the products of the democratic process and the values of the constitution, it is the constitution that will prevail. Other than the passing of some constitutional amendment (that is a rare and very difficult thing to do), the constitution will be given systemic priority and authority. By contrast, for much of its history, Canada did not have an entrenched bill of rights that superseded the normal outputs of the democratically elected branch of government; Parliament was supreme in such matters.[14] However, in 1982, the Constitution was amended and a Charter of Rights and Freedoms introduced. Although the Constitution took presumptive precedence over any acts of provincial and federal legislatures, the Constitution itself contained a provision whereby many sections of the Charter could be bypassed by a simple vote of the relevant provincial or federal legislature.[15] In effect, Canada has opted for a less strong commitment to constitutionalism in the name of democracy than the United States.

In dealing with any trade-off between democracy and other governmental norms, the most pressing issue will be the theoretical and practical basis on which this done. Whereas democracy can claim its epistemic and normative mandate from popular participation (ie, the values and opinions of electors), any mode of

---

[12] Martin Loughlin, *Against Constitutionalism* (Cambridge, Harvard University Press, 2022) and Hutchinson, above n 8.

[13] Andreas Follesdal, 'Tracking Justice Democratically' (2017) 31 *Social Epistemology* 324, 326. See also Ian Shapiro, *The State of Democratic Theory* (Princeton, Princeton University Press, 2003).

[14] However, there was and remains a constitutional set of arrangements as regards federalism. See Constitution Act 1867, ss 91–92.

[15] Constitution Act 1982, Sch B of Canada Act 1982 (UK), s 33. It should be noted that reliance on this section has been mixed. While the federal government has never utilised s 33, numerous provincial legislatures have done so. See Peter Biro (ed), *The Notwithstanding Clause and the Canadian Charter: Rights, Reforms, and Controversies* (Montreal, McGill-Queen's University Press, 2024).

constraint on that process will need to ground itself in a different and presumably more reliable or authoritative set of norms and practices. So, if democracy is to be supplemented or disciplined by reference to some other set of values, it will be vitally important to offer a convincing account of both the source and authority of the standards that will be used to check the policies and outcomes of the democratic process through which those standards are to be identified and applied. This challenge goes to the heart of the legitimacy debate in democratic societies.

Accordingly, while the existence of non-democratic public institutions within a democratically governed society is problematic, there is no compelling reason to suggest that they are entirely illegitimate. For instance, many advanced industrial societies, including the United States and Canada, rely on a central bank or reserve to manage a country's currency and monetary policy. While the head of such bodies is appointed by a democratically accountable executive, the institution itself operates as a free-standing agency that expects and insists upon its independence from political agendas and partisan interference. Although many disagree with some of their decisions and occasionally their general political orientation, these bodies seem to have no major legitimacy issues. In large part, this is because the matters that they deal with are seen to be technical (even if they might be more than that) and do not raise directly moral and contestable issues; reserve management and bank-clearing systems are not the stuff of popular controversy as compared with abortion and euthanasia. That said, there is a general expectation that, because they are non-democratic institutions in a democratic society, their officials will fulfil their responsibilities in a principled and professional way.

When it comes to the Constitution and related legal matters, the extraordinary power to determine its meaning and application has been delegated to courts. The nature of courts is that they are considered the third branch of government. They comprise a group of professionals (ie, judges) who make claim to a range of privileges and protections in offering final and definitive meaning to the Constitution. Some courts have achieved this elevated status by virtue of a constitutional provision (eg, Supreme Court of Canada),[16] but others have managed to secure their position as a result of some long-accepted precedent of their own making (eg, Supreme Court of the United States).[17] Of course, there is no absolute reason why courts should have the final say on the meaning of the Constitution; it could be a responsibility of the legislative branch or another elected agency. However, the established practice has been to hand over this crucial power to a legal body. While its members are appointed by the executive branch of government from the ranks of qualified lawyers, the courts are largely unaccountable in their power and scope of action in regard to the Constitution.

---

[16] Constitution Act 1982, s 52(1). It must be remembered that legislative branches can end-run the courts in a large range of matters. See above n 10.

[17] See, eg, *Marbury v Madison* (1803) 5 US (1 Cranch) 137.

As such, courts are unelected and unrepresentative institutions that are entrusted with the enormous and decisive task of determining what limits should be placed on the elected government in the name and authority of democracy. Some contend that it is this very fact that they are unelected and unrepresentative that enables them to rise above internecine politics and serve the broader and less partisan ambitions of constitutional justice; the courts are viewed as a much-needed check on the ideological excesses of popular government that work to advance the substantive values of republican democracy. While it is conceded that there will be mistakes and missteps along the way by individual judges and in specific cases, the overall trend is assumed to be towards ensuring that society becomes more, not less, just as a result of judicial review over the long haul. However, this begs the question of whether there is a professional and non-political mode of fulfilling their constitutional responsibilities.

Curial Legitimacy

In terms of legitimacy, this institutional transfer of power to courts in order to oversee the operation and effect of the Constitution raises significant issues. In the starkest terms, it poses two foundational dilemmas – how to justify the exercise of non-democratic power in a society that is committed to democratic governance; and how to maintain people's trust in the work of courts in divisive times. In order to address these dilemmas, it will be necessary to critically explore and evaluate the expectations, forbearance and behaviour of a society's citizens. If there is a need for principled engagement in the democratic sphere, this is doubly true for non-democratic institutions. This challenge will have to be met not only if the legitimacy of courts is to be preserved, but also if the more general legitimacy of democracy at large is to be maintained – what will courts need to do to preserve and legitimise their role and its performance in a society that holds serious aspirations to being democratic in name and practice?

In order to assess the legitimacy of courts in fulfilling their constitutional duties at any particular point in time, it is important to look to the basic indicators of broad expectations, social assent and behavioural conformity. In making this inquiry, it will be useful to recognise that there are two axes along which the courts' authority and power can be measured:

- *Substantive* – this speaks to the substantive merits and appeal of individual decisions. People will consider such substantive decisions to be legitimate and, therefore, acceptable if they align with or, at least, do not clash too severely and deeply with their ideological leanings and political preferences. One or two deviations might be tolerated, but a series of decisions (or even one particularly controversial and significant decision) that goes directly against their fundamental beliefs or ideals will severely test the legitimacy of the courts more generally.

- *Procedural* – this speaks to the general interpretive methods and means used by judges to reach their decisions. If people perceive that judges are acting in an appropriate and professional manner, people are more likely to accept or, at least, put up with decisions that they do not fully agree with. In particular, although what it means for the judges to act professionally and appropriately is vague and contested, it will be especially important for people to be convinced that judges are above the political fray and acting in line with the law. If judges are seen as simply politicians in fancy dress, people will begin to question whether the courts are worthy of their respect and support.

Of course, these two measures do not operate independently of each; they interact and affect each other in significant and subtle ways. As the American Supreme Court itself put it, 'the Court's power lies … in its legitimacy, a product of substance and perception that shows itself in the people's acceptance of the judiciary as fit to determine what the nation's law means and to declare what it demands.'[18] However, once people's attention is drawn to the workings of the courts by a controversial decision or incident (eg, judicial misbehaviour), they will pay more attention to other decisions reached and look more critically at the general methods relied upon by the courts to perform their constitutional duties.[19] There is no dependable or sure-fire standard by which to evaluate whether courts are maintaining the confidence of people and thereby being a legitimate branch of government in people's eyes. Moreover, the more divisive a society, the more that people's sense of the courts' legitimacy will vary and conflict. Even when a society is more homogenous in its opinions and values, questions of legitimacy may still arise, albeit in a more restrained and less immediate style.

Not all constitutional cases raise issues of legitimacy: many cases are very technical in their orientation and presentation, so they are not understood to be openly political in their substance. Indeed, much of the time, people are oblivious to what courts are doing on a regular basis. Cases like *Brown* and *Roe* are the exception, not the rule. The more people like or approve of a decision substantively, the more likely that they will think that the method to reach that decision was acceptable and proper. Similarly, the more proper and correct that people perceive the courts' approach to be, the more accepting people will be of the decision itself. Indeed, the courts themselves have often been acutely aware of this tension between substance and procedure. This has resulted in courts making trade-offs between the two in

---

[18] *Planned Parenthood of Southeastern Pennsylvania v Casey* (1992) 505 US 833, 865. See also Brandon Bartels and Christopher Johnston, 'On the Ideological Foundations of Supreme Court Legitimacy in the American Public' (2013) 57 *American Journal of Political Science* 184, 185. Some suggest that the substantive factor is primary and almost exclusive. See Terri Peretti, *In Defense of a Political Court* (Princeton, Princeton University Press, 1999) 161–88.

[19] James Gibson and Michael Nelson, 'Reconsidering Positivity Theory: What Roles do Politicization, Ideological Disagreement, and Legal Realism Play in Shaping U.S. Supreme Court Legitimacy?' (2017) 14 *Journal of Empirical Legal Studies* 592. See also Robert Post and Neil Siegel, 'Theorizing the Law/Politics Distinction: Neutral Principles, Affirmative Action, and the Enduring Legacy of Paul Mishkin' (2007) 95 *California Law Review* 1473, 1473–74 (2007).

order to maintain overall legitimacy. This, of course, is viewed by some people (and judges and jurists) as a prudent course of action, whereas it is criticised by other people (and judges and jurists) as being more of a sell-out and a threat to the courts' legitimacy.[20]

This is all illustrated by the furore occasioned by the recent decision in *Dobbs* in which a conservative-controlled Supreme Court overturned the 1973 *Roe* decision to establish a constitutional right to abortion. As with *Roe*, the response to *Dobbs* was swift, divided and antagonistic. But this time the tables were turned. As the pro-choice forces lambasted the work of the Court in gutting pregnant women's rights, the anti-choice lobby was gleeful in its success.[21] Predictably, legal academe was also divided, but its response was more restrained and jurisprudential. For some, the Court and its decision in *Dobbs* was viewed as simply correcting a constitutional misstep that was based on weak and unconvincing reasoning in *Roe*. For others, the *Dobbs* Court was to be chastised for riding roughshod over an established, if shaky, precedent of the earlier *Roe* Court.

In recent years, as the American Supreme Court has become more dominated by conservative-appointed Justices and has revisited some hotly contested issues (eg, abortion, gun control and Medicare), popular support for it has fragmented and fallen. In the past 20 years, strong confidence and approval in the work and rulings of the Supreme Court has steadily fallen from around a disappointing 50% of people to a troubling 25%; the figures are even more depressed for young people and persons of colour. This trend is also complemented by the fact that the strong disapproval rating (as opposed to an indifference) has been climbing at an equal pace and intensity.[22] If these statistics were understood in purely political terms, they would not be surprising or unexpected; modern American society is sharply and antagonistically divided in its politics. However, mindful that the power and authority of the Supreme Court depends on it being perceived as non-political in its workings, these statistics strongly suggest that the Supreme Court's legitimacy is in jeopardy – almost 75% of people do not hold a high opinion of the Supreme Court and its role in American governance.

---

[20] Tara Grove, above n 11 at 2245 ('the Justices may feel pressure to sacrifice the legal legitimacy of their judicial decisions in order to preserve the sociological legitimacy of the Court as a whole') and Lawrence Lessig, *Fidelity & Constraint: How the Supreme Court Has Read the American Constitution* (Oxford, Oxford University Press, 2019) 213 ('getting it right is important, but appearing non-political can be much more important').

[21] *Dobbs v Jackson Women's Health Organization* (2022) 597 US 215. Compare, eg, Lauren McEwan, 'Feminist Women's Health Center Speaks Out Against Anti-Abortion Arguments in Dobbs v Jackson' (*Feminist Women's Health Center*, 2021) https://feministcenter.org/blog/feminist-womens-health-center-speaks-out-against-anti-abortion-arguments-in-dobbs-v-jackson/ with Tom Shakely, 'A New Day at Last: U.S. Supreme Court Reverses Roe v. Wade' (*Americans United for Life*, 24 June 2022) https://aul.org/2022/06/24/a-new-day-at-last-u-s-supreme-court-reverses-roe-v-wade/.

[22] See, eg, 'Do you approve or disapprove of the way the Supreme Court is handling its job' (*Gallup*, 2024) https://news.gallup.com/poll/4732/supreme-court.aspx and Joseph Copeland, 'Favourable views of Supreme Court fall to historic low' (*Pew Research Center*, 21 July 2023) www.pewresearch.org/short-reads/2023/07/21/favorable-views-of-supreme-court-fall-to-historic-low/.

As the stakes go up and the public response becomes more intense, there is even greater institutional pressure on Supreme Courts to act (or be seen to act) in a judicial way. In order to consolidate their legitimacy, they must be able to set aside their own work and decisions from those of their other governmental partners as being not only of a different style and form, but also of a different quality and character. In particular, Supreme Court judges must do more (or less) to ensure that their decisions and reasoning are not simply understood as partisan politics in judicial garb. Of course, this challenge is especially difficult because what is considered to count as 'acting judicially' is itself a contested and divisive topic.[23] Moreover, there is an obvious tension between what acting judicially means in the public realm and in the academic world. Indeed, each seems to have very different understandings and expectations from the other. If the popular perception is that judges must act and appear to be studiously non-political to be legitimate, the juristic response is that judges can act politically as long as they do so objectively and neutrally. Nevertheless, both combine in their appreciation that courts must not step too far outside their understood roles if they are to retain a necessary or workable degree of social legitimacy.

It also worth noting that people's satisfaction with the courts' work may be as much about a comparative lack of confidence in the work of legislatures as anything else: the work and identity of judges is much less appreciated than that of politicians. While judges surround themselves with a certain detachedness and aloofness, politicians are under greater and more intense public scrutiny. For instance, in Canada, the Supreme Court's reputation and, therefore, legitimacy has remained fairly steady and consistent: 74% of Canadians hold favourable opinions on the Court and almost 70% have higher amounts of confidence in the institution relative to legislatures and politicians. This support is equally balanced in terms of gender, but decreases as people age However, it increases with the extent of education received and income.[24] All in all, perhaps because the Canadian Supreme Court has tended to follow a more middle-of-the-road approach than its American counterpart, Canadians are little troubled by the legitimacy of courts in challenging and curtailing legislative and executive power.

Conclusion

Like almost all ideas and practices in and around governance, legitimacy is a contested and politicised one. There is no simple or agreed-upon definition of

---

[23] See ch 8.

[24] See 'Canadians have a more favourable view of their Supreme Court than Americans have of their own' (*Angus Reid Institute*, 17 August 2015) www.angusreid.org/supreme-court/ and 'Canadian Supreme Decisions: Public's View of the Supreme Court' (*Ipsos*, 4 July 2001) www.ipsos.com/en-ca/canadian-supreme-decisions-publics-view-supreme-court/. There is no available data for how race and ethnicity affect support.

what will or will not count as the legitimate exercise of power and authority. In polities that are democratic (or claim to be), the pursuit of popular legitimacy is even more important and consequential. This challenge becomes particularly acute when power and authority are vested in an institution (ie, a Supreme Court) that lacks any obvious or settled basis for its validity of having a recognised democratic status – why and how should unrepresentative and unelected officials be granted so much influence over other branches of government that have a clearer, if constrained and questionable, status as a democratically authorised and accountable grounding? In the next few chapters, I will examine and evaluate the leading attempts by jurists to explain and justify how this question can be successfully answered. And, in the process, I will begin to flesh out the force and thrust of the critical claim that constitutional law is politics.

3

By Way of Apology:
Constitutional Law and Theory

In recent decades, constitutional lawyers have not only continued to debate and disagree over the merit and correctness of various constitutional decisions by Supreme Courts. Indeed, the scope for engagement is almost limitless as Supreme Courts have chosen or been obliged to become entangled in the knotty thickets of heated political and moral controversies, like abortion, affirmative action, voting rights and physician-assisted suicide. However, the focus has been as much about the overall judicial theories and methods that have been relied upon by different judges as the decisions themselves. The literature has been varied and passionate in its contestation and conflict. Indeed, it is fair to say that constitutional theory has become something of a popular blood sport. At the heart of these exchanges is the compelling issue of whether there exists a solid and detectable, if elusive, basis for judicial decision-making that can act both as a realistic hedge against ideological and undemocratic unruliness by judges or anyone else and as a democratically acceptable complement to the work of elected legislators and executives. In so many ways, this fraught and unresolved jurisprudential inquiry remains the ground zero of constitutional law and scholarship.

The courts' legitimacy, therefore, can be defended on the basis that, while some of the courts' constitutional decisions might not meet with whole-hearted public approval, people are reassured by legal experts that the courts are acting in line with the appropriate professional expectations – the process of judicial review might occasionally produce disliked decisions, but that process can be assumed to be functioning in a proper and defensible manner. The price to be paid for the legitimate practice of constitutional law and decision-making in which 'justices are not merely politicians in robes'[1] might well be the occasional decision that fails to garner wide and unified public satisfaction. If people perceive that judges are acting in an appropriate and professional manner, they are more likely to accept or, at least, put up with decisions that they do not fully agree with. Alternatively, if judges are seen as simply politicians in fancy dress, people will begin to question whether the courts and their decisions are worthy of their respect and support. Legitimacy casts a long shadow over the work of Supreme Courts.

[1] Richard Fallon, *Law and Legitimacy in the Supreme Court* (Cambridge, Harvard University Press, 2018) x.

In this chapter, therefore, I will distil the jurisprudential literature that has sought to provide the appropriate and proper methods and practices that Supreme Courts should follow if they are to maintain a sufficient degree of public approval and legitimacy. First, I will lay out the political, social and intellectual context that prevailed after the Second World War and framed the jurisprudential task to be performed. The next three sections will introduce some of the leading American voices that have tended to dominate the debate about legitimacy in and around constitutional law and judicial decision-making – Herbert Wechsler introduced the disciplining metric of 'principled reasoning' that has come to permeate traditional approaches to normative accounts of constitutional law; Alexander Bickel addressed more directly how judicial review could be squared with the institutional demands of a modern democracy; and Ronald Dworkin continued the challenge of demonstrating that judicial decision-making was a special type of political analysis, but one that could be rightly distinguished from more partisan practices of political reasoning. Throughout the chapter, my ambition is to present these jurisprudential interventions in their best light in order to make any criticism of them more plausible and persuasive.

From One War to Another

The years after the Second World War were good ones for the United States and Canada. While the United Kingdom was struggling to recover from the social and economic ravages of a six-year war, the United States and Canada were thriving in terms of growth and prosperity. Fuelled in part by huge increases in immigration, both countries were asserting themselves as serious domestic and global nations. Canada put much of its efforts into reducing its ties with the United Kingdom and establishing for itself a strong and independent style of national government; it also began to lay the foundations for a broad welfare state. In contrast, the United States was more determined to utilise its domestic and economic strength in policing the world as the self-proclaimed champion of global democracy. However, in the 1950s and onwards, both Canada and the United States engaged in further belligerent actions (principally in Korea and Vietnam) as part of the united and cold front against China, Russia and Communist regimes generally.

Apart from the difficulties that came with burgeoning and more diverse populations, Canada and the United States had to deal with internal and structural challenges of disenfranchised minorities. A more homogenous Canada was less willing to confront the problems of its oppressive traditions against its indigenous and immigrant inhabitants, especially the Chinese.[2] However, the United States was soon faced with increasing pressure to remedy the long-standing wrongs of

---

[2] See, eg, Daniel Paul, *We Were not the Savages, First Nations History: Collision Between European and Native American Civilizations*, 4th edn (Halifax, Fernwood Publishing, 2022).

its historic racist and apartheid practices that still prevailed. After all, many black Americans had fought and died for their country in a war that was, in part, an effort to check a racist and fascist state, Germany. As such, it was difficult for the American government to remain entirely insensitive to the discriminatory conditions and grievances of black Americans generally. The push for desegregation was gathering momentum. Although many southern states were intransigent and unapologetic, the federal government began to take initiatives to deal more positively with the so-called race problem. As is so often the case in the United States,[3] it soon brought the Supreme Court and the Constitution into play. Although the Court's historical record was far from reassuring on race, there were signs that things might be different this time round in the 1950s.

The history of the American Supreme Court's interpretive stance on its constitutional responsibilities, let alone its performance on individual decisions on race, was a serious impediment to progress. Its 1896 decision in *Plessy v Ferguson* (that sanctioned a separate-but-equal defence) stood as a direct barrier,[4] but its overall approach to the Constitution was as much or more of a significant obstacle. During the New Deal of the 1930s, the Supreme Court had initially struck down government attempts to introduce social legislation; the main line was that the New Deal initiatives ran counter to the Constitution's guarantees of liberty and freedom. However, the progressive opposition to this was based on the alleged fact that the Court's Justices had allowed their own political and partisan preferences to contaminate constitutional law. In the famous words of Justice Holmes, 'the Constitution does not enact Mr. Herbert Spencer's Social Statics.'[5] The problem was that this push-back relied upon an account of judicial decision-making that, while successful in condemning the rightward lurch of the Court, managed to frame the Constitution in almost timeless and non-political terms: it was premised too closely on the idea that constitutional law should stand apart from and above the political and social values of the times. In a post-war and changing world, this kind of inorganic approach had more downs than ups.

Also, the realist assault on traditional formalism (ie, rules do not speak or apply themselves without judicial judgment on substantive values) and its obvious implications for constitutional law and decision-making meant that reliance on the notion of a fixed or detached Constitution was no longer tenable. So, the Supreme Court (and its juristic apologists) had to find a more legitimate and acceptable way to drag the Constitution into the second half of the twentieth century. As a result, a concerted effort was made to turn to an understanding of law as being a rational method through which social values and facts could be better understood and integrated into judicial work; the disciplines of economics, sociology and moral

---

[3] Alexis de Tocqueville, *Democracy in America*, vol 1 (Phillips Bradley (ed), New York, Alfred Knopf, 1945) 280 ('scarcely any political question arises in the United States that is not resolved, sooner or later, into a judicial question').

[4] *Plessy v Ferguson* (1896) 163 US 537.

[5] *Lochner v New York* (1905) 198 US 45, 75.

philosophy became more pertinent and relevant.[6] Consequently, when the newly minted Warren Court was faced in the mid-1950s with the desegregationist challenges presented by *Brown*, it sought to finesse any high-flying rhetoric about the Constitution's self-evident or transcending truths. Instead, it took a much more pragmatic and modest stance that relied upon available research into the psychological and social effects of segregated education – considering 'public education in light of its full development and its present place in American life throughout the Nation, ... to separate [black children] from others of similar age and qualifications solely because of their race generates a feeling of inferiority as to their status in the community that may affect their hearts and minds in a way unlikely to ever be undone.'[7]

Although the *Brown* decision was predictably divisive (and had a long and contested life in its attempted implementation), it put into play the idea that constitutional law was not a set body of rules that endured unchanged over the years. While there was little consensus on this, the idea of constitutional law as a doctrinal process, like the common law, that might evolve and change with the times began to gain currency. Indeed, the Warren Court gambled that the legitimacy of the Constitution would be better achieved and maintained by a Supreme Court that reflected the more modern views, albeit conflicted and often opposed, of a fresh generation of Americans; there was little professional reason as opposed to political will to insist that what was thought to be constitutional and just in the last decade of the nineteenth century (eg, the *Plessy* decision) was still appropriately considered to be constitutional and just in the mid-twentieth century. In a manner of speaking, the Supreme Court mined the strong contemporary sense that, after the sacrifices and abominations of Hitler's Nazism and Stalinesque communism, it was essential that the United States showed itself to be the very epitome of a democratic society.

In jurisprudential terms, the accompanying drive in legal academe was to combat the realist contagion and to ground constitutional law as a professional pursuit that stood apart from rank politics. To do this, the prevailing mind-set was to refocus attention on the general processes through which decisions were made rather than how individual rules were applied or substantive decisions reached. The ambition was to persuade officials and, as importantly, people that democratic legitimacy might be better sustained by developing and defending a range of 'decisions which are the *duly arrived at* result of *duly established* procedures'.[8] The thrust of this so-called Legal Process trend was that, provided these processes and procedures were respected and followed, the legitimacy of official institutions,

---

[6] Morton Horwitz, 'The Warren Court and The Pursuit of Justice' (1993) 50 *Washington and Lee Law Review* 5.

[7] *Brown v Board of Education of Topeka* (1954) 347 US 483, 492–94. For a socio-historical account of *Brown*, see Allan Hutchinson, *Is Eating People Wrong?: Great Legal Cases and How They Shaped the World* (Cambridge, Cambridge University Press, 2020) ch 5.

[8] Henry Hart Jr and Albert Sacks, *The Legal Process: Basic Problems in the Making and Application of Law* (Cambridge, s.n., 1958) 113.

especially the Supreme Court, might be maintained in a changing world and bring a much-needed stability. While this approach held an obvious appeal to lawyers and judges, the basic gambit was that reasonable men (and it was largely, of course, white and older men) acting reasonably would produce reasonable results. As such, this pitch built on the general view, at least among the elite, that the Constitution and its attendant doctrines were, despite disagreement and dissension, at their core 'necessary, right, and good'.[9] Notwithstanding the social turmoil that often followed, the law-changing decisions of the Warren Court were well served by this juristic line of defence.

As part of this focus on process as a response to the realist critique, these constitutional jurists still kept faith with the belief that there was a discernible and important distinction between the proper professional practice of law and its unacceptable political downgrading or degradation. If this were not the case, they argued that there would be no basis for people to accept as legitimate those decisions that fell outside their own preferred comfort zone. The central conceit was that constitutional law had its own body of principles that animated and distinguished it: these were not rules, but generalised norms that could be weighted and shaded as circumstances and facts dictated. Accordingly, rather than preach a discredited black-letter characterisation of constitutional law or accept that legal rules were a mere front for rule by unelected officials, these post-realist jurists offered a vision of constitutional decision-making that cast judges as the educators of an engaged and conscientious society in regard to the meaning and relevance of the Constitution's own lasting principles. The Court led, but only by virtue of its elevated and professional stature above and beyond the political branches of government.

This jurisprudential exercise was portrayed as a noble and high-minded undertaking in that the courts were viewed as a complementary partner in realising the larger democratic aspirations of republican governance. Yet, even within the elite ranks of legal theorists, this way of proceeding did not garner universal approval. Again, *Brown* proved to be a lightning rod. Whereas most were approving (or, at least, tolerant) of its progressive motivations and results, others had severe doubts about whether the decision could be squared with the primary and overriding principles of constitutional law that knitted it together in a consistent and mutually reinforcing whole: the existential struggle at the heart of constitutional law was between principle and politics, between form and substance, and between legal correctness and social justice. While there was growing agreement that a legitimate understanding and practice of constitutional law must be principle-driven, there was ample disagreement about the nature, content and ordering of these operative principles. So, it was not so much that constitutional jurists did away entirely with crude politics in constitutional law; it was whether they managed to keep it cabined within a disciplinary framework of principled decision-making.

---

[9] Lon Fuller, 'Positivism and Fidelity to Law: A Reply to Professor Hart' (1958) 71 *Harvard Law Review* 630, 642.

Although the leading constitutional theorists of the post-war decades (ie, Herbert Wechsler, Alexander Bickel and Ronald Dworkin) were committed to this principled account of constitutional law and decision-making, they all shared another significant, if unfortunate tendency – they were apologists for the existing substance and form of constitutional law and decision-making. It was not that they felt obliged to defend each and every decision of the courts or each and every judge's approach. But it was that they felt a deep commitment to the system as a whole: they blended the prescriptive and the descriptive. Theirs was a bootstrap manoeuvre in that, in offering an account of what constitutional courts should do to meet their institutional responsibilities, they could not resist making the claim that this is what they actually were doing. As neatly framed by a more contemporary fellow-traveller, they sought to provide 'an account that fits the … the decisions by the U.S. Supreme Court, while justifying the practice these data reveal'.[10] While the performance of this apologistic task demonstrated the jurists' extraordinary ingenuity and dexterity, it was no more convincing for that.

A Proper Herbert

When the 50-year-old Herbert Wechsler gave his Holmes Lecture in early April 1959, he was returning to Harvard from Columbia Law School where he had been a professor for over 20 years. He had been a visiting professor there in the 1956/57 academic year (at the same time as HLA Hart). During his limited time at Harvard (that Dean Griswold unsuccessfully tried to make permanent), Wechsler was beginning to formulate his own views on the jurisprudential dynamics of constitutional law in the post-*Brown* era. While heavily influenced by Hart and Sacks' Legal Process approach, he was also keen to stymie the more radical and disruptive influence of legal realism's claims about law's indeterminacy. He was on many counts, therefore, a middle-of-the-road jurist. While accepting that constitutional law was inevitably and inescapably about political choices among competing values, he insisted that its central problem was 'not the substance, but the method of decision' that was relied upon by judges.[11] For him, process was the parent to substance and its guardian.

As such, Wechsler was more prepared to place a demanding burden on adjudicative reasoning that asked judges not only to be rational and reasonable, but also to be principled in their reasoning. Her began his lecture – 'Toward

---

[10] Lawrence Lessig, *Fidelity & Constraint: How the Supreme Court Has Read the American Constitution* (Oxford, Oxford University Press, 2019) 2. For a more critical assessment of this manoeuvre, see Roberto Unger, 'The Critical Legal Studies Movement' (1983) 96 *Harvard Law Review* 561, 575 ('generalize from particular doctrines and intuitions, then hypostasize the generalizations into moral truth, and finally use the hypostasis to justify and correct the original material').

[11] Herbert Wechsler, 'Toward Neutral Principles of Constitutional Law' (1959) 73 *Harvard Law Review* 1, 23.

Neutral Principles of Constitutional Law' – by distancing himself from the previous year's Holmes Lecture by Learned Hand. He confessed that he had 'not the slightest doubt respecting the legitimacy of judicial review' and rejected Hand's position.[12] In his eyes, the Supreme Court has an institutional obligation to determine the meaning of the Constitution and to decide cases in line with that interpretation whether or not it involved the powers of the federal or state governments. For him, therefore, the key issue became 'what, if any, are the standards to be followed in interpretation.'[13] And it was to this task that he devoted the bulk of his lecture.

Emphasising the priority of 'an exercise of reason' over 'an act of willfulness', Wechsler recommended that the Supreme Court must never simply 'function as a naked power organ', but must studiously avoid '*ad hoc* evaluations'. In particular, he maintained that any resort to principles was not simply an instrumental ruse or 'manipulative tool' as it might be for politicians. Instead, the Court must 'decide on grounds of adequate neutrality and generality, tested not only by the instant application but by others that the principles imply'. This did not mean that no special weight was to be given to the text of the Constitution, the history of the Constitution or the precedents developed. Nevertheless, he contended that 'where they do not combine to make an answer clear – itself a matter to be judged, so far as possible, by neutral principles – by standards that transcend the case at hand.' Legitimacy, therefore, was assured not by whether decisions are liked or agreed with but because their decisions are 'asserted to have ... legal quality' that is conferred by the judicial obligation 'to be ... entirely principled'.[14]

In order to give these abstract recommendations some practical bite and illustration, Wechsler ran through some recent cases. In line with his admonition that 'the critic's role is the sustained, disinterested, merciless examination of the reasons that courts advance',[15] he pointed out where they did or did not meet his proposed interpretive standards of neutrality and generality.[16] However, he ran into serious difficulty when he focussed his critical attention on the particularly controversial areas of the constitutionality of racially restrictive covenants and segregated schools. For instance, he cavilled over 'why is the enforcement of the private covenant a state discrimination rather than a legal recognition of the freedom of the individual.' Further, he condemned some decisions,

---

[12] ibid at 2. See also Learned Hand, *The Bill of Rights* (Cambridge, Harvard University Press, 1958).

[13] Wechsler, above n 11 at 10–11.

[14] ibid at 11–12, 15, 17, 19. Wechsler tweaked this slightly a couple of years later when he wrote that 'the demand of neutrality is that a value and its measure be determined by a general analysis that gives no weight to accidents of application, finding a scope that is acceptable whatever interest, group, or person may assert the claim'; Herbert Wechsler, *Principles, Politics, and Fundamental Law* (Cambridge, Harvard University Press, 1961).

[15] Wechsler (n 11) at 20.

[16] For example, he took the Supreme Court to task in *Carter v Carter Coal Co* (1936) 298 US 238 and *United States v Butler* (1936) 297 US 1 where he concluded that 'some of the principles affirmed by the Court were strikingly deficient in neutrality'; Wechsler (n 11) at 23.

like *Shelley* and *Black*, as '*ad hoc* determinations of their narrow problems, yielding no neutral principles for their extension or support'.[17]

Nevertheless, Wechsler's real problems began to come to light in his critique of *Brown*. Professing to be supportive of its outcome, he threw up his hands at the fact that he saw no available or convincing neutral principle that was capable of resolving the selective and inconsistent thrust of the Court's analysis. As such, he concluded that *Brown* was not a decision that in its all-important reasoning met the Wechslerian exacting standard of judicial legitimacy and appropriateness:

> For me, assuming equal facilities, the question posed by state-enforced segregation is not one of discrimination at all. Its human and its constitutional dimensions lie entirely elsewhere, in the denial by the state of freedom to associate, a denial that impinges in the same way on any groups or races that may be involved. I think, and I hope not without foundation, that the Southern white also pays heavily for segregation, not only in the sense of guilt that he must carry but also in the benefits he is denied …. But if the freedom of association is denied by segregation, integration forces an association upon those for whom it is unpleasant or repugnant …. Given a situation where the state must practically choose between denying the association to those individuals who wish it or imposing it on those who would avoid it, is there a basis in neutral principles for holding that the Constitution demands that the claims for association should prevail?[18]

But this is not at all convincing. Contrary to Wechsler's protestations, choosing to understand *Brown* in terms of freedom of association and not racial equality is the most profound of political decisions on its own terms. When considered in light of the historical context around racism in America, that choice becomes not only political, but also very partial; it is not at all clear why a social evil should be perpetuated simply because there was a failure of imagination among legal theorists to identify a faux-neutral principle. So, while Wechsler's effort to pitch white and black suffering as being on a par speaks for itself today, these arguments around *Brown* point up to some of the obvious challenges of Wechsler opting to hang his constitutional hat on the importance and primacy of neutral principles as a standard for legitimate judicial review:

- What counts as a principle?
- Can there be a truly neutral principle?
- Why is a neutral principle about politics not itself a political stance?
- What is so special anyway about neutrality or disinterestedness in matters of constitutional or social justice?

---

[17] Wechsler (n 11) at 29, 31. See *Shelley v Kraemer* (1948) 334 US 1, 14–23 and *Black v Cutter Labs* (1956) 351 US 292.

[18] Wechsler (n 11) at 34. It is worth noting that Wechsler was an assistant attorney-general in charge of the War Division during much of the Second World War. His responsibilities included overseeing internments on the West Coast and martial law in Hawaii. Although he opined that this internment was an 'abomination', he admits that, 'though in the line of duty as a lawyer I participated in the effort to sustain it in the Court'; ibid at 27. See *Korematsu v United States* (1944) 323 US 214.

- What is gained by putting neutral principles above substantive justice?
- Why is the style of reasoning more important than the substance of the result?[19]

While a requirement of principled decision-making might work, if it all, to contain the rare rogue judge with a penchant for arbitrary or capricious decision-making, it had little purchase for most judges. As such, Wechsler provided the icing on the constitutional cake, but he had little to say about the substantive ingredients and mix of that cake. His was, at bottom, a stylistic demand that could be met by most judges who took a conscientious and professional approach to their craft. In short, there was nothing in Wechsler's imperative for making decisions based upon neutral principles that would cramp the political leanings or constitutional agendas of judges. Indeed, framed in Wechslerian terms, an incorporation of neutral principles might enable those judges with a strong or even radical set of political values to clothe their judgments with a false appearance of impartiality and disinterestedness.[20]

All that said, there were so many motifs in Wechsler's work that would, for good and bad, influence the development of thinking about constitutional law and decision-making for many decades – that judicial review is a respite from the crude and unprincipled realm of legislative politics where there is no obligation 'to support its choice of values by the type of reasoned explanation that ... is intrinsic to judicial action';[21] that, even if judicial review is unavoidably about making value choices, legitimacy could be maintained by ensuring that decisions were based on principles *of* the Constitution, as Wechsler's lecture intimated, not simply *about* the Constitution; and that a reliance on principles, albeit differently and more substantively defined than Wechsler's for neutrality, would offer a genuine bulkhead that could protect judicial review from the disruptive infiltration of realist ideas; and that the formal style of judicial decisions could be as important as or, sometimes, more important than the substantive result of the decision made.

So, Wechsler can be read as offering an invitation to follow his lead and provide a more principled and rigorous defence of judicial review. Although Wechsler himself did not change or dilute the strength of his commitment to neutral principles as a panacean remedy for the ills of constitutional decision-making, others were not slow to take up the challenge that he had implicitly laid down. There was no shortage of jurists who, although criticising Wechsler's ideas and proposals, made serious efforts to supplement and thereby better realise his theoretical and rationalising ambitions. The two most well-known and influential exponents were Alexander Bickel and Ronald Dworkin.

---

[19] I will deal much more extensively with each of these difficulties and criticisms throughout the book, especially in chapter 4. However, for a useful summary of the immediate response to Wechsler's defence of neutral principles, see Reva Siegel, 'Equality Talk: Antisubordination and Anticlassification Values in Constitutional Struggles Over Brown' (2004) 117 *Harvard Law Review* 1470, 1489–97.

[20] An example of this might be Chief Justice Robert's opinion in support of a race-blind approach. See *Students for Fair Admissions, Inc v President and Fellows of Harvard College* (2023) 600 US 181.

[21] Wechsler (n 11) at 16.

In a Bickel

Like Herbert Wechsler, Alexander Bickel clerked at the Supreme Court; he with Justice Felix Frankfurter and Wechsler with Justice Harlan Stone.[22] Before that, he had immigrated to New York from Romania in 1939 as a 14-year-old. After graduating from Harvard in 1949, he worked for the US State Department in Europe. On his return to the United States in 1952, he was responsible for drafting the memo by Justice Frankfurter that demanded successfully that *Brown* should be reargued. He then joined the Yale law faculty and remained there until his early death in 1974 at 50. By any standards, his was a fruitful and influential career in constitutional law and theory. Along with Wechsler, he became 'probably the most creative constitutional theorist of his generation'.[23] Like Wechsler, Bickel emphasised the importance of principled reasoning in meeting the Supreme Court's legitimacy challenge. But, unlike Wechsler, he went beyond the idea that such judicial reasoning should be normatively neutral or politically unaligned in content or direction. He put some substantive political flesh on the bare Wechslerian skeleton.

The special focus of Bickel's work was a more in-depth appreciation of how judicial review could be squared with the institutional demands of a modern democracy. From the get-go, he fully accepted that judges could not avoid becoming embroiled in political disputes and that, on face value, the Supreme Court was more of a threat than a helpmate to society's democratic ambitions and commitments. Indeed, in a famous phrase, he highlighted 'the counter-majoritarian difficulty' as the central challenge of constitutional law and jurisprudence: judicial review runs so fundamentally against the basic precepts of democratic governance that it might actually 'weaken the democratic process'.[24] Accordingly, in order to offer any kind of justification for a judicial finding of unconstitutionality on the part of the legislative or executive branches of government, Bickel was adamant that there must be a disciplined mode of judicial performance that could fit safely

---

[22] A pervasive problem is that many professors at the leading law schools, including and especially legal and constitutional theorists, have clerked for Supreme Court judges. While it is not always the case (as the critical scholars, Duncan Kennedy and Mark Tushnet, were also Supreme Court clerks), young and talented students are still encouraged to become judicial clerks. This has a general tendency to co-opt budding theorists and to encourage them to defend and rationalise the work of the courts; they become apologists for that judicial process, not potential and detached critics of it.

[23] John Ely, *Democracy and Distrust: A Theory of Judicial Review* (Cambridge, Harvard University Press, 1980) 71. For a similar endorsement, see Anthony Kronman, 'Alexander Bickel's Philosophy of Prudence' (1985) 94 *Yale Law Journal* 1567.

[24] Alexander Bickel, *The Least Dangerous Branch: The Supreme Court and the Bar of Politics* (Indianapolis, Bobbs-Merrill, 1962) 21–23. This difficulty has been evaluated to be 'the central obsession of modern constitutional scholarship'. Barry Friedman, 'The History of The Counter-Majoritarian Difficulty, Part One: The Road to Judicial Supremacy' (1998) 73 *New York University Law Review* 333, 334. Also, it is fair to report that the counter-majoritarian difficulty has late 18th century origins. See Jesse Choper, 'The Supreme Court and The Political Branches: Democratic Theory and Practice' (1974) 122 *University of Pennsylvania Law Review* 810.

and convincingly within the broader understandings of democracy and popular rule. He took Wechsler's basic theme and ran with it:

> judicial review is the principled process of enunciating and applying certain enduring values of our society ... the root idea is that the process is justified only if it injects into representative government something that is not already there; and that is principle, standards of action that derive their worth from a long view of society's spiritual as well as material needs and that command adherence, whether or not an immediate outcome is expedient or agreeable.[25]

Bickel set about developing this 'root idea' by relying upon two principal and extended themes – principled reasoning and passive virtues. As regards the former, it is immediately apparent that he understood principled reasoning in a much broader context and with a much richer meaning than Wechsler. For Bickel, although Wechsler's argument for neutral principles did encourage greater coherence and consistency in judicial decisions and respected the values embedded in the Constitution itself, he construed neutral principles as being only one part, albeit a very important one, of a more flexible and prudent account of constitutional law and decision-making. An exclusive reliance on them would not only be detrimental to the overall role of the Supreme Court as the dependable guardian of the Constitution's fundamental and enduring values, but it would also be counter-productive to an overall advancement of democratic rule: 'no viable society can be principle-ridden.'[26] As such, Bickel was much more functional and strategic than hidebound or idealistic in his account of constitutional law and judicial review. Indeed, mindful of the Supreme Court's always parlous democratic legitimacy, he was cognisant that a Wechslerian abstractness had a 'tyrannical tendency' and could lead to a 'a dictatorship of the self-righteous'.[27]

The second aspect of his constitutional account was that the Supreme Court should recognise that discretionary inaction was sometimes the better part of constitutional valour. While Wechsler concentrated on how the Supreme Court should use its power and authority, he did not address the neglected issue of when it should do that. Bickel addressed and made a mainstay of his account the idea that there are numerous occasions when it is unwise and even undemocratic to decide cases. So, as well as being able to validate or invalidate legislation or executive action in line, the courts can and should sometimes do neither. In the very act of refusing to decide, Bickel claimed to have hit upon 'the secret of [the Supreme Court's] ability to maintain itself in the tension between principle and expediency'.[28] These so-called passive virtues – doctrines such as standing, mootness and ripeness – will allow the Supreme Court to maintain an important and

---

[25] Bickel, *Least Dangerous*, above n 24 at 58.
[26] ibid at 59–64.
[27] Alexander Bickel, *The Morality of Consent* (New Haven, Yale University Press, 1975) 12, 142.
[28] Bickel, *Least Dangerous*, above n 24 at 69.

ample legitimacy.[29] Moreover, a modest and restrained judiciary would fulfil a more appropriate role in in a supposedly democratic republic and allay genuine fears about the courts overstepping their political mark: 'it is quite wrong for the Court to relieve [legislators] of this burden of self-government.'[30]

For Bickel, therefore, democracy required a robust balancing act between satisfying the short-term contingent views of the majority and, at the same, defending the longer-term values that preserve the overall and underlying democratic values of society. Whereas elections and representative democracy were able to do the former, it was for an institution like the Supreme Court to ensure that the latter was also safeguarded: 'the Court should declare as law only such principles as will – in time, but in a rather immediate foreseeable future – gain general assent.'[31] The role of the courts was both defended and justified in the fact of its non-democratic identity and *modus operandi*: the judges were to be 'teachers to the citizenry' and to be engaged in 'a continuing colloquy' with them.[32]

For all this fine-sounding rhetoric and appeals to fundamental values, there was a clear and relatively conservative subtext to Bickel's writings. Although he put constitutional law and reasoning front and centre within the debate over democratic practice and theory, his brand of democracy verged on the aristocratic and was almost condescending in its thrust and organisational imperatives; he paid little more than lip service to popular participation. For him, judges and jurists were teachers, and citizens were pupils and listeners; judges are people with 'the leisure, the training, and the insulation to follow the ways of the scholar in pursuing the ends of government'.[33] This results in less of a conversation between equals and more of a civics lesson. Also, like Wechsler, Bickel makes a serious mistake in thinking that democracy is primarily about majoritarianism. While the legislature and elected officials have more of a democratic mandate than courts, this does not mean that those governmental actors have an entirely legitimate and defensible mandate. There is a democratic deficit all across the different branches of government; politicians' legitimacy is far more tentative and tenuous than Wechsler, Bickel and many others, both inside and outside of academe, assume; it is simply a different kind of democratic shortfall than hobbles courts.

Bickel's elitist portrayal of democratic practice and ideals is revealed in his response to the Warren Court as it got into its liberal stride on civil rights and related matters in the 1960s. In his later work, he attacked that Court for what he saw as its misuse of history, its sloppy reasoning, and sometimes what he liked to identify as arbitrary results (ie, results that he did not approve of or did not align

---

[29] ibid at 111–198. See also Alexander Bickel, 'The Supreme Court 1960 Term' (1961) 75 *Harvard Law Review* 40.

[30] Bickel, *Least Dangerous*, above n 24 at 156.

[31] ibid at 239.

[32] ibid at 69, 240.

[33] ibid at 25–26.

with his political leanings).[34] His championing of passive virtues and his treatment of constitutional law as a process of common law development reflected a Whiggish and almost Burkean attitude. For him, constitutional law should eschew a purely rationalist approach by building on as it extended its own traditions and values: 'we do well to remain attached to institutions that are often the products more of accident than of design, or that no longer answer to their original plans, but that challenge our resilience and inventiveness in bending old arrangements to present purposes with no outward change.'[35] Not surprisingly, therefore, he challenged the legitimacy of the liberal and substantive work of the Warren Court not directly, but by focussing on what he perceived as its argumentative and justificatory failings (ie, it did not 'act rigorously on principle'[36]).

That said, Bickel's measured and modest recommendations about how Supreme Court judges should act continues to have its devotees. Yet there is something slightly misleading about it as a means by which to avoid politically charged issues in constitutional law. The decision to remain passive in the face of political divisions is itself also a highly political position; it takes a stance by refusing to take a stance. In striving to negotiate a cautious response to 'the tension between principle and expediency', the judges must exercise political judgment about the where and when of passivity; fence-sitting is a political tradition in itself.[37] As such, following on from Wechsler, Bickel developed further the need for a principled approach to constitutional decision-making. In doing so, he leavened the austere fundamentalism of Wechsler's approach with a helping of political and pragmatic expediency. Unfortunately, as much as he improved on the Wechslerian initiative, he threw in a few additional problems of his own. Again, it was another effort to finesse politics that managed to hide in plain sight the politics of judicial review.

Getting Political

Ronald Dworkin has had a massive influence over contemporary jurisprudence and constitutional theory. After a storied student career, he turned down a clerking offer with Justice Frankfurter. Instead, he opted to stay in New York and work for Justice Learned Hand. Indeed, in 1957, he researched and helped

---

[34] Alexander Bickel, *The Supreme Court and the Idea of Progress* (New York, Harper & Row, 1970) and Alexander Bickel, *Morality*, above n 27. For an approving commentary, see John Moeller, 'Alexander M. Bickel: Toward a Theory of Politics' (1985) 47 *Journal of Politics* 113.

[35] Alexander Bickel, *Reform and Continuity: The Electoral College, the Convention, and the Party System* (New York, Harper & Row, 1971) 3.

[36] Bickel, *Least Dangerous*, above n 24 at 69.

[37] If Cass Sunstein is an academic advocate of this approach, then Chief Justice Roberts is a judicial disciple of a Bickelian institutionalism. See, eg, Cass Sunstein, 'Constitutional Personae: Heroes, Soldiers, Minimalists, and Mutes' (2015) 262 *Publishers Weekly* 49 and *National Federation of Independent Business v Sebelius* (2012) 567 US 519.

to draft Hand's Holmes Lecture on *The Bill of Rights*.[38] After a short spell at a New York law firm, Dworkin went on to become a Yale law professor where he crossed constitutional swords with both Alexander Bickel and Robert Bork. On Hart's retirement in 1969, he occupied the Chair of Jurisprudence at Oxford University at the young age of 38. Throughout his prolific academic career until his death in 2014, he championed an unrelenting anti-positivist jurisprudence and an account of constitutional decision-making that insisted that 'justice plays a role in fixing what the law is'.[39]

Dworkin's self-imposed challenge was, much like Wechsler's and Bickel's, to demonstrate how judicial decision-making can be distinguished from 'the ad hoc in politics' by its reliance upon a more principled and disciplined mode of legal reasoning. Although he was not given to recognising the influence of his teachers and mentors, his work can be profitably understood as drawing together different jurisprudential elements from others – like Hart, he made philosophy the motor of his jurisprudential theorising, but distanced himself from its prevailing positivistic rendering; like Hart and Sacks, he looked to the courts as an avenue for reasoned elaboration, but rejected the prominent role of policy in adjudication; like Wechsler, he emphasised the need for principled decision-making, but claimed not to be hampered by the false allure of neutrality; and, like Fuller, he insisted on the unavoidable moral element to law and its adjudicative function, but abandoned the notion that this moral dimension was limited to procedural values rather than substantive commitments. In short, Dworkin developed a theory of law that carried on the prevailing legal process tradition, but added a significant and particular political twist to it – judicial decision-making was a special type of political reasoning, not something different from or a stark alternative to it.

Dworkin's formative years as a jurist were during the heyday of the Warren Court from 1953 to 1969. In sharp contrast to Bickel, he thought that the work of the Court in addressing civil rights and offering liberal solutions was the apogee of American constitutional law. But, for him, it became important to show how this liberal period was not simply an aberration or respite from the Supreme Court's overall conservative tradition and pedigree. He set himself the enormous philosophical task of not only defending how such judicial decision-making was preferable as a matter of partisan politics, but also explaining why this way of proceeding brought into force the real or true meaning of the Constitution: 'a proposition of law is true if it flows from principles of personal and political morality that provide the best interpretation of the other propositions generally treated as true in contemporary legal practice.'[40] On this basis,

---

[38] Ironically, in light of his later writings, Dworkin contributed to the strength of Hand's critique of a robust version of judicial review in a democratic republic. See Hand, *Bill of Rights*, above n 12.

[39] Ronald Dworkin, *Justice in Robes* (Cambridge, Belknap Press, 2006) 35.

[40] ibid at 14.

he claimed to offer and defend a more 'noble vision'[41] of what law both was and could be:

> members of a genuine political community ... accept that they are governed by principles, not just by rules hammered out in political compromise [;] ... their political rights and duties are not exhausted by the particular decisions that their political institutions have reached, but depend, more generally, on the scheme of principles those decisions presuppose and endorse.[42]

Dworkin's account of democracy (and the integral role of the judiciary), therefore, was different from that of both Wechsler and Bickel. For him, while a majoritarian conception of democracy presupposes that 'it is always unfair when a political majority is not allowed to have its way', a constitutional conception of democracy requires the majoritarian procedures to be constrained 'out of a concern for equal status of citizens, and not out of any commitment to the goals of majority rule'.[43] So, because democracy is about more than counting preferences, judicial review can play a vital and necessary role in advancing and protecting 'a constitution of principle that lays down general, comprehensive moral standards that government must respect'.[44] Understood in this way, Dworkin is able to note that judicial review would be neither undemocratic nor anti-democratic because it advances the overall project of democracy: 'a judge who is insulated from the demands of the political majority whose interests the [constitutional] right would trump is, therefore, in a better position to evaluate the argument'.[45]

In order to perform this democratic-reinforcing and democratic-defining role, Dworkin maintains that judges will need to make decisions that are 'deeply and thoroughly political ..., but not a matter of personal or partisan politics'.[46] Appearing to abandon the pretence of neutrality, he believes that this can be done by adopting a view of 'law as integrity' in which 'law is structured by a coherent set of principles about justice and fairness'.[47] He advocated a judicial approach that both emboldened and disciplined judges by asking them to combine the twin virtues of fit (ie, decisions must be consistent with the existing body of principles and precedents) and justification (ie, decisions must make the political best out of those principles and precedents). In vigorously pursuing such a constructivist course of action, the judges as unelected officials would not only be meeting the institutional and power-separating demands of a constitutional democracy, but would also be defending and advancing the substantive quality of a liberal

---

[41] Ronald Dworkin, *Life's Dominion: An Argument About Abortion, Euthanasia, and Individual Freedom* (New York, Vintage Books, 1994) 122.

[42] Ronald Dworkin, *Law's Empire* (Cambridge, Belknap Press, 1986) 211.

[43] Ronald Dworkin, *Freedom's Law: The Moral Reading of the American Constitution* (Cambridge, Harvard University Press, 1996) 17.

[44] Dworkin, *Life's Dominion*, above n 41 at 119.

[45] Ronald Dworkin, 'Hard Cases' (1975) 88 *Harvard Law Review* 1057, 1062.

[46] Ronald Dworkin, *A Matter of Principle* (Cambridge, Harvard University Press, 1985) 146.

[47] Dworkin, *Law's Empire*, above n 42 at 244.

democracy as administrators of justice. In Dworkin's hands, constitutional decision-making was presented as both a professional and political enterprise in equal measure. As such, it was meant to merit popular acceptance and could achieve political legitimacy.

Pitched at this level of philosophical abstraction, Dworkin's theory of constitutional law and decision-making has much to recommend it. However, the political devil is in the operational detail. He maintains that, if this judicial task is performed properly, it will manifest itself in a Constitution that incorporates those 'moral standards' and 'principles' that comprise a left-liberal version of democratic politics (ie, his own preferred political values). Accordingly, Dworkin contended that constitutional decisions or developments that did not reflect such a general thrust would not only be undesirable and undemocratic, but would be flat wrong as a matter of constitutional truth and validity. Even at face value, this is a wildly audacious claim to defend; it stretches credulity to think that the Constitution always has one right answer to any particular dispute and that this answer aligns with the jurist's own vision of democratic and constitutional justice. Any serious grasp of basic legal insights suggests that the gap between general principle and specific application cannot be easily or uncontestably closed: principles compete with each other and their weighting is variable in changing contexts and circumstances.[48]

Even the most cursory grasp of constitutional history reveals that Dworkin's characterisation of judicial review as being a reliable (let alone a primary) forum for the advancement of progressive or even liberal politics was woefully mistaken; it confounds any reasonable sense of history or politics. Except in the 1960s and 1970s, the courts have consistently been conservative and establishment-favouring bodies. The Warren Court was very much the exception that proved the rule: judges as a whole are not in the serious business of advancing a consistently liberal agenda. Indeed, the evidence is that they often do quite the opposite.[49] As both a leading jurist and strategic thinker, Dworkin made a calculated gamble that the Supreme Court was more likely to deliver the liberal goods than not. And, it has to be said, he lost that wager: he (and those liberals that he influenced) were throwing good political and jurisprudential money after bad. By lionising the Warren Court as the epitome of constitutional law-making, Dworkin was doing a grave disservice to the liberal and progressive cause. The reactionary performance of the Supreme Court in the decade since Dworkin's death in 2013 has made that assessment accurate in depressing and emphatic ways.

---

[48] Jack Balkin, *Living Originalism* (Cambridge, Belknap Press, 2011) 44 ('Although the persuasive power of principles may originate from how we expect they will apply when we argue for them, their jurisdiction, their scope, their weight, and the kinds of practices they regulate can shift over time.').

[49] See, eg, Mark Tushnet, *Red, White, and Blue: A Critical Analysis of Constitutional Law* (Cambridge, Harvard University Press, 1988) and Adam Cohen, *Supreme Inequality: The Supreme Court's Fifty-Year Battle for a More Unjust America* (New York, Penguin Press, 2020).

Indeed, Dworkin's writings must bear some responsibility for shoring up the legitimacy of the Supreme Court in troubled times. Although he would be horrified by the recent conservative turn in law and politics and would have undoubtedly condemned it as a willful betrayal of the American constitutional tradition, he contributed to the widespread sense that it is the Supreme Court, not the legislature or executive branch of government, that is the final and most favoured guardian of constitutional values. Insofar as liberals and progressives now want to abandon or severely limit the role of judges and courts in democratic politics,[50] Dworkin's apologistic jurisprudence has made that possibility more remote. Even though he claimed to be a democrat at heart and justified his legal theory in democratic terms, his work has had the perverse effect of not only making an unelected and largely unaccountable body – the Supreme Court – the central pivot of American democracy, but also providing legitimacy to its conservative rendition of the Constitution itself. This is both a tragedy and a travesty for all concerned.

Conclusion

Consequently, Herbert Wechsler, Alexander Bickel and Ronald Dworkin's efforts to provide the Supreme Court with a much-needed way of proceeding that can confer legitimacy on their decisions and the development of constitutional law fails. Despite the reasonable motivations of this jurisprudential triumvirate, the unifying rationale for relying upon a principled mode of decision-making to confront and meet the democratic objections to judicial review cannot succeed – it hides or elides the inescapable political and partisan dimensions of judicial decision-making in constitutional law. Indeed, it can be argued that these jurists' failed efforts to offer a solution to the democratic challenge had the effect of preparing the ground for the rise and contemporary ascendancy of originalism as the principled basis for grasping and developing the content of American constitutional law.[51] So, I next turn to the range of constitutional theories that have established themselves in contemporary constitutional discourse and demonstrate their efforts to make good on the promise of principled reasoning as an escape from and as a seawall against the tides of raw political contestation that threaten to flood and saturate constitutional law.

---

[50] Jonathan Gould, 'Puzzles of Progressive Constitutionalism' (2022) 135 *Harvard Law Review* 2053, 2100 ('A more systemic critique contends that progressives have more to fear from the Court than its current composition. On this view, progressives should seek to disempower the Court in order to advance both their agendas and democracy more broadly'.)

[51] See ch 4.

4

In Search of Principles:
From Origins to Equilibrium

For those who defend the need for and possibility of principled reasoning, it is championed as a convenient and convincing way to meet two pressing needs. It is assumed by its proponents to stand between and be distinguishable from two other important styles of argumentation. First, principled reasoning is contrasted with an implausible practice of impersonal rule-based adjudication as a viable basis for judicial decision-making and law's development. If this is ever possible, it is certainly not so in matters of constitutional law when political values and social interests are so evidently in play. Secondly, it is viewed as a hedge against open-ended political haggling; this is considered to be presumptively invalid for the judicial application and development of constitutional law. The underlying justification is that 'only opinions which are grounded in reason' and which possess 'the underpinning of principle' can 'carry the weight which has to be carried by the opinions of a tribunal which, after all, does not in the end have the power either in theory or in practice to ram its own personal preferences down other people's throats'.[1] This is a considerable weight for principled reasoning to carry in a world in which constitutional law looms larger and larger in resolving matters of significant political, moral and social conflict.

As such, therefore, depending on where the jurist's allegiances lie, principled reasoning is understood to be either located in the attractive sweet-spot between an unconvincing practice of rule-based reasoning and open-ended politicking or it falls precipitously through the substantial gap between those established judicial ways of proceeding. The problem is that, as important as principled reasoning is considered to be, it is not up to the challenge that it is supposed to meet. Almost all good faith arguments can claim to be principled in selection and implementation; there is little about principled reasoning that places any real check on judges when they are fulfilling their constitutional role.[2] Furthermore, the claim to be engaging in principled reasoning does not mean that such exponents are acting in a neutral or apolitical fashion; there is no place to stand or work from that can exempt itself

---

[1] Henry Hart Jr, 'The Supreme Court, 1958 Term – Foreword: The Time Chart of the Justices' (1959) 73 *Harvard Law Review* 84, 99.

[2] The condition of 'good faith' is no small issue. For an extended discussion of what that entails, see ch 5.

from political affiliation or infiltration. In short, no matter what the kind of content or identity of principled reasoning that is relied upon, it cannot provide the type of convincing answers to the thorny questions of validity and legitimacy that permeate constitutional decision-making and doctrinal development.

In this chapter, therefore, I will take the traditional efforts to address the legitimacy problem in constitutional law and judicial decision-making to task. I begin by surveying and categorising the raft of theories that have been offered to operationalise the nature of principled reasoning and to demonstrate how a particular theory completes the traditional project. The next section takes a deeper dive into this reliance on principled reasoning and exposes its flaws and failings. After that, I concentrate on and reject the claim that such reasoning can be done in a neutral manner that transcends or obviates dependence on a particular or partisan view of constitutional justice. Next, I take strong issue with the current back-to-basics preference for originalist approaches to constitutional law that claims to deliver a detached and true accounting of what the Constitution demands in difficult or divisive cases. Finally, I examine the contemporary responses to originalism as they seek to put a more organic and progressive understanding of constitutional law on a better footing. Throughout the chapter, my objective is to clear the jurisprudential ground for a more convincing account of what it means to take seriously the idea that law is inescapably political in all its manifestations.

A Raft of Theories

Alexis de Tocqueville was nothing else if not prescient. He famously warned that 'there is almost no political question that does not sooner or later resolve itself into a judicial question'.[3] Since he first stated this in the 1830s, it has become more, not less, the case: the Supreme Court has not only been at the centre of American politics, but it has consolidated its position as the primary and most authoritative voice on the resolution of the contested political and social issues of the day. It might also be added that 'political questions' do not so much transmute themselves into 'legal questions', but also remain political in nature and resolution when they become legal questions; the venue and discourse changes, but the basic politicalness of the question remains. In a society that holds itself out as being committed to and acting as the standard bearer of democratic governance, this means that the fundamental task for theorists and practitioners is to explain and justify how to square the centrality and primacy of the Supreme Court with the basic tenets and thrust of democracy. In short, as phrased by the Supreme Court itself, 'the Court's legitimacy depends on making legally principled decisions under circumstances

---

[3] Alexis de Tocqueville, *Democracy in America* (Stephen Grant tr, Indianapolis, Hackett Publishing, 2000) 122.

in which their principled character is sufficiently plausible to be excepted by the nation.'[4]

Not surprisingly, much constitutional scholarship over the past 50 years has been preoccupied with devising and developing appropriate interpretive methodologies that can be relied upon by judges to fulfil their constitutional responsibilities. While there is an underlying and widely shared assumption among judges and jurists that the Constitution is, at its heart, 'necessary, right, and good',[5] this is where any agreement stops; there is widespread disagreement over the particular and precise ways in which the Constitution is or can be 'right' and 'good'. As such, there are a large number of different theories that claim to provide and defend an account of how and what the Constitution means both in general and in specific instances. Although there is a raft of explanatory and predictive theories on offer to guide judges, these proposed frameworks are also intended to work as life-rafts to protect judges who feel adrift and vulnerable on a broad swirling sea of constitutional politics. By following a certain theory, it is recommended that judges can act in a principled and professional manner that avoids the dangerous currents and stormy waves of political contestation. However, with the proliferation of competing constitutional theories and accounts, the challenge is to decide which theories are worth following and which are not.

In the principled spirit of Wechsler, Bickel and Dworkin, these different theories look to the imperatives of formal objectivity and substantive justice: there is a felt need to provide some method or technique by which judges can give meaning to the Constitution that is both capable of giving substantive direction and consistency to decisions reached and that is itself not reducible to only their own (or an enabling jurist's) political and moral commitments. Indeed, at the core of many of these modern efforts is the audacious claim that it is judges' non-democratic status (ie, being unaccountable and unrepresentative) that guarantees the institutional and intellectual detachment necessary to ensure that fundamental and contested matters of political justice are addressed and resolved in an impartial and legal way. As such, judges are heralded as better placed and, therefore, better able to protect democracy against its own excesses: it is their very detached and professional nature that underwrites their democratic legitimacy and commitment. Of course, few jurists recommend that the adoption of their theories can relieve judges entirely of the need to make controversial choices. In the contemporary milieu of constitutional adjudication, there is nothing wholly formulaic or mechanical about their operation.[6] However, the reliance on one method over another will have a significant orientating effect on the evidence used, the arguments made and, particularly, the results reached. In this important sense, constitutional theories count.

---

[4] *Planned Parenthood of Southeastern Pennsylvania v Casey* (1992) 505 US 833, 866.

[5] Lon Fuller, 'Positivism and Fidelity to Law: A Reply to Professor Hart' (1957) 71 *Harvard Law Review* 630, 642.

[6] Some do get very close to maintaining such a possibility. In particular, variants of originalism do suggest that constitutional interpretation can be done in a largely formalistic manner. See pp 55–58.

So, whether by way of grand theorising or through case-by-case criticisms, judges and jurists have sought to understand and handle the tensions between power and principle, politics and personnel, tradition and change, and much else besides in accounting for the performance and perils of constitutional adjudication. Some of the leading and most popular accounts on offer within the constitutionalist canon include:[7]

- *Deep Moralists* – While accepting that a principled approach is essential, these adherents contend that this cannot be done in an entirely 'general' or 'neutral' way. For them, constitutional adjudication demands that judges make political and moral choices, but not of a partisan or personal kind. The law is considered to possess its own deep political morality that undergirds and informs the Constitution: it is for judges to identify it, develop it consistently and apply it to the particular matter at hand.[8] Although this obliges judges to confront and negotiate the world of ideological contestation, this is a task that cannot and should not be shied away from. But, by making such choices in a principled and professionally mandated way, they can work with and within the important tension between the law as it is and the law as it ought to be.

- *Originalists* – Unpersuaded that the moralist task can be completed without playing politics of the most basic and unmitigated kind, these jurists advocate a way of proceeding that builds on the idea that the Constitution had an objective and stable meaning when enacted and that this should govern judicial review going forward. Although there is much internal debate about how that original meaning is to be fixed and applied today, the predominant thrust is to give substantive and practical bite to the text's sweeping and abstract declarations by determining what they meant in the founding society at that time.[9] If people do not like the results of that adjudicative responsibility, originalists insist that it is for politicians, not judges, to amend or update the Constitution.

- *Organicists* – Distinguishing themselves from those who want to fix the Constitution with a stable and unchanging meaning, they look beyond such bygone values and pre-commitments. Instead, they posit a Constitution that is dynamic in character and adaptable to the changing social, political and technological context.[10] Treating the Constitution as a living tradition that can evolve and

---

[7] Some jurists who provided helpful typologies of constitutional theories that still remain relevant today are Philip Bobbitt, *Constitutional Fae: Theory of the Constitution* (New York, Oxford University Press, 1982) and Thomas Baker, 'Constitutional Theory in a Nutshell' (2004) 13 *The William and Mary Bill of Rights Journal* 57. I have drawn my classificatory scheme from earlier work. The text represents a revised and reworked scheme from Allan Hutchinson, *Democracy and Constitutions: Putting Citizens First* (Toronto, University of Toronto Press, 2021) ch 2.

[8] See, eg, Ronald Dworkin, *Law's Empire* (Cambridge, Harvard University Press, 1986).

[9] See, for example, Antonin Scalia, *A Matter of Interpretation: Federal Courts and the Law* (Princeton, Princeton University Press, 1997).

[10] See, for example, David Strauss, 'Common Law Constitutional Interpretation' (1996) 63 *University of Chicago Law Review* 877 and Wilfrid Waluchow, *A Common Law Theory of Judicial Review: The Living Tree* (Cambridge, Cambridge University Press, 2007).

grow, they rely upon the Constitution's broad principles and update them in a way that better responds to the conditions and conundrums of contemporary society. It is not that this results in an anything-goes approach, but encourages one that trades off in a principled way tradition and innovation within the natural limits of the Constitution.

- *Pragmatists* – Abandoning the grander and overambitious claims of the deep moralists, the originalists and the organicists, these jurists reject any dogmatic allegiance to any overarching interpretive methodology or basic constitutional compact. They hold that the work of judges is bounded by established legal doctrines, but not narrowly or legalistically so. Drawing upon established and practical traditions of legal argumentation, it is expected that judges will act in good faith and strive for reasoned justice under law. Emphasising judicial modesty and institutional restraint, they urge a prudent reliance upon received notions of justice and common sense.[11] As such, these jurists recommend that judges must be self-consciously reasonable about the approach they adopt, the reasons that they give, the decisions that they reach, and the innovations that they propose.

- *Dialogists* – There has been a turn to 'dialogue theory' as an alternative justification for judicial review. Judges and jurists have begun to accept that some reliance upon contested political commitments is not only inevitable, but also desirable. The basic recommendation is that the courts and the legislature should engage in an institutional conversation about the Constitution and its requirements on particular and pressing issues of the day. They aim to demonstrate that courts and legislatures have complementary roles that enable legislation to be carefully tailored to meet the government's political agenda and the Constitution's underlying values. Understood in this way, the hope is that judicial review on constitutional grounds brings 'a certain measure of vitality to the democratic process, in that it fosters both dynamic interaction and accountability amongst the various branches'.[12] In this way, it is asserted that courts and legislatures will be dialogic partners, not antagonists, in an institutional partnership to advance shared democratic goals.

- *Democratists* – Disenchanted by what they consider to be the failed efforts of almost all constitutional theories to confront successfully the counter-majoritarian dilemma, these jurists insist that the only way that courts can act legitimately is by hewing to the direct goals and ambitions of democracy itself. They recommend that judges must only and always act to ensure that representative channels of democracy are kept open so as to close the existential gap

---

[11] See, for example, Cass Sunstein, *Constitutional Personae* (New York, Oxford University Press, 2015) and Richard Fallon, *Law and Legitimacy in the Supreme Court* (Cambridge, Harvard University Press, 2018).

[12] *Bell ExpressVu Limited Partnership v Rex* [2002] 2 SCR 559, [62]. See also, for example, Mark Tushnet and Bojan Bugarič, *Power to the People: Constitutionalism in the Age of Populism* (New York, Oxford University Press, 2021).

between citizens and their elected representatives.[13] By doing so, it is maintained that judges can gain both political legitimacy as well as constitutional guidance from seeking to give expression to the marginalised and excluded voices of the citizenry in contributing to the ideological debates that shape government policy and practice.

For all their variety and range, each of these theories are connected by and share the basic idea that there is available a principled basis for both making arguments and reaching results that can meet the challenge of not reducing constitutional adjudication to 'ad hoc politics'.[14] Moreover, they each manage to succeed to a greater or lesser degree. But, most tellingly, they each are unable to claim that a preferred theory is somehow entirely successful at meeting the basic challenge. Indeed, whether one theory is better or worse than another is not simply based on their intellectual cogency and normative rigour. The ultimate criterion of choice is political in that a judge's selection of one theory to the exclusion of others is political – does that theory produce the kind of results that will more often than not align with that judge's or jurist's own sense of justice?

Underlying the different theories is an account of 'principled reasoning' that will make or break it as a theoretical construct. Each theory depends upon a convincing explanation of what principled reasoning is and how it can bridge the existential gap between juristic theory and judicial practice. Most pointedly, it must be able to do so in a way that does not itself fall foul of the imperative to do law and not politics. Within the self-defined parameters of modern jurisprudence, this is a fundamental demand for and requirement of any constitutional theory. If it is not able to do that, a particular theory will necessarily fail as a viable and valid account of constitutional adjudication in a democracy from both a descriptive (ie, what judges are doing) and prescriptive perspective (ie, what judges should be doing). Not surprisingly, it is my critical claim that the project of defining and justifying what is and is not principled reasoning is fated to fail on many different levels and in many different ways: it is a profoundly and fatally flawed enterprise. Accordingly, it is to a demonstration of this that I now turn.

A Principled Failure

For a standard of argumentation that is intended to carry so much weight in jurisprudential matters, 'principled reasoning' is a decidedly elusive and fragile

---

[13] See, for example, John Hart Ely, *Democracy and Distrust: A Theory of Judicial Review* (Cambridge, Harvard University Press, 1980) and Patrick Monahan, *Politics and the Constitution: The Charter, Federalism, and the Supreme Court of Canada* (Agincourt, Carswell, 1987).

[14] Herbert Wechsler, 'Toward Neutral Principles of Constitutional Law' (1959) 73 *Harvard Law Review* 1, 31. There are some overlaps between the different theories. For example, Jack Balkin offers an innovative blend of originalism and organicism. See Jack Balkin, *Living Originalism* (Cambridge, Belknap Press, 2011).

notion. That said, the basic idea is clearly meant to be that, by making reasoning conditional on being principled, it is supposed to underwrite the validity and force of conclusions reached that are in line with its demands. As such, it seems clear that principled reasoning is warranted to be superior to a kind of reasoning that involves a certain moral or value-laden dimension; it is a mode of persuasion or justification that provides a normative and animating basis for guiding reasoning or actions.[15] So, principled reasoning can be contrasted with calculated exercises in rationalisation, rule-fixated resolutions and other means of persuasion that are intended to be self-serving and spurious.

In the more jurisprudentially oriented language of constitutional legitimacy, principled reasoning is something that does not fall foul of the imperative to avoid mere politicking or ad hoc justification. By relying upon principled reasoning, its proponents contend that the outcomes reached not only become more compelling in themselves, but also respect and preserve the special character of constitutional decision-making in a democracy. It is assumed that a preference for reasoning that is principle-based will result in outcomes that are considered to be more ethically good than bad. In particular, a principle is said to be something that entails a willingness to act honestly in line with it, even if this leads to uncomfortable or inconvenient places; it cannot be 'reduced to a manipulative tool'.[16] By bestowing this virtuous quality on judicial decisions and judgments, constitutional law will become and be viewed as more legitimate: the fragile underpinnings of constitutional law will be reinforced and better able to resist criticism and even condemnation.

In asking principled reasoning to fulfil such an onerous responsibility, it might reasonably be assumed that the abstract identity of principles generally would be easily identifiable and broadly appreciated. However, this is not the case. It is not so much that principled reasoning does not exist, but that its nature is so wide and indeterminate that it fails to act as the effective disciplinary device that it is intended to be: it is unreliable in its vaunted capacity to distinguish principled reasoning in law from non-legal or other political modes of reasoning. In short, the identity and identification of principles is far from definitive or decisive. Of course, this might be part of the deceptive allure of the favoured reliance on principled reasoning – it lends itself to multiple meanings; it can be utilised to encompass and support a range of possible outcomes; and its efficacy depends on the very implicit kind of political choices that it is supposed to finesse.

Discussion about the role of principles in understanding law generally and their centrality to judicial decision-making is fairly commonplace. One particular focus is on how principles are said to be different from rules. An initial problem is that

---

[15] There is also the important category of reasoning that is motivated by 'bad faith'. I will deal with this problem at much greater length in a later chapter. See ch 5.

[16] Herbert Wechsler, above n 14 at 15. Indeed, some have refused to acknowledge that evil 'may have as much coherence and inner logic as good ones'. Fuller, above n 5 at 636.

certain norms are not easily identified as either a rule or a principle (eg, the protection of free speech). Also (and more importantly for my purposes), although some jurists place considerable reliance on this distinction,[17] the difference between rules and principles is not so obvious or significant. While principles tend to be broader and more general (eg, no one should profit from their own wrong) than more tailored and specific rules (eg, speed limits on roads), neither function in an all-or-nothing or conclusive way: they are both subject to discretionary weighting. Rules and principles both allow for exceptions, neither can fix decisively the scope of their operation, and both have to be traded off against other competing standards. Indeed, as Herbert Hart insisted, it is not that rules and principles are entirely different species, but that they both are differing parts of the same species – 'variable legal standards'.[18] Nevertheless, it can be concluded that legal principles are generalised norms that are obviously intended to be evaluative and judgmental in content and application.

What does this mean in the effort to explain and understand the nature and operation of principled reasoning in constitutional law? There are four particular implications that warrant consideration. First, there is the traditional conundrum that, even if it might be possible to isolate one ruling principle, there is considerable leeway in how such generalised norms can be applied in any specific and concrete context. So, if it is agreed that a certain principle can or should be controlling, it does not self-apply: there is always some gap that needs to be filled between the governance of the abstract principle and its authoritative application in practice. It is the existence of this gap that reintroduces the personal element of judicial choice; it reduces the sway of politics, but it does not eradicate it. As such legal principles can only get you so far, they must be supplemented by the judge's values to bridge that gap between general norms and specific circumstances. This does not mean that judges act in an arbitrary or irrational fashion, only that these values cannot be explained or justified by resort to any detached and objective methodology. The fact that Dworkin had to go to such lengths to meet this challenge by postulating an 'imaginary judge of superhuman intellectual power and patience',[19] Hercules, says much about the mortal possibility of fulfilling this task with any degree of precision, impartiality or predictability.

Secondly, it is not simply any principle that can count for adjudicative purposes, but only those that are legally and constitutionally-based in their derivation and source. As Wechsler noted, it is 'the kind of principled appraisal, in respect of values that can reasonably be asserted to have constitutional dimension, that alone is in the province of the courts'.[20] So judges cannot rely on any old principle that they like: a preferred principle must be found and anchored in

---

[17] See, for example, Ronald Dworkin, *Taking Rights Seriously* (London, Duckworth, 1977) 22–28 and Ronald Dworkin, *Law's Empire*, above n 8 at 15–20.

[18] HLA Hart, *The Concept of Law*, 2nd edn (Oxford, Clarendon Press, 1994) 130–33, 259–63.

[19] Ronald Dworkin, *Law's Empire*, above n 8 at 239 and Ronald Dworkin, *Justice in Robes* (Cambridge, Belknap Press, 2008) 55–56, 67–68.

[20] Wechsler, above n 14 at 16.

the available constitutional doctrines and legal traditions. This condition seems to follow from the general purpose of relying upon principled reasoning in order to avoid trespassing on the perilous territory of open-ended political disputation. As such, there is an obligation to defend any principle relied upon as being part and parcel of extant legal doctrine. But that is a very low threshold to meet.

The problem is not locating principles within extant legal doctrine, but recognising that there are too many principles buried within the rich confines of constitutional law. Indeed, on almost all issues of constitutional constitution, there is more than one principle that can claim such an adequate and proven pedigree. As well as it being difficult to distinguish principles from other types of norms, there is no definitive way to separate legal principles from more general moral and political principles. The fact is that the doctrinal resources of law are so ample, so capacious and so multi-dimensional that the range of principles available are prolific and abundant; it is possible to generate any number of principles at any number of levels in legal doctrine to support a range of positions and outcomes.[21] The jurisprudential problem is that, because there are too many principles on offer, there needs to be an available meta-principle or method to resolve any competition or contradiction between them. But no such meta-principle or method exists.

Of course, mainstream jurists will claim that a proper and appropriate theory of constitutional interpretation will narrow down the genuine options sufficiently so that there will remain one pre-eminent and overriding principle to rely upon.[22] This is an important and bold assertion, but it is overambitious and unsustainable. Each of the theories on offer will be able to reduce the source, scope and kind of principles that might be settled upon as decisive and determinative. But, apart from the difficulty of being able to cash-out its meaning in particular and detailed settings, it is almost always the case that principles tend to travel in pairs – for every principle, there is a counter-principle in play. So, for example, a classic tension that runs throughout constitutional doctrine is that between freedom and equality. Indeed, even the most extremist judges have to accept that, on some occasions, each must give some weight and significance to the other: libertarians leaven their commitments to freedom with some measure of equality, and some progressives temper their championing of equality with some recognition of freedom's worth. Accordingly, while the moralist, the organicist, the pragmatist, the dialogist and the democratist can contribute to a narrowing of the range of principles available, they cannot eliminate entirely the need to make the kind of value-based judgments that the reliance on principles is supposed to obviate.[23]

---

[21] See, for example, Mark Tushnet, 'Following the Rules Laid Down: A Critique of Interpretivism and Neutral Principles' (1983) 96 *Harvard Law Review* 781, 805–14 and Allan Hutchinson, above n 7 at ch 8.

[22] I will deal fully with the neutral argument in the next section. See pp 9–11.

[23] The one main candidate that might be seen to make a better job of meeting this challenge is originalism. I will deal with this directly and fully in the last section of this chapter. See pp 55–58.

Thirdly (and perhaps most critically), the resort to constitutional principles for adjudication does not resolve political disputes, but simply shifts them to a different level of abstraction. Despite the assertions of constitutional theorists and judges, it is difficult to understand how a controlling principle can achieve the required quality of generality that would allow it to apply effectively to contested or ideological issues (like abortion) and avoid having a built-in propensity to favour one set of interests over others. There seems to be no or very few principles that could strike either a theoretical or operational balance that could be acceptable to all political or moral sides of a dispute. Moreover, such an aspiration smacks of a certain otherworldliness. The assumption seems to be that there is some obvious and intuitive worth to those principles that transcend or go beyond familiar and contested stances on controversial issues, like racial equality or same-sex marriage. Indeed, the belief that there could be some principle that would reconcile or placate the competing values in play seems far-fetched. Accordingly, no judge can claim to be reasoning or speaking from such a general or unaligned standpoint. While not arbitrary or capricious, the judicial or juristic justifications espoused are clearly partial and favour some immediate social interests over others.

Finally, within the Wechslerianesque frame of reference, an implicit consequence of criticising judges for their failure to act in a principled manner is that they are then condemned as being nothing more than crude or cynical ideologues; they are castigated as being beyond the judicial pale because they have abandoned principle or professional argumentation entirely and are fulfilling their judicial duties in bad faith by making decisive resort to ideological prejudices. In short, under the traditional view, there is an unnecessary and self-defeating Hobson's choice – judges can be principled, even if they occasionally fall short of meeting that exacting standard, or they can be 'manipulative', in that they make no attempt to be principled.[24] But this is less about being principled or unprincipled; it is simply an exercise of faux-reasoning. As such, for traditional jurists, the principled/unprincipled contrast is a self-serving distinction that directs and validates jurists' choice to adopt a (pseudo-) principled approach over any other explanation or account of judicial behaviour and decision-making. In short, if the alternative is being ideological in the crudest sense, then principled reasoning might be the only and best way to go.

Lost in Neutral

The upshot of all this is the basic claim that constitutional adjudication earns its legitimacy by requiring that judges keep in check their partisan political preferences by resort to the formal discipline of principled legal reasoning. So, although

---

[24] Wechsler, above n 14 at 15. Of course, there will be occasions when the allegation of bad faith and manipulativeness might be warranted. See ch 5.

constitutional litigation might be awash in the muddy waters of politics and power, jurists recommend that judges can keep relatively dry and clean by wearing their institutional wetsuits of abstract neutrality. But this is an unconvincing argument. As well as the stated deficiencies with principles generally as a jurisprudential barrier against judicial decision-making becoming a political project, the suggestion that some principles can be normatively neutral in both content and application is simply unsustainable: 'the demand of neutrality is that a value and its measure be determined by a general analysis that gives no weight to accidents of application, finding a scope that is acceptable whatever interest, group, or person may assert the claim.'[25] If it ever made any sense, it is no longer credible or reasonable to imagine that there is a general principle that can receive the support and approval of competing interests and groups such that a highly charged dispute (eg, abortion, euthanasia, and affirmative action) will be amenable to a resolution that cuts across and unifies those interests and groups.

No abstract realm of higher order impartiality is available that can confer a neutral status (ie, not politically aligned) on constitutional principles. There is no neutral justification or universally fair territory on which to stake such an ontological claim. Indeed, despite the protestations of their defenders, so-called neutral principles are more of a hidden rhetorical and political gesture than anything else: it is the historical and social context in which that principle functions that gives a neutral principle its bite and bias. Of course, the obvious problem is that this is exactly the political stance against which the reliance upon a purportedly abstract principle defines itself and that gives content and power to it. In short, contrary to its proponents, principle is not an escape from a substantive context, but depends on it fully for particular meaning and force: 'principles and substance come always mixed.'[26] To be blunt, whatever the intentions or goals of those who defend reliance on neutral principles, what is done in the name of general principle is simply another mode of partisan pleading dressed up in principled garb; it falls well short of being a credible justification for dealing with the difficult constitutional challenge that it is supposed to meet.

Standing on principle, therefore, is simply another way of sitting on some substantive ground and pretending that it is more solid and unaligned than it actually is. A compelling example of this claim to being neutral and its shortcomings is the recent Supreme Court decision in *Students for Fair Admission*. It involved the constitutional validity of programmes for college admissions that took into account an applicant's race in order to produce a racially balanced class and to address past discrimination. In invalidating such programmes, the majority argued

---

[25] Herbert Wechsler, *Principles, Politics, and Fundamental Law* (Cambridge, Harvard University Press, 1961).
[26] Stanley Fish, *The Trouble with Principle* (Cambridge, Harvard University Press, 2001) 9. See also Morton Horwitz, *The Transformation of American Law, 1870-1960: The Crisis of Legal Orthodoxy* (New York, Oxford University Press, 1992) 265–68; Fred Schauer, 'Neutrality and Judicial Review' (2003) 22 *Law and Philosophy* 217, 234; and Ronald Turner, 'On Neutral and Preferred Principles of Constitutional Law' (2014) 74 *University of Pittsburgh Law Review* 433.

that the Constitution mandated a colour-blind approach so that any consideration of race was determined to be unconstitutional whether its purpose was intended to be ameliorative or not: 'eliminating racial discrimination means eliminating all of it' and that 'equal protection cannot mean one thing when applied to one individual and something else when applied to a person of another color.'[27] While this appeal to color-blindness has some superficial claim to appearing to be a neutral principle, the fact is that, when it is put in the prevailing social context, it operates to legitimate existing racial equalities: 'ignoring race will not equalize a society that is racially unequal' and 'deeming race irrelevant in law does not make it so in life.'[28]

In short, the seeming justice of an abstract principle can be entirely turned on its head by the relevant practical context of application; neutrality becomes a cover for, not a flight from, politics. Consequently, it is hard to see how the judicial resort to principles resolves political disputes in any neutral, impartial or objective way. It simply shifts the contested territory to a different level of abstraction (ie, from rules to principles). Despite the assertions of jurists and judges, posited and controlling principles fail to achieve the vaunted quality of generality or to be sufficiently 'disinterested'[29] that would allow them to settle impartially and authoritatively ideological issues, like abortion and affirmative action. Moreover, even those jurists who eschew neutrality and talk in terms of principles of being 'deeply and thoroughly political' are making exactly the same jurisprudential manoeuvre when they make this conditional on the proviso that such principles must not be reducible to 'personal or partisan politics'.[30] Such claims about objectivity and impartiality are on all fours with those that defend the resort to neutral principles as being a successful avoidance technique that elides political contestation. In both cases, the politics can be hidden, but they cannot be done away with.

Accordingly, each and every neutral principle relied upon cannot avoid having a built-in propensity to favour one set of social interests over others, even if what those are might change from one circumstance to another. As well, there is a certain otherworldliness to the traditional view of the principles/politics dichotomy. The assumption seems to be that there is some obvious and intuitive worth to a proposed principle that transcends or goes beyond familiar and contested stances on controversial issues (eg, same-sex marriage or religious tolerance). But there are no or very few principles that could strike a theoretical or operational balance that could be acceptable to (or, at least, not offend) both sides of a politicised or

---

[27] *Students for Fair Admissions v Harvard* (2023) 600 US 181, 15 (Roberts CJ). I also pursue a similar line of argument in the context of the recent abortion decision in *Dobbs*. See ch 5.

[28] ibid at 17 (Sotomayor J), 25 (Jackson J). It is ironic that this is exactly the same category of reasoning that prevailed in *Plessy v Ferguson* (1896) 163 US 537. There, the possibly neutral principle of 'separate, but equal' was used to perpetuate racial discrimination.

[29] See Wechsler, above n 14 at 31–34.

[30] Ronald Dworkin, *A Matter of Principle* (Cambridge, Harvard University Press, 1985) 146.

moralised dispute. Indeed, it can also be added that the general pretence that there exist neutral principles that can resolve issues of pressing political import (eg, racism, sexism, homophobia, etc) is itself the most political of assertions; it only gains any popular traction by ignoring social reality and treating political issues as somehow neither political nor divisive.

Originalist Sin

Among the constitutional theories on offer, it is originalism – that the Constitution is to be given the original meaning that it had when adopted – that has seized pole position in the constitutional theory race.[31] Its appeal as a convincing response to the democratic dilemma is that its back-to-basics approach appears not only to insulate judges from charges of political inappropriateness, but also to deliver a detached and true accounting of what the Constitution demands in difficult or divisive cases. As such, originalists claim to occupy the high ground of truth and objectivity in the struggle to rise above or capture the lower turf of constitutional politics. Understood in this way, originalism is seen to be a self-contained jurisprudence that has all the answers to all the cases that come before the courts. Moreover, it does this by providing a prophylactic means against justices getting their hands dirty in the cloying mud of contemporary political contestation. Accordingly, originalism is intended to work as both a solid basis for decision-making and as a realistic hedge against ideological unruliness.

Nevertheless, the extravagant boldness of originalism's formalistic claims means that its vulnerability to a political exposé is proportionately greater and that any subsequent uncovering will be all the more ruinous for it. And that is the case. Despite the protestations of its juristic and judicial champions, originalism cannot come close to living up to its own central claims. But no theory could. Although it has revived the long-dormant argument that the Constitution has a fixed and determinative meaning, it is unable to make good on its ambitious, but fatally flawed jurisprudential project; it fails in almost all the claims that it makes. In short, originalists preach legal theory, but practice political ideology. As its most trenchant contemporary critic phrases it, originalism 'is simply convenient rhetoric, used by conservatives to make it seem that their decisions are a product of

---

[31] The progenitors of this modern development of originalism as the purported gold standard of constitutional interpretation are Robert Bork and Edwin Meese. See Robert Bork, 'Neutral Principles and Some First Amendment Problems' (1971) 47 *Indiana Law Journal* 1 and Edwin Meese, 'Toward a Jurisprudence of Original Intent' (1988) 11 *Harvard Journal of Law and Public Policy* 5. Justice Scalia is quite simply the godfather of modern constitutional law and theory – 'The Constitution is not a living document. It is dead, dead, dead.' Katie Glueck, 'Scalia: The Constitution is "dead"' (*Politico*, 29 January 2013) www.politico.com/story/2013/01/scalia-the-constitution-is-dead-086853. For a more extensive account, see Antonin Scalia, above n 9 and Randy Barnett, *Restoring the Lost Constitution: The Presumption of Liberty* (Princeton, Princeton University Press, 2004).

something other than their political views'.[32] In terms of making a principled and neutral contribution to constitutional discourse, there are, at least, three difficulties with the originalist programme of constitutional interpretation – hermeneutical; historical; and ideological.

On the hermeneutical front, originalists claim is that it is possible to isolate and identify not only a general and common consensus among the founding generation on the Constitution's meaning and scope, but also to do so with specificity and precision in regard to contemporary and contested issues of political moment. But this undertaking is thoroughly permeated with major challenges. In particular, to have any possibility of success, it has to rely on subjective creativity as much as objective retrieval. In short, the problem of identifying original meaning, whether based on the founders' intent or on the public meaning at that time of the language used, cannot work as a sufficiently rigorous hermeneutical algorithm that can explain and justify what to do in difficult and hard cases. Moreover, the hermeneutical task certainly cannot be done in the entirely objective way that originalists must demonstrate in order to justify their interpretive imperialism. Of course, it might be feasible to recommend that there is an overall normative trend and general milieu that permeated the founding generation, but that leaves too much to be done before it could be counted on to resolve actual modern problems.

As regards history, it is apparent that originalists play fast and loose with historical materials to suit their own purposes.[33] Most importantly, there is no evidence that the founding generation thought that its views on what the Constitution meant or stood for were to be fixed or binding; that generation was as explicitly ideological and at odds within itself as any other generation of politicians and jurists. Indeed, if there was any consensus at all, there is some evidence that they did not think that their views of the Constitution were to be treated with any particular reverence or primacy.[34] Ironically, therefore, the founding generation's views that are the informing foundations of modern originalist interpretation were unsupportive of and even antagonistic to an originalist approach. Indeed, if the founding generation's views are to have any weight in modern constitutional discourse, they would point away from originalism's retrograde stance and towards a more dynamic approach. Accordingly, in contrast to today's originalists,

---

[32] Erwin Chemerinsky, *Worse than Nothing: The Dangerous Fallacy of Originalism* (New Haven, Yale University Press, 2022) 165. For my own extended critique, see Allan Hutchinson, *Toward an Informal Account of Legal Interpretation* (New York, Cambridge University Press, 2016) ch 5.

[33] Chemerinsky argues that originalists are often hypocrites (or, at least, fair-weather originalists) because they 'abandon the method when it fails to give them the results they want'. Chemerinsky, above n 32 at 139. See *Citizens United v FEC* (2010) 558 US 310 (campaign finance right). For a now classic illustration of methodological incoherence, see *District of Columbia v Heller* (2008) 128 S Ct 2783, 2790, 2790 n 6 (Scalia J) (examining text of Constitution and 'other founding-era documents' to determine scope of Second Amendment right) and ibid at 2831–36 (Stevens J, dissenting) (reviewing text and constitutional drafting history of Second Amendment).

[34] See, eg, Jefferson Powell, 'The Original Understanding of Original Intent' (1985) 98 *Harvard Law Review* 885 and Gordon Wood, *The Idea of America: Reflections on the Birth of the United States* (New York, Penguin Press, 2011).

the more credible view of the founders' understandings about the Constitution is that they did not valorise or venerate their own practices and political leanings. For them, the force of history was not static, inflexible or unjust. Instead, it was viewed as a vibrant and changing tableau of political and moral values.

In ideological terms, today's adherents of originalism are no different from earlier generations. If the leading jurists of the New Deal were focussed on establishing the primacy of democracy over dubious rights arguments and those of the Warren Court were enthusiastically devoted to identifying rights as institutional limits on democratic outcomes, the apologist jurists of today's Roberts Court are fully committed to reviving the conservative values of the late eighteenth century. This is no accident of history or legal theory. As an astute critic has noted, 'today's judges are not conservatives because they are originalists; they are originalists because [originalism] is conservative.'[35] Mouthing the frightening and infamous reasoning of Chief Justice Taney in *Dred Scott*, in opining that 'while [the Constitution] remains unaltered, it must be construed now as it was understood at the time of its adoption',[36] originalists seem to be content not only to run the risk of updating its racist underpinnings, but also to embrace other similar detestable moral values and political commitments. Governing contemporary America by reference to opinions and ideals from well over 200 years ago is hardly a non-political programme of constitutional law. Indeed, understood as the ideological programme that it is by both judges and jurists, originalism is a radical and reactionary approach that does neither the Supreme Court nor American society any good at all: it is the worst kind of politics masquerading as a vulgar farrago of constitutional pseudo-truths.

In conclusion, therefore, originalism's hermeneutical dimension (ie, what is the correct approach to access the true meaning of the Constitution?) and its historical dimension (eg, what are the historical grounds for adopting a history-based account of constitutional interpretation?) are conflated to sustain its ideological dimension (ie, what political interests and values are promoted by such a methodology?). This is a potent manoeuvre, but it cannot do what the originalists claim it does and needs it to do – finesse the 'law is politics' critique at the same time that it implements a particular ideology. For originalists, it is clearly the case that all that glitters jurisprudentially is not constitutional gold: it requires the insertion of the very politics that it eschews in order to meet its own self-imposed political agenda. As such, the originalist claim that the Constitution and its doctrines can be applied in a principled, correct and politically neutral way is itself thoroughly ideological in both operation and justification. But the real charm of originalism is not its theoretical cogency, but its capacity to promote the kind of conservatism that its supporters favour under the guise of technical

---

[35] Michael Waldman, *The Supermajority: How the Supreme Court Divided America* (New York, Simon & Schuster, 2023) 257. Of course, the same thing is true of liberal judges – they are not liberal because they are non-originalists, they are non-originalists because it better facilitates their liberalism.
[36] *Dred Scott v Sandford* (1857) 60 US 393, [404].

constitutional interpretation. This, of course, is the proof-positive that original-ism is simply one more political theory that is masquerading as legal theory.

The Modern Move

As originalism has begun to gain institutional and intellectual momentum as a favoured mode of constitutional interpretation and decision-making, there has been a concerted push-back against it. Many judges and mainstream jurists have taken aim at originalism as an account of constitutional interpretation that fails as a legal theory because it is simply a thinly veiled political stance. Although there is a wide range of serious and strong criticism advanced, there is also a felt need to defend an alternative non-originalist account of constitutional law. Indeed, on the basis that it is not possible to replace something with nothing, these jurists have re-entered the jurisprudential fray and sought to demonstrate how constitutional law can not only be done effectively without endorsing an originalist account, but also that such an alternative approach can deliver the validating and legitimating goods that originalism claims to have the corner on – that constitutional law is something that exists separately from political engagement and can be appreciated as a distinctly legal undertaking. Although this anti- or post-originalist project is pressing and pertinent, it has not achieved the success that its proponents seek or the legitimacy that they crave in defend-ing the exercise of judicial power and preferences through constitutional law in democratic societies.

In crafting these modern responses, there has been a marked tendency to function within the general Bickel-Wechsler-Dworkin project, albeit in a more stripped-down and modest manner. Indeed, while long on intent and intensity, their contributions fall short in that they are so thin and modest that they are unable to do the work that they claim to be doing (ie, demonstrating that constitu-tional law is something that can be done in a way that is law-bound and politically neutral). Indeed, a reasonable case can be made that their unintended effect is to support the very critical claim that they are most at pains to reject – that constitu-tional law is politics. There are three main and related strategies of contemporary mainstream critics – water-down what counts as valid constitutional law to almost nothing so the contrast with politics becomes non-existent; suggest significant changes that will make a difference and improve things, but avoid dealing with the fundamental challenge of a law-is-politics approach; and propose novel theo-ries about how to do constitutional law better that often collapse back into the first strategy. Taken together, the stances that they take and the arguments that they deploy may well be preferable politically than originalism in that they can allow for less conservative and more progressive results, but they have very little to recommend them as defences of the standard line that law is and should not be only politics.

The first strategy is exemplified by the work of Richard Fallon and Stephen Breyer. Adopting a pragmatic approach, they are content to defend a slightly reno-vated traditional understanding of judicial responsibilities.[37] Fallon holds to the view that the work of Supreme Court judges is 'law-bound', but not 'narrowly legal'.[38] Indeed, he reports that the great bulk of Supreme Court decision-making is, 'as I think most Americans do, … reasonably just'.[39] He is firmly opposed not only to on-the-fly and *ad hoc* decision-making, but also to any dogmatic allegiance to an overarching methodology. In the same way that he believes 'case specific judg-ments should yield to demands for the consistent application of sound interpretive principles', he also insists that there will be occasions when 'unshakeable convic-tions about the constitutional correctness of particular outcomes should instigate a reformulation or revision of prior methodological commitments'.[40] But he is very short on the details or the substance. The range of techniques and tools in the Fallonian judicial tool-box are so extensive and so multiple that almost anything short of outright manipulation or lying is acceptable. Hewing to the middle ground for its own sake, he offers no suggestions on how contentious issues – health care, abortion, campaign financing, gun control and the like – might be approached, let alone resolved. For him, the difference between legitimate and ille-gitimate decision-making is conflated and flaccid. In contrast to what he contends, therefore, Fallon's constitutional judges become, as he dismissingly puts it, 'merely politicians in robes'.[41]

Another self-proclaimed pragmatist is former Supreme Court Justice (and law professor) Stephen Breyer. Insisting that there is no one way to do it right or properly and being opposed to 'methodological purity and dogma,' his lodestar for constitutional judging is the development of a 'workable' body of constitutional law and decisions.[42] He is all about compromise and interest-balancing. Although he defends himself against the charge that a 'purpose-oriented approach is merely a matter of choosing which outcome [is] believed to be best in any given case', he proposes that constitutional decision-making is simply about 'judicial instinct, created, and honed by experience, that will typically tell the judge what considera-tions to use, and emphasize in a particular case'.[43] This seems a very thin diet for the modern constitutional judge in today's society. While his pragmatic, practi-cal and almost down-to-earth approach has much to recommend it as a candid account of judging, it is very hard to see how 'workability' can advance the tradi-tional project of keeping sufficiently distinct the realms of constitutional law and

---

[37] Their brand of pragmatism is rarely critical, nor does it push more deeply into some of the founda-tions of traditional jurisprudence. For a contrasting and more critical account of pragmatism, see ch 6.

[38] Richard Fallon, above n 11 at 93, xi.

[39] ibid at 29.

[40] ibid at 18.

[41] ibid at x.

[42] Stephen Breyer, *Reading the Constitution: Why I Chose Pragmatism, Not Textualism* (New York, Simon & Schuster, 2024) 255, 197–230.

[43] ibid at xvii, 262.

constitutional politics. Indeed, it might be ventured that, like Fallon, Breyer makes a convincing case in support of the opposite critical claim – constitutional law, no matter how skillfully disguised or practical, is politics all the way up and down.

The second strategy is associated with the work of Erwin Chemerinsky and Daniel Epps and Ganesh Sitaraman. Writing in 2019 after President Trump's recent appointments to the Supreme Court, Epps and Sitaraman lamented the fact that the Court had become increasingly and openly political in its performance and decisions; they provided a detailed and relentless account of how the Supreme Court's reputation and legitimacy was threatened and on a collision course with a constitutional crisis.[44] This situation, of course, was to get much worse with the abortion decision in *Dobbs* and the gun decision in *Bruen*. However, as compelling and extensive as their critique is, they maintain that it is possible for the Court to redeem itself and, at least, salvage its own legitimacy: 'radically changing the Supreme Court is necessary if we hope to preserve what is good about the Court.'[45] They propose a number of constitutionally friendly reforms to do this (ie, all federal appellate judges would be members of the Supreme Court and nine would be picked by lottery to handle individual cases; and a balanced bench of Republicans and Democrats would be mandated and effected by an elaborate selection process among sitting judges). For them, these reforms would ensure that constitutional judges can, with effort and conscientiousness, keep the constitutional faith. However, they refuse to recognise or accept that the present 'crisis' is not deviant or aberrational. Nor are they too explicit about 'what is good about the Court'. For them, constitutional law simply needs not to succumb to the temptation to treat constitutional law as always being an exercise in politics as much as anything. This is hardly a reassuring platitude.

From a different, but also highly critical position about the performance of the present Supreme Court, Chemerinsky similarly recommends that institutional changes must be made. A long-time champion of the Court and the traditional practice of judicial review, he has recently become disillusioned and is now convinced that a new Constitution is required.[46] Characteristically inventive and persuasive in the kind of changes that need to be made, he nevertheless still maintains that democracy should be subservient to constitutional law, not vice versa. More tellingly, he has little to say about the Court's composition and its judicial methodology; he fails to appreciate that, even with a new constitutional text, the same judges will use the same methods to fulfil their constitutional interpretive duties. While a new and more progressive Constitution will, of course, help, the judges are still highly likely to proceed much as they do now and follow their own political dictates. As such, Chemerinsky's changes will be little more

---

[44] Daniel Epps and Ganesh Sitaraman, 'How to Save the Supreme Court' (2019) 129 *Yale Law Journal* 148, 153–69.

[45] ibid at 206.

[46] Erwin Chemerinsky, *No Democracy Lasts Forever: How the Constitution Threatens the United States* (New York, Liveright, 2024).

than cosmetic: they will not do much to get at the basic dynamic that informs and moulds the Court's image of itself – the judges' underlying and formative self-understanding of what constitutional adjudication is and should be about as a professional and non-political enterprise.[47] Without more than he is prepared to advocate, the traditional model of feigned detachment and posited neutrality will continue to dominate.

The third strategy is evident in the work of Mary Ann Franks and Cass Sunstein. In a sweeping indictment, Franks condemns both liberals and conservatives for their commitment to reading the Constitution 'selectively, self-servingly, and in bad faith'.[48] She maintains that constitutional law has been utilised to advance very particular and partisan projects (ie, protecting and promoting white, male and vested interests). In this regard, her critical work is unapologetic and unyielding. However, she also insists that it is possible to 'have faith in the Constitution' by developing constitutional law along lines that uncover in good faith the true or correct meaning of the Constitution.[49] For her, this entails espousing 'an unflinching commitment to the principle of reciprocity expressed in the Fourteenth Amendment's equal protection clause'.[50] Of course, in recommending this, she is replacing one form of constitutional fundamentalism with another: there is one meaning to the Constitution and she knows what it is – 'one can only honour the Constitution by honoring equality' and by 'reorient[ing] our constitutional attention to those whose rights have been excluded, ignored, and subordinated'.[51] But, no matter how attractive her constitutional credo might or might not be, hers is not a jurisprudential ambition; it is a political or ideological aspiration. As Franks confirms, but fails to follow through on, there is no neutral, objective or non-ideological way to read the Constitution that can, by virtue of that fact alone, trump all others.

Sunstein takes a different and typically clever approach to meeting the constitutional challenge. Offering an unqualified dismissal of originalism as a serious mode of judicial practice or juristic endeavour, he is adamant that any viable approach to constitutional interpretation needs to be defended in terms of whether it makes constitutional law 'better rather than worse'.[52] To do this and also to accept the pluralism of both American politics and law, he asserts that 'the search for reflective equilibrium … is the only game in town'.[53] By relying on Rawls' theoretical manoeuvre that involves working the space between the interpreters' provisional

---

[47] Of course, originalists' commitment to their brand of constitutionalism would be sorely tried. If they kept faith with the main imperative of their approach (ie follow the new views of the amenders), this would result in a very different set of outcomes. But would they do that? I think that politics might well prevail over method at that point.

[48] Mary Anne Franks, *The Cult of the Constitution* (Stanford, Stanford University Press, 2020) xii.

[49] ibid at 21.

[50] ibid.

[51] ibid at 202, 204.

[52] Cass Sunstein, *How to Interpret the Constitution* (Princeton, Princeton University Press, 2023) 15.

[53] ibid at 11.

fixed normative points and the particular theories and landmarks of extant constitutional law, he claims to have hit upon a convincing way of proceeding that gives 'due respect for existing law'[54] and allows for just decisions going forward. Indeed, although there is no one fixed or stable account of what constitutional law is or can be, he maintains that, under his approach, 'the arc of history bends towards justice'.[55] As such, constitutional law will come to be appreciated as being a better (and even the best), not worse, site for achieving justice.

Sunstein's emphasis on being reasonable and open-minded is all well and good, but it runs into the same problems as Fallon and Breyer. It adopts a posture of reasonable middle-of-the-road moderation as a serious way to avoid politics. This might hide or soften the political slant of the choices to be made, but it cannot do away with them. 'Being reasonable' is a notoriously unreliable standard for resolving conflict. Moreover, his reliance on 'reflective equilibrium' as a neutral effort to validate outcomes is an epistemic sleight of hand: its obvious limitations are twofold. First, people's fixed points are given ethical worth and weight in the justificatory process simply by virtue of their present existence; there is no critical threshold to be crossed before they are taken seriously as valid or credible ethical and political stances.[56] Secondly, constitutional law's doctrinal resources are so capacious in extent and so diverse in substance that they can be squared with all manner of evaluative positions that span the existing political spectrum; there is no realistic or undisputed check that these resources can definitively put on their support for competing and clashing political choices.

Accordingly, each of these modern responses to the rising dominance of originalism and its reactionary political underpinnings is effective in exposing the faux-foundations in neutrality and efficaciousness of that approach. However, they are unable to do so in a way that completes and remains true to the traditional Bickel-Wechsler-Dworkin project. Indeed, they provide ample grist for the critical mill. The arguments that they use against originalism are so powerful and so effective that they do more than invalidate originalism as a theory and practice of constitutional interpretation. They also preclude those modern jurists from establishing the validity of not only their own preferred alternative accounts, but also the whole traditional project of showing that constitutional law can be done in a non-political, objective, impartial and neutral manner. They are, as it were, hoist by their own jurisprudential petards. In short, the tools and weapons used to undermine originalism also disable this modern group from continuing and completing their own self-imposed challenge – to show that constitutional law is not only reducible to political contestation, but is also defensible as a separate and professional practice at justice-seeking.

---

[54] ibid at 91.

[55] ibid at 134.

[56] See Norman Daniels, *Justice and Justification: Reflective Equilibrium in Theory and Practice* (Cambridge, Cambridge University Press, 1996) 21–46. Of course, the question of how people's political instincts and, as Rawls put it, 'sense of justice' arise and change remains a mystery; individuals with similar experiences and backgrounds can develop very different moral compasses.

Conclusion

It seems clear that any of the jurisprudential approaches on offer – moralist, origi-nalist, organicist, pragmatist, dialogist and democratist – might be supported politically for the purposes they fulfil and the results they help to produce. However, they do not work in the principled and non-political way that they are packaged and marketed to do so by their juristic creators and popular supporters. While some have more initial appeal than others and can make some superficial assertion to being a distinctive style of legal theory, they each ultimately fail to complete the traditional project that they claim to be part of and whose stand-ards that they claim to be judged by – that the practice of constitutional law is or can be something that is truly separate from political posturing. Although I have provided a theoretical response and condemnation of such a legitimating project, these abstract arguments and criticisms need to be explored and fleshed out further in a more practical and focussed setting. It is to this task that I now turn in the next couple of chapters.

5

The Good, the Bad and the Ugly: A Constitutional Reckoning

In so many ways, the Supreme Court's recent decision in *Dobbs* has put the cat among the pigeons.[1] It has brought about a political and social fallout that has generated a torrent of heated commentary and active protest. More importantly, it has had an immediate and negative impact upon the lives of women across the country. For good and bad, therefore, it has already joined that small set of cases that count as 'landmarks placed upon the trackless wilds of law'.[2] As such, it has also roiled the more secluded and precious waters of jurisprudential study. *Dobbs* has brought back into sharp focus the debate about not only what the Supreme Court decides in constitutional cases, but also how it goes about making those decisions – is there an objective method or way of proceeding (eg, principled reasoning) that can be relied upon to discover or produce constitutional decisions that are considered just and that amount to more than the preferred outcomes of those making such decisions?

The *Dobbs* opinions readily suggests that the different judicial perspectives are stark and unrelenting. That said, I do not want to take apart both sets of opinions analytically bit-by-bit. Nor do I want to suggest that one opinion is somehow better than the other either as a matter of law or politics. What I do want to do is expose and criticise the jurisprudential underpinnings of the opinions in terms of their argumentative structure and judicial philosophy. My focus will largely be on the fact that the majority and the minority each accuse the other of acting in an unprincipled and, therefore, indefensible and illegitimate manner. While the majority alleges that the minority flouts the settled modes of constitutional interpretation (ie, constitutional text and established national traditions), the minority asserts that the majority has ignored a settled precedent of constitutional law (ie, *Roe* and related 'substantive due process' holdings). However, these assertions of unprincipled behaviour speak to a much deeper and more telling divide between the Court's Justices. They provide clear evidence that politics are the driver of their legal opinions, not jurisprudential or judicial philosophies.

---

[1] *Dobbs v Jackson Women's Health Organization* (2022) 142 S Ct 2228.
[2] Samuel Warren, *A Popular and Practical Introduction to Law Studies* (London, A Maxwell, 1835) 434.

In this chapter, therefore, I will unpack the argumentative structure and normative dynamics that are present and revealed in *Dobbs*. After introducing *Dobbs* and framing its opinions in jurisprudential terms, I will highlight and examine the recognisably good (ie, that constitutional law and reasoning is a professional and principled activity, but one that does not always or only produce consistent or even just results), the presumptively bad (ie, that constitutional reasoning and law is inescapably political and ideological even when it is done in a principled way), and the evidently ugly (ie, that efforts at doing constitutional reasoning and law that would otherwise be legitimate can lose that estimable status if made in bad faith). Throughout the chapter, I will show that *Dobbs* is not only a decision to be reckoned with generally, but also evinces a need for a robust jurisprudential reckoning. Although extreme in its divided politics and judicial presentation, *Dobbs* is not an aberrational or special case. Indeed, if anything, it illuminates the deep and problematic footings of what might appear to be other more run-of-the-mill constitutional decisions. As such, it highlights generally rather than creates independently the failed challenge to keep constitutional law and constitutional politics apart.

The *Dobbs* Debacle

Roe v Wade represents one of those precedents that has reached landmark status, even if there is as much criticism of it as celebration. By way of Justice Harry Blackmun's leading opinion (in a 7–2 split) in 1973, although conceding that there was no explicit textual reference to a right to privacy, the Court recognised such a right and found that it was 'broad enough to encompass a woman's decision whether or not to terminate her pregnancy'. However, this was a right that was not absolute, but could be balanced against a state government's appropriate interests in protecting fetal life and health; a trimester approach was adopted. Moreover, because the right was considered 'fundamental', any restriction had to meet the demands of strict scrutiny. In an aspiration that reverberates through all the Court's jurisprudence, Justice Blackmun insisted that his and the Court's challenge was 'to resolve the issue by constitutional measurement, free of emotion and of predilection'.[3]

Not surprisingly, the immediate response to *Roe* was divided and passionate; there were unyielding partisans on either side of the issue. As with earlier iconic decisions like *Brown*,[4] there was not only heated debate about the result, but also stark disagreement among legal academics about the strength and kind of reasoning used to establish such a right and, therefore, the legitimacy of the

---

[3] *Roe v Wade* (1973) 410 US 113, 153, 150, 163, 155, 116.
[4] See *Brown v Board of Education* (1954) 347 US 483.

majority's holding.[5] Some praised the decision and took the organicist view that it was right and proper that the Constitution should evolve in line with society. But others railed against the decision on the basis that it betrayed the originalist underpinnings of constitutional interpretation.[6] As framed by the dissenting Justice Byron White, the problem was that there is 'nothing in the language or history of the Constitution to support … a new constitutional right for pregnant women', and therefore the decision amounted to 'an improvident and extravagant exercise of the power of judicial review'.[7] As such, Roe not only wreaked political and social havoc, it also set the jurisprudential battle lines for the coming half-century: the more progressive forces of an organicist constitution were pitted against the more conservative ranks of an originalist constitution.

Over the years, the opponents of *Roe* began to gain political ground. Inroads were made into women's fundamental procreative rights. In *Casey*, the trimester schema was abandoned in favour of a fetal viability test, and strict scrutiny was replaced by an 'undue burden' standard.[8] The Court became even more deeply divided. Whereas Justice Blackmun would have kept *Roe*'s approach fully intact, Justice Scalia would have done away with *Roe* as he maintained that such a right was not a liberty protected directly by the Constitution and there was a long-established tradition of permitting state governments to regulate and even proscribe it. As the protesting social voices against *Roe* were unrelenting and the Republican-appointed membership of the Court began to change, the push to overrule *Roe* became stronger and bolder.

In June 2022 (after an earlier leaked draft of Justice Alito's majority opinion), the Supreme Court published its decision in *Dobbs*. As anticipated, the Court's majority of five Justices overruled *Roe* and did away with any constitutional right that women might have to terminate their pregnancies; it was left to individual states to determine when, if at all, and how abortions might be permissible.[9] Again, as with *Roe*, the response was swift, divided, and antagonistic. This time, of course, the tables were turned. As the pro-choice forces lambasted the work of the Court in gutting pregnant women's rights, the anti-choice lobby was gleeful

---

[5] See Mary Ziegler, *After Roe: The Lost History of the Abortion Debate* (Cambridge, Harvard University Press, 2015). I will use the terms 'anti-abortion' and 'pro-choice'; other labels are loaded and controversial.

[6] Compare, eg, Ronald Dworkin, *Life's Dominion: An Argument About Abortion, Euthanasia, and Individual Freedom* (New York, Vintage Books, 1994) and Richard A Epstein, 'Substantive Due Process by Any Other Name: The Abortion Cases' (1973) 1973 *Supreme Court Review* 159, 185. For a hard-hitting account of progressive complacency and conservative activism, see Elizabeth Dias and Lisa Lerer, *The Fall of Roe: The Rise of a New America* (New York, Flatiron Books, 2024).

[7] *Roe*, above n 3 at 221–22. Even the supporters of the *Roe* outcome were troubled about the weakness of its reasoning and doctrinal cogency. See, eg, John Hart Ely, 'The Wages of Crying Wolf: A Comment on Roe v. Wade' (1973) 82 *Yale Law Journal* 920; Donald Regan, 'Rewriting Roe v. Wade' (1979) 77 *Michigan Law Review* 1569; Judith Jarvis Thompson, 'A Defense of Abortion' (1971) 1 *Philosophy and Public Affairs* 47; and Mark Tushnet, 'Following the Rules Laid Down: A Critique of Interpretivism and Neutral Principles' (1983) 96 *Harvard Law Review* 781, 805–14.

[8] *Planned Parenthood of Southeastern Pennsylvania v Casey* (1992) 505 US 833, 837.

[9] *Dobbs*, above n 1 at 2242.

in its success.[10] Predictably, legal academe was also divided, but its response was more restrained and jurisprudential. For some, the Court was viewed as simply correcting a constitutional misstep that was based on weak and unconvincing reasoning. For others, it was chastised for riding roughshod over an established, if shaky, precedent of the Court. Either way, as in the world at large, a legal landmark has been revealed to be less enduring than many realised or expected; it was torn down and might or might not be replaced by a *Dobbs*-like other.

Justice Alito's leading opinion was scathing in its general treatment of *Roe* and particularly Justice Blackmun's reasoning. Alito condemned *Roe* as being 'egregiously wrong', 'plainly incorrect', 'remarkably loose', 'deeply damaging', and 'exceedingly weak'.[11] The main thrust of the opinion was twofold – that the right asserted was supported neither by the text's wording nor by the nation's traditions and that *stare decisis* was not an insuperable barrier when it came to correcting constitutional errors. As such, Justice Alito was not prepared to treat abortion as a constitutionally protected right, but handed the issue back to state governments to regulate as they saw fit: the Court must 'heed the Constitution' and 'not fall prey to [*Roe*'s] unprincipled approach'.[12] By way of concurrence, Justice Kavanaugh insisted that 'because the Constitution is neutral on the issue of abortion, this Court also must be scrupulously neutral'.[13] Although Chief Justice Roberts joined the majority in the immediate resolution of the case, he took a more restrained and narrow approach: 'there is a clear path to deciding this case correctly without overruling *Roe* all the way down to the studs: recognize that the viability line must be discarded, as the majority rightly does, and leave for another day whether to reject any right to an abortion at all.'[14]

Of course, the three dissenting Justices were not at all persuaded that *Roe* was wrongly decided and should be overruled. Expressing both disagreement and dismay, Justice Breyer emphasised the need to respect established precedents and, thereby, the legitimacy of the Court. He rejected the majority's originalist approach and contended that 'the Constitution does not freeze for all time the original view of what those rights guarantee, or how they apply'. For him, it was vital that the Constitution was understood within a more organicist frame of interpretive reference. The challenge was to ensure that such an approach did not give Justices *carte blanche* to do whatever they wished, but that 'applications of liberty and equality can evolve while remaining grounded in constitutional principles, constitutional

---

[10] Compare, eg, Lauren McEwan, 'Feminist Women's Health Center Speaks Out Against Anti-Abortion Arguments in Dobbs v Jackson' (*Feminist Women's Health Center*, 2021) https://feministcenter.org/blog/feminist-womens-health-center-speaks-out-against-anti-abortion-arguments-in-dobbs-v-jackson/ with Tom Shakely, 'A New Day at Last: U.S. Supreme Court Reverses Roe v. Wade' (*Americans United for Life*, 24 June 2022) https://aul.org/2022/06/24/a-new-day-at-last-u-s-supreme-court-reverses-roe-v-wade/.

[11] *Dobbs*, above n 1 at 2240, 2243, 2245, 2265, 2270.

[12] ibid at 2235–36, 2239, 2243, 2248.

[13] ibid at 2305 (Kavanaugh J, concurring).

[14] ibid at 2314 (Roberts CJ, concurring).

history, and constitutional precedents'. As an almost half-century-old precedent that had been approved and followed by more than 20 cases, Breyer cautioned that *Roe*'s overruling would 'call into question this Court's commitment to legal principle' and that both women and the Court would pay 'a terrible price' for such recklessness.[15]

A Legitimate Problem of Principles

The aftermath of *Dobbs* is far from novel in either intensity or sweep. There has been a continuing and troubling history of bitter reactions to Supreme Court decisions. The reaction to the school desegregation decision of *Brown* in 1954 and the following years ran deep and volatile.[16] In particular, the Southern States refused to abide by it and engaged in outright resistance for many years and even decades.[17] Also, there was opposition to the decision and its reasoning within both academic and judicial circles; it was considered to be an improper exercise of judicial power that flouted established traditions of what counts as valid constitutional law and as appropriate judicial decision-making.[18] The other obvious decision that received a powerful backlash was *Roe* itself. On this occasion (and in contrast to *Dobbs*), it was the political right that orchestrated and engaged in a violent and prolonged protest for almost half a century. In both situations, whether made by the political left or right, the charge that the Supreme Court has acted politically became a partisan rallying cry. The liberal defenders of *Roe* celebrated it as good and valid constitutional law, but condemned *Dobbs* as bad and invalid constitutional law. Of course, the conservative opponents of *Roe* condemned it as bad and invalid constitutional law and defended *Dobbs* as good and valid constitutional law.[19]

In the past, although political disagreements ran strong and divided, there seemed to be some loose agreement that resorting to the Supreme Court would and should effectively resolve disputed matters. It was assumed that after any

---

[15] ibid at 2326, 2326, 2348, 2350 (Breyer J, dissenting).

[16] See 'The Case That Changed America: Brown v. Board of Education: The Southern Manifesto and "Massive Resistance" to Brown' (*Legal Defense Fund*) www.naacpldf.org/brown-vs-board/southern-manifesto-massive-resistance-brown/; see also Leslie Fenwick, 'The Ugly Backlash to Brown v. Board of Ed That No One Talks About' (*Politico*, 17 May 2022) www.politico.com/news/magazine/2022/05/17/brown-board-education-downside-00032799.

[17] See Richard Kluger, *Simple Justice: The History of Brown v Board of Education and Black America's Struggle for Equality* (New York, Knopf, 1976) and Charles Ogletree, *All Deliberate Speed: Reflections on the First Half Century of Brown v Board of Education* (New York, WW Norton & Co, 2004).

[18] See, for example, *The Conference of Chief Justices: Report of the Committee on Federal-State Relationships as Affected by Judicial Decisions* (1958) 104 Cong Rec A7782 and Herbert Wechsler, 'Toward Neutral Principles of Constitutional Law' (1959) 73 *Harvard Law Review* 1.

[19] Compare Erwin Chemerinsky, 'The Enormous Consequences of Overruling Roe v. Wade' (*Time*, 3 May 2022) https://time.com/6172956/consequences-overruling-roe-wade/ with Dan O'Donnell, 'The Brilliance of the Dobbs Decision' (*MacIver Institute*, 4 May 2022) www.maciverinstitute.com/perspectives/the-brilliance-of-the-dobbs-decision.

Supreme Court decision was handed down, both sides of the political aisles would accede, albeit reluctantly and critically, to the dictates of constitutional law. So, while there was understood to be underlying and sharp ideological differences in play, there was a deeper and more unifying commitment to the idea that the Constitution can stand, if not apart from prosaic politics, at least to the side of them. Properly interpreted by the Supreme Court, constitutional law was accepted to be a principled and reasoned refuge from the opportunistic hustle and bustle and arch-partisanship of the political arena; the courts could fulfil their constitutional role by bringing a measured, rational and non-ideological level-headedness to political contestation. While presidents, politicians and social activists played politics and got their hands dirty, the Chief Justice of the Supreme Court and his puisne associates were expected to take a more elevated stance and keep their hands unsoiled by that same political dirt. As such, the Supreme Court was viewed as a 'forum of principle', not another divisive arena of political haggling, by both the warring politicians and judges.[20]

In recent years, even that shallow and far from universal assumption has been eroded. Notwithstanding what many judicial apologists still maintain, the Supreme Court appears to be facing a full-on crisis of institutional legitimacy. Many citizens no longer concede that the Supreme Court is not a political institution. Indeed, it seems to be a reasonably common perception that it is or has become a political institution, which may explain the public's rapidly declining confidence in the Supreme Court.[21] As such, political activists have begun to direct their efforts to ensuring that judges are appointed who reflect and embrace their politics and to developing a litigation strategy that leverages that realisation. However, there can be little doubt that political conservatives have been much more effective and successful at doing this. In contrast, political liberals seem to have difficulty letting go of the idea that, whatever its present failings, the Supreme Court can actually live up to the traditional aspiration that constitutional law can be done in a way that grapples with politics, but in a way that does not collapse into partisan politics.[22] They seem willing to declare that 'constitutional interpretation is necessarily a normative enterprise, not a mechanical one',[23] but they maintain that it is possible to be normative without also being ideological.

In an important sense, political liberals and progressives have been unable to abandon the heady days of the 1970s when the Warren Court 'gave progressives a

---

[20] Ronald Dworkin, *A Matter of Principle* (Cambridge, Harvard University Press, 1985).

[21] Most adults in the United States are sceptic that Justices are not influenced by politics according to recent polls. See 'Public's Views of Supreme Court Turned More Negative Before News of Breyer's Retirement' (*Pew Research Center*, 2 February 2022) www.pewresearch.org/politics/2022/02/02/publics-views-of-supreme-court-turned-more-negative-before-news-of-breyers-retirement/ and Jeffrey M Jones, 'Confidence in the U.S. Supreme Court Sinks to Historic Low' (*Gallup*, 23 June 2022) news.gallup.com/poll/394103/confidence-supreme-court-sinks-historic-low.aspx.

[22] See Martha Minow, *In Brown's Wake: Legacies of America's Educational Landmark* (Oxford, Oxford University Press, 2010).

[23] Jonathan Gould, 'Puzzles of Progressive Constitutionalism' (2022) 135 *Harvard Law Review* 2054, 2084.

reason to see the judiciary as a friend rather than a foe'.[24] This is a dangerous and self-defeating belief; it is more wishful thinking than anything else. The Constitution's past, except for the Warren Court, has been largely conservative with small pockets of liberal alignment. Also, the whole constitutional enterprise has been played according to conservative rules and on their home turf. *Brown* and then *Roe* are both the talismans and the *bêtes noires* of liberal and progressive constitutionalism. While they are high watermarks of liberal achievement, they were bought at the enormous cost of portraying the Supreme Court as the exclusive or only place to seek liberal justice and hold back the conservative tide. Further, this meant that being for the Constitution entailed being for the Supreme Court as its primary expositor and guardian of its values. However, in defending the Supreme Court as a neutral institution, liberals, like Ronald Dworkin, were making a gamble that liberalism would prevail more than or as much as conservativism in constitutional battles. However, the fact is that, in such contests, liberalism, let alone progressivism, has come out second best in the long and medium term.

In so many ways, *Dobbs* will likely come to be seen as the occasion when the liberal chickens came home to roost. Emboldened by their savvier grasp of judicial politics, the conservative judges and activists have taken advantage of liberalism's naïveté. They have exploited the idea that the Supreme Court should be understood as a politically neutral institution and weaponised the Constitution as a force for advancing their own political agenda. In dealing with this challenge, liberals and progressives will need not only to change their strategy to constitutional law and litigation, but also to adopt an entirely different approach to thinking about and implementing what is involved in having a constitutional agenda. This is no easy task. But, if liberals and progressives are to reverse or even offset the conservative successes in constitutional law, they must be prepared to make bold and radical moves. By pursuing the same tried-and-untrue tactics, they will only be throwing good money after bad. If they do not take this stance, they will be handing over the future of constitutional law to an increasingly conservative politics for generations to come.

As the *Dobbs* decision shows, what makes a judicial decision good or bad is not based on an internal technical assessment (ie, does it best conform with existing legal doctrine in small and/or large ways?), but is validated by an external normative evaluation (ie, does it reach and defend a stance that is politically desirable and defensible in terms of prevailing social and political contexts?).[25] As such, the appropriate and pressing questions are not about whether judges act judicially, but whether what it means to act judicially can be understood in more openly political terms. In saying this, I am not suggesting that there is no difference between

---

[24] Larry Kramer, 'Popular Constitutionalism, circa 2004' (2004) 92 *California Law Review* 959, 964.
[25] See ch 6.

judges and politicians. However, I am suggesting that the difference is not as large or as significant as most scholars and popular commentators contend. Moreover, no matter how desirable maintaining the traditional distinction between judges and politicians would be, it is simply not achievable or realisable – judges cannot fulfil their roles in deciding constitutional issues without resorting to or relying on controversial and disputed political values. The Supreme Court is inevitably and unavoidably political. In other words, acting judicially is another way of acting politically.

As obvious and uncontroversial as this principled requirement seems, it places very little restraint on the judges' argumentative efforts. Indeed, this is where the jurisprudential rubber hits the road. The resources of constitutional law are so ample, so capacious, and so multidimensional that principles are prolific and abundant; it is possible to generate any number of principles at any number of levels to support a range of positions and outcomes.[26] The jurisprudential problem is, therefore, that there are too many principles, not too few, with no available meta-principle to resolve any tension or contradiction. Because of this profligacy, both the majority's and minority's doctrinal stances are entirely defensible in strictly legal terms. Most significantly, they both can easily claim to be above the threshold of doctrinal integrity that is reasonably demanded of judges in constructing legal judgments; the judgments are sufficiently polished and professional instances of the judicial craft. At face value,[27] therefore, each of the opinions given in *Dobbs* can claim to be principled and, therefore, legitimate. However, they are each far from decisive in being able to persuade those with different principles and normative commitments.

Whereas the majority draws upon the principled idea of a fixed and originalist Constitution, the minority rests its case on the principled appeal to an evolving and organicist Constitution. While there is nothing that necessarily follows from those initial commitments, they tend to lead in a doctrinal direction that plays out predictably – the majority rejects a right to abortion (as it was not recognised in the constitutional text or traditions) and the minority defends it (as it was recognised as being an evolving development in established precedent).[28] Both majority and minority, in claiming the particular principled ground that they

---

[26] Tushnet, above n 7 at 813. The inferences that I draw from this observation are different from those of Tushnet. See Allan Hutchinson, *Democracy and Constitutions: Putting Citizens First* (Toronto, University of Toronto Press, 2021) ch 8.

[27] It is not that there is nothing to choose between the two sets of opinions in terms of either their constitutional merit or democratic legitimacy. See pp 73–76. For instance, although the *Dobbs* majority treated the absence of the word 'abortion' as highly significant, there is also no mention of the words 'fetus' or 'prenatal life' that the majority recognised as a competing interest that could and should be weighed by the states. See *Dobbs*, above n 1 at 2242.

[28] ibid at 2242–43, 2245 (Alito J, majority) and at 2319–20 (Breyer J, dissenting). For a qualified defence of the *Dobbs* majority, see Randy Barnet and Lawrence Solum, 'Originalism After *Dobbs, Bruen, and Kennedy*: The Role of History and Tradition' (2023) 118 *Northwestern University Law Review* 433.

did, strongly assert that the other is acting in an unprincipled, abusive and opportunistic manner. Indeed, they each condemn the other as engaging in a crude power grab: 'the Court must not fall prey to such an unprincipled approach'[29] and '[the] majority's pinched view of how to read our Constitution … is hypocrisy.'[30] In short, the assertion of being unprincipled is simply a convenient way to castigate those who disagree with the particular principles being relied upon in the reasoning or result. The problem, of course, is that if opposing approaches to constitutional argument can qualify as principled, then the idea of principled reasoning is doing little work at all.

As such, the majority's judgment does not prevail because it is somehow a better or more cogent example of constitutional reasoning. Although it might be considered so in some juristic and judicial quarters, Justice Alito's opinion prevails because it garnered the support of more judicial colleagues than the minority did. As evidenced by *Dobbs*, the Rule of Law is often little more than the Rule of Five (even if those judges claim to be offering better or more valid legal arguments). It is a numbers game as much as anything else. Indeed, Justice Breyer's warning can be directed against him and his dissenting colleagues as much as it can be at the majority – 'to reverse prior law "upon a ground no firmer than a change in [the Court's] membership" would invite the view that "this institution is little different from the two political branches of the Government".'[31] On another day (perhaps on 22 January 1973, when *Roe* was decided?), the three Justices of the minority might be able to acquire two or more votes and be susceptible to the same charge.

So, if the measure of principled reasoning does not explain the relative and opposite justifications of the majority's and minority's opinions, what does? Is there some persuasive account of constitutional reasoning that can salvage the judicial enterprise and confer legitimacy on their work? Or is it all simply a matter of political manoeuvring dressed up as legal reasoning? I will offer some initial answers to those questions. Of course, the jurisprudential challenge is to produce an account that allows for some disagreement between Justices in approach and outcome, but does not validate all approaches and outcomes. If that were the case, then the account offered would not be doing the kind of heavy lifting that is expected or required. However, the fact that all judges are obliged to deal with a constitutional text and doctrine that can be traced back over more than two centuries does not augur well for any approach that seeks to be more progressive and modern in its outlook.

---

[29] *Dobbs*, above n 1 at 2248 (Alito J, majority).

[30] ibid at 2325 (Breyer J, dissenting). Although Justice Kavanaugh stresses that the rolling back of *Roe* is a one-off, ibid at 2310 (Kavanaugh J, concurring), Justice Thomas hints that the overruling of *Roe* might presage other corrective interventions on 'substantive due process', ibid at 2301–02 (Thomas J, concurring).

[31] ibid at 2350 (Breyer J, dissenting).

Breaking Bad

There is nothing about the reasoning employed by the majority and minority in *Dobbs* that would permit them to claim conclusively that their decision was more valid or legitimate simply by virtue of the style and force of their reasoning. Of course, each chastises the other and contends that their opponents are either 'unprincipled' or guilty of 'hypocrisy'.[32] As such, the debate over whether the majority or minority is more compelling and decisive in terms of their principled reasoning is a sleeveless errand; each can claim to have met and exceeded any threshold requirement for competent and professional reasoning. Moreover, numerous issues with each approach make it impossible to draw a clear, authoritative connection between reasoning and decision. So, while both are entirely acceptable examples of professional competence, both are also unable to convince that their reasoning is authoritatively superior to the other.

The majority opinion's reliance on an originalist approach drawing exclusively on 'the constitutional text, history, or precedent' flatters to deceive in its claim to be both grounded and insulated from political contamination.[33] Indeed, the shakiness of this approach is not difficult to reveal – its use of history is too selective and too self-serving; it is unsupported by the Court's own jurisprudence as being the only and exclusive mode of constitutional reasoning; it is unable to account for some important decisions, especially *Brown*; and it offers no convincing evidence that the Founders would have expected their own substantive views to be given enduring priority. As the minority states, 'the Constitution does not freeze for all time the original view of what those rights guarantee, or how they apply' and 'one result of today's decision is certain: the curtailment of women's rights, and of their status as free and equal citizens.'[34] In short, the majority's decision needs to be buttressed by something other than the innate strength of its legal reasoning if it is to assert unassailable authority or appeal.

Reaching a similar conclusion, the minority opinion's energising force depends on the extent to which its evolutionary and organicist rendition of constitutional reasoning can be defended. Again, the fragility of this approach is not difficult to reveal – it places enormous power and trust in each generation's judges; it imposes no fixed or reliable constraints on what the judges can or should do; it is unsupported by the Court's own jurisprudence as being the only and exclusive mode of constitutional reasoning; and its reliance on precedential authority is not easily squared with its emphasis on growth and responsiveness. As the majority states, 'the Constitution does not grant the nine unelected Members of this Court the unilateral authority to rewrite the Constitution to create new rights and liberties'[35]

---

[32] ibid at 2248, 2319 (Breyer J, dissenting).
[33] ibid at 2266 (Alito J, majority).
[34] ibid at 2326, 2318 (Breyer J, dissenting).
[35] ibid at 2248.

and 'the Court must not fall prey to such an unprincipled approach.'[36] In short, the minority's decision does not make itself authoritative and superior by dint of its legal arguments alone.

Consequently, the only credible way to explain what went on is that the majority and minority each made a decision to rely on a legal technique that would produce what in their eyes was a more desirable outcome. What gets these opinions over the decisional line, leaving aside the numbers issue, is their commitment to a particular political and/or moral stance. Of course, each side might seek to argue that it was their commitment to a certain style of argumentation – originalist or organicist – that tipped the scales one way or the other in reaching the conclusion that they did. But this position is very hard to maintain. It would seem that it is only jurists (as opposed to the general public) who hold to this naïve and romanticised view of judges as political innocents who eschew the temptations to act politically. It is certainly not the case that most politicians, including and especially appointing presidents, pay no attention to a judge's political leanings. While judges might not be appointed only for their politics or their identity, it is a rare appointee whose general political views run counter to the politics of the appointing president.[37]

A much more plausible account is that the mode of reasoning chosen, organicist or originalist, is compatible generally with reaching the kind of result that such proponents would approve of in terms of its political or moral salience. It is not that every decision would result in such compatibility, but that it will most often be the case, especially in areas of overt moral and political controversy. To put it bluntly, in *Dobbs*, the majority was set on overruling *Roe* and coming up with the best set of reasons to do that, whereas the minority was equally determined to stand by *Roe* and opt for a reasoning strategy that leaned strongly in that direction. So, insofar as the anti-abortion position is more easily achieved by an originalist and thereby conservative style of reasoning, the majority took such a line. Insofar as the pro-choice stance is more straightforwardly attained by an organicist and thereby more progressive mode of reasoning, the minority adopted this approach. While this phenomenon is more readily apparent in *Dobbs* (and *Roe*), it is a staple feature across the case law of constitutional law.

Any account of judging that wants to be taken seriously, especially by the legal community at large, needs to accept that the craft skills of legal argument and judicial reasoning are not just self-serving exercises in convenient ideological window dressing. Even if legal techniques fail to explain all that judges do, it is equally fallacious to assume that they have no influence at all. The better argument is that,

---

[36] ibid at 2306 (Kavanaugh J, concurring).

[37] This is not to say that judges always follow the wishes of their appointing president (eg, Earl Warren) or that judges do not change their political allegiances over time (eg, Harry Blackmun). See Allan Hutchinson, *Toward an Informal Account of Legal Interpretation* (New York, Cambridge University Press, 2016) 104–22. However, in recent years, some presidents have been more openly ideological in their choices.

as a piece of legal reasoning, the more it will convince others about the validity of the decision reached. Judges are never fully restrained nor are they ever fully free; freedom and constraint are mutually dependent and can only be made sense of in light of the other. In *Dobbs*, the majority and minority opinions were both good and bad depending on your political allegiance. However, it must also be remembered that the claim that the Constitution and its doctrines can be applied in a principled, correct, and politically neutral way is itself a thoroughly ideological claim.[38] Both originalism and organicism are themselves as much political ideologies as interpretive theories; they do not work as a hedge against ideology, but as a professional conduit for its implementation.

Unfortunately, the organicism that is wielded by the *Dobbs* minority does not put enough distance between itself and the philosophical underpinnings of originalism. While the minority rejects originalism, it unnecessarily hobbles itself by seeking to remain in the business of espousing constitutional truths, albeit of a less fundamentalist and ahistorical character. This seems a strategic and philosophical error on its part. In seeking to overturn a long-established decision, like *Roe*, and its entrenchment of a fundamental constitutional right, the majority has a much steeper jurisprudential hill to climb. Whereas the majority must justify a major shift and reversal in constitutional doctrine that takes away a recognised right, the minority only has to offer a justification for why such a radical break is inadvisable and should not be made. This is not to suggest that the minority's stance is not a political one, but that the nature of that politics and its attendant rationalisation in principled terms is much easier to defend and promote in *Dobbs* than the majority's far-reaching and almost militant upheaval of constitutional law. The minority took the stand that it did not only because of its free-standing commitment to precedent, but also because it would lead to a more politically preferable result. Like the majority, it would not have permitted precedent to prevent the recognition of what it considered to be important constitutional rights.[39]

If politics are considered to be as much a part of judicial decision-making as legal reasoning (as they are), then traditional scholars will no doubt raise the criticism that such a law-and-ideology approach will undermine the constitutional authority of the courts and fatally compromise their institutional legitimacy – how can judges, as unelected officials, retain popular support and deference if they are seen to be acting as politicians countermanding the decisions of elected legislators? If *Dobbs* is anything to go by, pretending that courts act only in a principled and not political way does not promote the cause of democracy. Indeed, Supreme Court opinions that hide behind such a pretence cause irreparable harm to the legitimacy of judicial review. Apart from their strengths and weaknesses as judicial opinions, the bitter back-and-forth between the majority and the minority only adds fuel to an already fierce fire. If encouraging or restoring public support is the

---

[38] See *Dobbs*, above n 1 at 2305 (Kavanaugh J, concurring) (describing the Constitution as 'neutral' and as 'neither pro-life nor pro-choice').

[39] See, eg, *Brown*, above n 3; *Obergefell v Hodges* (2015) 576 US 644; and *Roe*, above n 4.

aim, then *Dobbs* has failed on its own terms. The fact that both popular support of and opposition to the decision are based on its political outcome and consequences offers further evidence of why constitutional decision-making cannot be defended as being an entirely principled and professional exercise; it must also be characterised as a political and partisan performance to some extent.

Turning Ugly

In his concurrence, Justice Kavanaugh offered comments about his own and all other Justices' approach to the constitutionality of abortion rights. He noted that 'amidst extraordinary controversy and challenges, all of [the more than twenty Justices of this Court since 1973] have addressed the abortion issue in good faith after careful deliberation.'[40] This is an important and revealing assertion that, if true, is extremely important in evaluating the work of the Supreme Court – disagreement and dissent are to be respected as long as judges are acting in good faith. However, there are several reasons to question whether this sweeping claim is supportable, especially in regard to the majority opinion that Justice Kavanaugh was very much part of. Of course, challenging the idea of whether judges are acting in good faith is a very serious matter, but it is one that deserves to be aired and explored in light of some of the surrounding features and context of the *Dobbs* decision. There are, at least, three particular issues that warrant attention: (1) the institutional and democratic assumptions that inform the opinion; (2) the disregard of any appreciation of how the members of the majority might appreciate the influence of their own identities and values; and (3) the public statements made by the Justices at the time of their appointment to the Supreme Court.

What amounts to good or bad faith is itself a matter of considerable debate and disagreement. However, in general terms, it seems reasonable to suggest that one of the core ideas is the notion that people at bottom are expected to be as honest and authentic as they can when accounting for the things that they do. Bad faith might include hiding the real reasons for their actions, offering justifications for what they are doing that are insincere and misleading, or relying on irrelevant details and motivations.[41] At its most extreme, this involves fraud and deceit, but it also encompasses the lesser failings of hypocrisy, trickery and disingenuity. As regards judicial decision-making, this premise would recommend that relying on reasons that were not disclosed, that claimed a false lack of knowledge or that set aside earlier commitments without good reason would all count as sufficient to undermine the integrity and uprightness of opinions given. In *Dobbs*, this would

---

[40] *Dobbs*, above n 1 at 2310 (Kavanaugh J, concurring).

[41] This can be distinguished from the usage of 'bad faith' in existential philosophy where it is more about self-deception. See Jean-Paul Sartre, *Being and Nothingness*, special abridged edn (New York, Citadel Press, 1965). This explanation still has some jurisprudential relevance. See Duncan Kennedy, *A Critique of Adjudication: Fin de siècle* (Cambridge, Harvard University Press, 1997) 191–205.

seem to be a genuine possibility when the majority's opinion is placed in a wider context. Indeed, Justice Kavanaugh's insistence that he and his colleagues were acting in good faith might well be a statement not itself made in good faith.[42]

First, the majority pleads a certain naïveté or ignorance at the likely effect of the *Dobbs* decision on American society: 'we do not pretend to know how our political system or society will respond to today's decision overruling *Roe* and *Casey*'.[43] This is not a claim that is easy to accept at face value. It does not require any prescience or insight to grasp that, especially after a draft opinion was leaked seven weeks before the release of the actual decision, there would be social and political turmoil. Many states were pushing to ban abortion services entirely or with only minimal exceptions; state legislation was primed to be activated if a favourable decision was forthcoming. Although the precise situation was fluid, it was known to everyone that it would be much more difficult for women to obtain abortions if the *Dobbs* decision came out the way that it did; this is precisely what the minority noted with concern.[44] As such, it seems disingenuous for the majority to pretend that the consequences of the opinion were not known or knowable.

Secondly and as a corollary of this, the majority's claim that abortion is an issue best left to the states' democratic procedures also seems less than candid or consistent. The thrust of the argument is that, because 'the Constitution is neutral on the issue of abortion, ... the people and their elected representatives [can] address the issue through the democratic process'.[45] Moreover, the decision is promoted by the majority as allowing women to use their 'electoral or political power' in lobbying for legislation.[46] Leaving aside the fact that *Dobbs* undercuts women's power over themselves, let alone the electoral process, this defence appears somewhat hypocritical. The traditional stance is usually that constitutional rights are so important and fundamental that they need to be insulated from the vagaries of the political and democratic process.[47] However, in this case, a right that was recognised as a constitutional right for nearly 50 years is now seen to almost benefit from being put back into the political arena. For those not persuaded that the Constitution is or should be 'neutral on the issue of abortion',[48] this is cold comfort. As importantly, it is, at best, selective and inconsistent for the majority to take this stance.

---

[42] *Dobbs*, above n 1 at 2310 (Kavanaugh J, concurring).

[43] ibid at 2279 (Alito J, majority).

[44] ibid at 2318–19 (Breyer J, dissenting). All states, except for New Mexico, North Carolina and Alaska, have regulated abortion in some way. There are nine states with what amounts to outright abortion bans. The strictest states are Texas, Arkansas, South Dakota and Oklahoma; abortion is completely outlawed except when the life of the mother was in imminent danger. See 'Abortion in the United States Dashboard' (*Kaiser Family Foundation*) www.kff.org/womens-health-policy/dashboard/abortion-in-the-u-s-dashboard/.

[45] *Dobbs*, above n 1 at 2305–06 (Kavanaugh J, concurring).

[46] ibid at 2277 (Alito J, majority).

[47] A good example of this is the rhetoric deployed by the same majority over gun rights. See *New York State Rifle & Pistol Association Inc v Bruen* (2022) 142 S Ct 2111, 2131.

[48] *Dobbs*, above n 1 at 2305 (Kavanaugh J, concurring).

Thirdly, the majority remain adamant that their opinion must be based exclusively on legal arguments. In particular, they protest that it would be illegitimate for them to 'allow our decisions to be affected by any extraneous influences such as concern about the public's reaction to our work', 'social and political pressures' or 'based on our own moral or policy views'.[49] But this grand assertion of principle seems to be almost willfully unaware of or insensitive to what might be their own views and any pressures working on them. Indeed, it cannot be ignored that all five of the majority were practising Catholics or had direct Catholic backgrounds.[50] While this cannot be decisive in accounting for their moral or policy views (and it has to be recognised that one of the dissenting minority judges was Catholic), it is surely improbable and unrealistic to think that this played no part at all. Similarly, four of the five Justices who joined the majority were men and, therefore, had no direct personal experience of women's reproductive experiences. On both counts, it is hardly going too far to expect that some recognition or, at least, explanation of how these factors played no part in their decision would be offered; it cannot simply be assumed and asserted. Again, the failure to speak to or even mention these telling facts raises reasonable doubts about the integrity and trustworthiness of the majority's opinion.

The fourth and perhaps most telling issue is the circumstances under which each individual Justice of the *Dobbs* majority became a member of the Supreme Court and their relevance to any questions of good faith performance. That the appointment process has a marked political dimension is uncontestable. Presidents appoint judges whose political leanings, if not always fully in synch with their own, do not run counter to them. Some might want to go as far as the fictional Irish bartender, Martin Dooley that 'th' Supreme Courts follows th' iliction returns'.[51] However, this is not entirely accurate: it is more often the case that the Court does not reflect the substantive voting preferences of the winning President, but that the appointment of judges tends to follow the election returns at that time. As history shows, while almost all judges tend to remain reasonably consistent in their political orientation, there are a handful that buck that trend; *Roe's* Justice Harry Blackmun is often considered exhibit one in this regard.[52]

Nevertheless, as the membership of the *Dobbs* court reveals, it is reasonable to assume that much can be learned about judges and their political leaning

---

[49] ibid at 2278 (Alito J, majority), 2306 (Kavanaugh J, concurring).

[50] While it is possible to be a Catholic and take a pro-choice stance, it is a fundamental tenet of Roman Catholicism that abortion is sinful and should be prohibited. Chief Justice Roberts is Catholic. Also, President Biden might be one of those Catholics who supports a pro-choice position politically. Either way, some explanation seems necessary.

[51] Finley Peter Dunne, *Mr. Dooley's Opinions* (New York, Harper and Brothers, 1906) 26.

[52] Along with Justices Hugo Black and David Souter, Justice Blackmun is one the exceptions that prove the general rule – among the great bulk of the Supreme Court, there is some ideological shift, but that shift is of contestable or limited significance; only three judges have crossed over the ideological divide between right and left. See Lee Epstein, Andrew D Martin, Kevin M Quinn and Jeffrey A Segal, 'Ideological Drift Among Supreme Court Justices: Who, When, and How Important?' (2007) 101 *Northwestern University Law Review* 1483, 1485–86.

by reference to their appointing president; the majority and Chief Justice were Republican appointees, and the minority were each Democratic appointees. In recent years, under the presidency of Donald Trump and with the support of a Republican-dominated Senate, the alignment of judges with their appointing president has become more doctrinaire; Trump made no bones about the fact that he was working to ensure that federal judicial vacancies were filled by card-carrying conservatives who were often originalist in their judicial philosophies and opposed *Roe*. And, of course, President Biden took a similar tack in filling a vacancy on the Supreme Court by replacing a retiring judge with a Democratic appointee, Ketanji Brown Jackson. Presumably, the belief was that this would bear partisan fruit for many years and even decades to come.

None of this is surprising, although many constitutional jurists seem intent on playing down the significance of judges' political affiliations when it comes to explaining or criticising their judicial performance and output in terms of principled reasoning. However, while all judges are vulnerable to the same observations when examining the link between their political leanings and their judicial decisions, there are some telling and disturbing differences when it comes to the appointments of the *Dobbs* majority. While all five Justices were appointed by Republican presidents, certain statements were made by them during their Senate confirmation hearings that raise disturbing doubts about their good faith in handling the divisive issue of abortion and the continuing validity of the *Roe* precedent. Indeed, at a minimum, these declarations offer some credible evidence that they were not entirely proceeding with integrity and honesty when *Dobbs* and related matters came before them.

As expected, a particular focus of the Senate confirmation hearings was the candidate's attitude towards the controversial decision of *Roe*. While each of them was typically circumspect in addressing this and related issues, there was a general sense in which they intimated that it was a settled constitutional precedent and, therefore, deserving of constitutional weight. Appointed to the Court in 1991 by President George Bush, Justice Thomas was deliberately evasive on *Roe* as he maintained he could not 'comment on that specific case' and 'maintain [his] impartiality'.[53] He also added that 'I think it is inappropriate for any judge who is worth his or her salt to prejudge any issue or to sit on a case [where] he or she cannot be impartial.'[54] Appointed to the Court in 2006 by President George W Bush, Justice Alito did not hide his conservative views: he maintained that *Roe* was entitled to 'considerable respect' and that he would separate his 'personal views' from what he did as a judge and keep 'an open mind'.[55] So, although far from

---

[53] 'The Nomination of Judge Clarence Thomas to be Associate Justice of the Supreme Court of the United States: Before the S. Comm. on the Judiciary' (1991) 102d Cong 262 www.govinfo.gov/content/pkg/GPO-CHRG-THOMAS/pdf/GPO-CHRG-THOMAS-1.pdf.

[54] ibid at 293.

[55] 'Confirmation Hearing on the Nomination of Samuel A. Alito, Jr. to be an Associate Justice of the Supreme Court of the United States: Before the S. Comm. on the Judiciary' (2006) 109th Cong 455, 531, 454 www.govinfo.gov/content/pkg/CHRG-109shrg25429/pdf/CHRG-109shrg25429.pdf.

categoric in their support for *Roe*, both Justices Thomas and Alito did not suggest that they would overrule it if a suitable occasion arose. Until 2021, that occasion (and the needed numbers) did not arise.

The appointments of the three remaining members of the majority were very recent. They took place during the presidency of Donald Trump who was publicly open about his intention to appoint Justices who were opposed to the *Roe* ruling. However, at their confirmation hearings, all three judges were not only cautious and guarded in their comments, but also gave reassurances that overruling *Roe* was not at all part of their immediate judicial philosophy. Denying that he had been asked by the President about his views, Justice Gorsuch remarked about *Roe* that 'a good judge will consider it as precedent of the U.S. Supreme Court worthy as treatment of precedent like any other'. He also insisted that his 'personal views [had nothing] to do with the judge's job'.[56] Justice Kavanaugh was also cagey in answering questions, but did confirm that *Roe* was 'settled as precedent'.[57] Finally, Justice Barrett was also difficult to pin down, but she did go so far as to say that:

> the substantive due process clause says that there are some liberties, some rights that people possess that the state can't take away or can't take away without a really good reason. So the right to use birth control, the right to an abortion are examples of rights protected by substantive due process.[58]

Taken at face value, the overall import of the three recent appointees' Senate hearings would not give rise to the expectation that they would become part of a majority that would overrule *Roe* at the earliest opportunity. But that is exactly what they did. Of course, as all lawyers know, it is not wise to take statements at face value. Although one might be forgiven for thinking that judges who are under oath might be relied upon to speak truthfully, the fact is that recent events have undermined the mild reassurances that those three judges offered. It might be said that they knew that they were under the ideological microscope and were simply engaging in a practised political strategy that treated anything other than outright lies as being close enough to truth. But, while Justices Thomas and Alito

---

[56] 'Confirmation Hearing on the Nomination of Hon. Neil M. Gorsuch to be An Associate Justice of the Supreme Court of the United States: Before the S. Comm. on the Judiciary' (2017) 115th Cong 77, 195, www.govinfo.gov/content/pkg/CHRG-115shrg28638/pdf/CHRG-115srg28638. pdf. It is also worth noting that, while a doctoral student at Oxford, he wrote a thesis on abortion and its (im)moral foundations.

[57] 'Confirmation Hearing on the Nomination of Hon. Brett M. Kavanaugh to be an Associate Justice of the Supreme Court of the United States: Before the S. Comm. on the Judiciary' (2018) 115th Cong 297, www.govinfo.gov/content/pkg/CHRG-115shrg32765/pdf/CHRG-115shrg32765.pdf. Prior to his hearing, Justice Kavanaugh told Republican Senator Susan Collins in a closed meeting that he was 'no threat' to Roe and that his 'don't-rock-the-boat' juridical style should demonstrate to her that confirming his nomination was a safe bet for women's fair access to abortion services. See Carle Hulse, 'Kavanaugh Gave Private Assurances. Collins Says He "Misled" Her' (*New York Times*, 24 June 2022) www.nytimes.com/2022/06/24/us/roe-kavanaugh-collins-notes.html.

[58] 'Amy Coney Barrett Senate Confirmation Hearing Day 2 Transcript' (*Rev*, 13 October 2020) www. rev.com/blog/transcripts/amy-coney-barrett-senate-confirmation-hearing-day-2-transcript. At their confirmation hearings, each of the minority judges obviously signalled that they considered *Roe* to be settled precedent.

might somehow claim that their views had shifted over time (although there is no evidence of that), the three recent recruits have no such excuse. At a minimum, it can reasonably be concluded that they were playing fast and loose with the truth – they were open and ready to overrule *Roe* if the occasion and judicial numbers presented themselves. That opportunity occurred very quickly. In the case of Justice Barrett, it was within 18 months of her appointment.

For those committed to the Court's legitimacy, these facts are not in any way reassuring or comforting. Indeed, they can be appreciated to have underlined and exacerbated a very uncomfortable state of affairs. Reasonably viewed and taken together, they cannot be brushed aside as being little more than the predictable carping of cynical critics. As judges and lawyers like to remind people, it is not only that justice should be done, but that it should be seen to be done.[59] These facts need to be responded to, if not by the majority Justices themselves, at least by mainstream defenders of the Court. At a minimum, these nagging misgivings about the *bona fides* of the majority not only speak to the legitimacy and, there-fore, the validity of the *Dobbs* decision itself, but also to the overall reputation and standing of the Supreme Court. After all, as Justice Kavanaugh suggests, there is much riding on the fact that the majority 'have addressed the abortion issue in good faith after careful deliberation'.[60] If they did not, it is important that jurists and commentators call them to account.

Conclusion

When it comes to constitutional law and doctrine, it is surely the case that there is no final or determinative word. Like most law, it is a work-in-progress that is always moving, but never arriving anywhere in particular. However, why its particular temporary destinations are set and how it intends to get to them is of the most crucial significance. In criticising the *Dobbs* decision, I have recommended that there are three standards that any Supreme Court must be judged by if it is to engender the kind of public and professional respect that it seeks and requires – the soundness of the legal reasons that have been offered; the political principles that guide their decision-making; and the integrity and good faith with which they operate. Although both the majority and the minority have little to divide them in terms of the first two (even though many will be more or less partial to the opposing political ideologies that animate the legal arguments), there is, at best, considerable uncertainty about whether the majority can or has lived up to the demands of the third standard. Indeed, it would seem that it has not.

---

[59] *R v Sussex Justices, ex parte McCarty* [1924] 1 KB 256, 259.
[60] *Dobbs*, above n 1 at 2310 (Kavanaugh J, concurring).

6

The Politics of Law:
A Clearer and Deeper Dive

One of the key fault-lines in jurisprudence continues to be the extent to which adjudication can or should be considered a political or ideological practice. There are almost no contemporary jurists who assert that adjudication can be performed without any reliance on contested values and choices. However, there are many who do maintain that, while a resort to such values is inevitable, this task can be accomplished without a vertiginous descent into an ideological free-for-all. The division among these jurists is over whether this resort is a penumbral and marginal occurrence (eg, Hartian-style positivists) or whether that resort to political values is pervasive, but can be carried out in a neutral and objective way (eg, Dworkinian-style naturalists). As I have explained, these basic stances play out in and across constitutional law and scholarship. In effect, these traditionalists are all neo-formalists to one extent or another because they think that adjudication is largely, if not exclusively, a professional and contained undertaking that is significantly different from an open and ideological exercise.

There is, of course, a small group of critical scholars (whom I count myself among) who reject any compromise with the idea that 'law is politics'. Instead, they argue that adjudication is always and everywhere a thoroughly ideological act – it is politics up, down and sideways. Although diverse in their approaches and methods, such critical theorists insist that adjudication is not only political in the circumstances that give rise to it and in the consequences that follow from it, but also is inescapably political in its operation and performance. Whether following, changing or developing the law, adjudication is understood as 'a forum of ideology'.[1] Consequently, any efforts to appreciate or understand adjudication and law generally are themselves unavoidably ideological projects. In short, therefore, critical legal theory dismisses most traditional accounts of adjudication as being little more than a vain attempt to confer a vestige of institutional legitimacy on a profoundly political process that inescapably tends to advance and favour some

---

[1] Duncan Kennedy, *A Critique of Adjudication: Fin de siècle* (Cambridge, Harvard University Press, 1997) 63. In constitutional law, the leading critical scholar is Mark Tushnet. See Mark Tushnet, *Red, White, and Blue: A Critical Analysis of Constitutional Law* (Cambridge, Harvard University Press 1988) and Mark Tushnet, *Power to the People: Constitutionalism in the Age of Populism* (New York, Oxford University Press, 2021).

social interest over others. Although this is a general feature of law and adjudication, this is nowhere more true than in the domain of constitutional law.

In this chapter, therefore, the main focus will not be on re-entering and re-fighting this law/politics debate; this has been much of the force and thrust of the preceding chapters. Instead, I will concentrate on explaining and clarifying exactly what is and is not meant by the assertion that 'law is politics' as well as pursuing its practical implications for jurisprudence and constitutional law. In the first section, I give a more sophisticated and nuanced account of what is meant by 'politics' and show how it can be better understood as an illuminating account of constitutional law. The next section offers an extended critique of principled reasoning in line with the critical claim that law-is-politics. The next three sections play out this law-is-politics critique in a Canadian social and political challenge over what can be done and by whom to tackle climate change issues – the first section sets up the political problem; the second section looks at how the courts approach the issue; and the third section drives home the inescapable political nature of judicial decision-making in constitutional law. Throughout the chapter, the ambition will be to demonstrate that the critical claim that 'law is politics' is not simply another jurisprudential posture or contribution, but is a practical and, of course, political intervention in substantive matters that are often decisive for society generally.

Law's Politics

The major thrust of a critical theory of law and adjudication is that, despite the claims of judges and their academic apologists, constitutional law and judicial decision-making are simply professional exercises in political decision-making and persuasion; it is judicial politics masquerading as objective law. Put succinctly, 'the content of the law and how it is applied is largely a function of who is on the bench and their values'.[2] Accordingly, academic theorists and judges have difficulty letting go of the idea that, whatever its contingent and occasional failings, judges can actually live up to the jurisprudential aspiration that law can be done in a way that grapples with politics, but in a way that does not itself collapse into politics *tout court*. They seem willing to declare that, while legal interpretation 'is necessarily a normative enterprise, not a mechanical one',[3] it is still possible to be normative without also being ideological. In contrast, I maintain that, while this is more acute and evident in the work of supreme or final courts of appeal, it is no less present or pervasive in lower courts. Also, and again, although the political

---

[2] Erwin Chemerinsky, *Worse than Nothing: The Dangerous Fallacy of Originalism* (New Haven, Yale University Press, 2022) 24.

[3] Jonathan Gould, 'Puzzles of Progressive Constitutionalism' (2022) 135 *Harvard Law Review* 2053, 2085.

character of adjudication is ever-present across all branches of law, even if more understated, it is at its most obvious and apparent in constitutional law.

Stated in these broad and sweeping terms, a law-is-politics critique may seem to be too blunt and too crass by far to be convincing; it can be more easily dismissed by its antagonists when expressed in such stark and unconditional terms. Consequently, it is important to offer several riders and provisos in defending a more nuanced account of this critical approach. In this way, the detractors might be more effectively rebuffed. Accordingly, there are four main clarifications or elucidations that need to be added to the charge that law-is-politics – that the politics at issue are broad and deep and, therefore, not reducible to only crude partisan or party politics; that legal reasoning is not entirely a bad faith enterprise when understood from a critical perspective; that the sharedness of the judicial values relied upon is not in itself a negation of their core politicalness; and that the critical alternative to traditional legal theory's account of legal reasoning and judicial decision-making is not a nihilistic free-for-all. In regard to each, I will emphasise that, although there is no objective fact-of-the-matter when it comes to politics, there is something more achievable than a series of foot-stomping, tub-thumping and visceral outbursts when it comes to political exchange and debate.

First, it essential that the reference to politics in law-is-politics is not to be understood in a narrow and parochial sense. It is about much more than a loose collection of issues that comprise piecemeal and expedient agendas for the purposes of periodic elections and the like. In the critical playbook, as well as encompassing those matters, it is about a much broader and deeper set of values and normative commitments. Politics is as much structural and systemic as it is personal and discrete – the nature of the individual, the organisation of society, the relationship between an individual and society, the role of government, institutional legitimacy (including the courts' own), the distribution of power, democratic dynamics, and the like. Many of these are dealt with in an unspoken and perhaps unappreciated manner; they are more assumed than admitted. However, these values are what animate and inform much of the debate about the issues that are to be dealt with in more prosaic contestation (eg, taxes, abortion, gender, education, sexuality, immigration, law and order, climate change, etc). Whether it is about the nature of private obligations or public arrangements, these deep-seated commitments orient people in a general direction when confronted with particular and substantive social challenges, moral controversies or ideological confrontations.

Also, I am using 'ideology' in a standard and neutral sense. In this defence of law-is-politics, I use it to refer to a roughly integrated set of beliefs and ideas, both shallow and deep, that help to explain and justify a general understanding of society, its constituent components, its appreciation of justice and the dynamic interaction of its various components. In particular, I am not intending to talk about ideology in the pejorative Marxist meaning as a set of normative commitments through which the powerful deceive and, therefore, subjugate the less powerful by impressing on them the supposed justness of present social arrangements. On this view, ideology is a clouding of reality, not a formative part of it. My use of 'ideological' is different in that it is not about the contested notion of 'false consciousness'.[4] For my present purposes, therefore, 'political' and 'ideological' are used largely inter-changeably; they are both intended to refer to the same group of constituting ideas and normative justifications for those ideas. In short, politics is something that shapes the characterisation of the problems of social power as well as informing people's take on particular problems within a society.

Secondly, there is nothing in the law-is-politics stance that commits critics to the position that legal reasoning and professional argumentation are meaningless or irrelevant endeavours. In short, that it is all a sham. This representation relies upon a neglected distinction between anti-formalists and informalists. Both reject the formalist idea that law should and can be applied by judges without any or, at least, very minimal resort to ideological preferences. However, the anti-formalist insists that any appreciation of adjudication begins and ends with judges' ideo-logical commitments (ie, consult one's own ideological compass, choose a desired outcome, and rationalise it in terms of the existing legal doctrines and decisions).[5] In contrast, the informalist takes a more sophisticated and less cynical approach. For the informalists (and, therefore, me), it is not that law is something separate and distinct from ideology or that law is nothing other than disguised ideological posturing. When understood properly from an informalist perspective, therefore, legal interpretation and judicial decision-making are applied exercises in law-and-ideology; it is both constrained and unconstrained in equal measure. As a couple of astute jurists observe, 'constitutional law shares this instability, vibrating constantly between the professional logic of reason and principle and the intui-tive, implicit, and contextual logic of fundamental social values'.[6] Importantly, the informalist insists that this instability is neither temporary nor resolvable in any settled way.

Accordingly, rather than treat legal reasoning and ideological argument as separate and antithetical practices, adjudication is treated as being both a thor-oughly professional craft as well as a thoroughly ideological exercise; law is a result of the combination of legal technique and political vision, particularly at the level

---

[4] Karl Marx, *The German Ideology* (first published 1845, London, Lawrence & Wishart, 1974). The best introduction to ideology remains Terry Eagleton, *Ideology: An Introduction*, new edn (London, Verso, 2007). However, I should say that there is a certain 'false consciousness' in play in the judicial and juristic community about the supposed apolitical and technical nature of the legal reasoning that they rely on.

[5] It is far from easy to identify any serious legal theorist or constitutional scholar who consistently runs such an anti-formalist line. Mainstream writers tend to label some of their critics as falling into such a camp so that they can be more easily dismissed without taking their critiques seriously. See, eg, Richard Fallon Jr, *Law and Legitimacy in the Supreme Court* (Cambridge, Harvard University Press, 2018) 13, 49, 120.

[6] See Robert Post and Neil Siegel, 'Theorizing the Law/Politics Distinction: Neutral Principles, Affirmative Action, and the Enduring Legacy of Paul Mishkin' (2007) 95 *California Law Review* 1473, 1501. For my own extended efforts to map out and defend an informalist position, see Allan Hutchinson, *Toward an Informal Account of Legal Interpretation* (New York, Cambridge University Press, 2016).

of supreme courts. So, the informalist does not insist that adjudication cannot occur in a law-contained, principled, and good-faith reasoned way. It can. What the informalist critic emphasises is that such a law-contained, principled, and good-faith reasoned way of judging in constitutional law cannot be accomplished and effectuated without resort to or reliance upon contested and political values: an informalist-influenced judge or jurist is not encumbered by any pretence that their institutional duties can be fulfilled by a neutral or detached method of professional performance.

Any account of judging (including and especially a critical one), therefore, that wants to be taken seriously by the broader legal and popular community needs to accept that the craft-skills of legal argument and judicial reasoning are not only self-serving exercises in convenient ideological window-dressing. A poorly reasoned opinion is unlikely to garner the support and approval of the legal community as a respected precedent whatever its political substance or slant.[7] Consequently, while legal considerations and reasoning techniques do not explain all that judges do (and they do not), it is equally fallacious to assume that they have no influence or effect at all. Indeed, it is the case that the better and more compelling an argument is as a piece of legal reasoning, the more likely it is that it will convince others about the decision reached. But legal craft alone cannot and does not carry the day. What makes a judicial decision good or bad is not based only on an internal technical assessment (ie, does it best conform with existing legal doctrine in small and/or large ways?), but a good decision has to be validated by an external normative evaluation (ie, does it reach and defend a stance that is politically desirable and defensible in terms of prevailing social and political contexts?).

Thirdly, the fact that judges and jurists share much the same values does not defeat or deflect the claim that law is politics. At its most extreme, it is often suggested that, when a judicial decision is unanimous and succeeds in receiving widespread approval, it can be assumed that politics are not in play and that the decision (and, as importantly, the values on which it is based) garners a certain objectivity. However, the fact that a professional or popular grouping possess a shared outlook cannot in itself definitively resist the law-is-politics charge: the sharedness might give the impression that politics has been sidestepped or dodged, but that is all it does. As with religion, so with law – the lack of disagreement within a group about foundational commitments does not grant those values any special or cogent authority outside of that group. Similarly, it is unpersuasive when it is claimed that moderation and reasonableness avoid charges that they are political: the middle-of-the-road is no less of a political position than either side of the political street. Moreover, even when there is a general sharedness of views and values, it does not mean that they will cash-out the same for everyone all of the time in specific controversies. Accordingly, the existence of shared values is no

---

[7] This was part of the problem with *Roe*, but only part of the problem. See ch 5.

less a sign of apoliticalness than a sharp conflict; shared and accepted values are as political as unshared and contested values.

The fourth caveat about the critical defence of the claim that 'law is politics' is that the alternative to traditional legal theory's account of legal reasoning and judicial decision-making is not a nihilistic free-for-all in which might always gets its way Although politics is always and everywhere a contestable matter with no final or fixed resolution, the engagement in politics does not need to be a descent into ideological mayhem in which there is no basis at all for principled or coherent engagement. Indeed, it is not only possible to be more reasoned and principled in politics than it is usually assumed by judges and jurists, but it also seems a desirable requirement for citizens in a society that considers itself committed to the ideals of democracy and justice. The robust and principled defence of contested positions within political debate is not the exclusive province of the formalist judge or jurist; democratic politics can be carried out in better (and worse) ways. This caveat and the nature of the critical position demand a more extended defence.

Principles, Philosophy and Politics

When it comes to talking about political and moral values, the ideas of Oliver Wendell Holmes, Jr are often attributed to the critical theorist. In particular, his philosophical scepticism that 'deep-seated preferences cannot be argued about' is considered to be a fair summary of the critics' stance.[8] This is mistaken. The critical theorist (or at least this one) has a more subtle and pragmatic approach to political values and any engagement about them. It might well be accurate and telling to assert such a position when it comes to beer and other beverages – 'you cannot argue a man into liking a glass of beer.'[9] However, such a relativistic approach holds little water or weight when it comes to people's deep-seated preferences in the political realm. It is not a straightforward choice between arbitrary acceptance or rejection; there are many other options that can be defended and promoted. Indeed, while there are evaluative dead-ends and argumentative cul-de-sacs to be avoided, there still exists the practical possibility of a reasoned exchange occurring. Indeed, this can engender, on occasion, a better understanding of opposing views and even an occasional moderation of views. As such, the critical informalist is more optimistic and sanguine than the Holmesian sceptic.

The critical theorist insists that debate about deep-seated preferences can be principled, but not in any final, fixed, or neutral way. In other words, philosophy and theory are themselves not an escape from nor a collapse into stark politics; there are more dialogic approaches to be identified and taken. Most importantly,

---

[8] Oliver Wendell Holmes, 'Natural Law' (1918) 32 *Harvard Law Review* 40, 41.

[9] ibid. Holmes also contended that '[t]o have doubted one's own first principles is the mark of a civilized man.' Oliver Wendell Holmes, 'Ideals and Doubts' (1915) *10 Illinois Law Review* 1, 4.

from a critical standpoint, it must be emphasised that, in addressing these deeper value-commitments and their political framework, there is no sub-strata that can be excavated and cleared that will provide solid and objective ground on which to stand. There is no place to reach that will obviate the need for justification and contestation. While people may well reach agreements on some of these basic premises, they do not offer an external or uncontestable platform that can legitimate them or put them beyond dispute. Such agreement between people is nothing more than that; it can and will shift and change as circumstances and conditions also shift and change across time, place and topic. Moreover, even if there was a shared consensus or compromise on these deeper values, they will not be capable of being applied automatically or easily when specific issues have to be dealt with in specific situations. In short, there is no Context of contexts that can render contingent commitments into absolute truths and that will withstand interrogation and engagement – it is politics all the way down.[10] But that politics need not be undebatable or beyond scrutiny; democracy can provide a space within which politics can be pursued in a tolerant and civilised manner.

Unfortunately, a Wechsler-inspired view of law and politics manages to negate the possibility of such democratic engagement outside of courts – it relies upon a very partial and self-serving account of the volatility and superficiality of politics when compared and contrasted with law. Insisting that judges should be principled in character and application, traditional theorists recommend that, in order to act legitimately, courts must not act as a 'naked power organ': they must be able to distinguish their work from 'the *ad hoc* in politics' where unprincipled, transient and self-serving ideological allegiances are the order of the day. To achieve this, Wechsler contended that courts 'are obliged to be entirely principled' and thereby be neutral in their dealing with politics.[11] This general approach was adopted by Lon Fuller who viewed the task of judges as being to identify and engage with the law's overall purposive enterprise that we 'inevitably help to create as we strive (in accordance with our obligation of fidelity to law) to make the [law] a coherent, workable whole'.[12] More recently, of course, Ronald Dworkin also developed a defence of the courts as being 'a forum of principle' that is obliged to be political, but to be guided in that duty by reference to the law's own objective politics, not their own ideological preferences.[13] These different approaches seem to unite in the unappetising prospect that it is principled judicial reasoning or the political abyss.

---

[10] For a fuller defence of this pragmatic stance, see Allan Hutchinson, *The Province of Jurisprudence Democratized* (New York, Oxford University Press, 2008).

[11] Herbert Wechsler, 'Toward Neutral Principles of Constitutional Law' (1959) 73 *Harvard Law Review* 1, 12, 19. See also Cass Sunstein, *Constitutional Personae* (New York, Oxford University Press, 2015).

[12] Lon Fuller, 'Positivism and Fidelity to Law: A Reply to Professor Hart' (1957) 71 *Harvard Law Review* 630, 667.

[13] See Ronald Dworkin, *A Matter of Principle* (Cambridge, Harvard University Press, 1985) 146. See ch 3.

In this stark Wechslerianesque scenario, it is not at all surprising that judicial decision-making, especially in constitutional matters, is treated as being preferable to politics. The traditional role of the courts is understood to be a principled and reasoned refuge from the opportunistic hustle-and-bustle and arch-partisanship of the political arena. Unlike politics, the courts are thought of as bringing a measured, rational and non-ideological level-headedness to the cynical mud-slinging antics of ideological politics. This is increasingly the way that contemporary politics are viewed. So, if politicians and social activists are entitled to play politics and get their hands dirty, the judges must adopt a clean-hands approach. For traditional jurists, therefore, there is a crunch question, even if this dichotomous understanding is a compelling rendition of the prevailing state of affairs – can judges (and their juristic supporters) actually achieve and pull off this 'clean hands' ambition? In contrast to the traditional answer of 'yes', my critical and informalist stance takes the position that it is simply not possible to do adjudication without judges getting their hands dirty. However, it also maintains that political debate and practice need not be as dirty or as gut-based as the traditionalists suppose: foot-stomping is not the only or inevitable posture of the respectable politician.

A critical stance argues that not only is adjudication not as principled (ie, not thoroughly politically infused) as its apologists claim, it also insists that politics is or, at least, need not be as unprincipled as jurists suggest. Good political or ideological argument is no more or less arbitrary than any other kind of argument. Of course, ideological argument can be arbitrary and opportunistic, but it can also be as principled and as reasonable as any other mode of reason, including legal reasoning. In short, legal adjudication has no corner on being principled or, at least, aspiring to be principled. Indeed, in law and politics, what does and does not count as 'principled' is both more and less constraining than is generally proposed. As well as it being difficult to distinguish principles from other types of generalised norms, there is no definitive way to separate legal principles from more general moral and political principles – law is politics The fact is that the doctrinal resources of law are so ample, so capacious and so multi-dimensional that the range of principles available are prolific and abundant; it is possible to generate any number of principles at any number of levels in legal doctrine to support a range of positions and outcomes.[14] The jurisprudential problem is, therefore, that there are too many principles, not too few, with no available meta-principle or method to resolve any tension or contradiction between them.

In short, under the traditional view, there is an unnecessary and self-defeating Hobson's choice – judges can be principled, even if they occasionally fall short of that exacting standard, or they can be 'manipulative', in that they make no attempt to be principled.[15] For traditional jurists, this is a self-serving distinction that, of course, directs and validates jurists' choice to adopt a (pseudo-) principled

---

[14] See ch 4.
[15] Wechsler, above n 11 at 15.

approach over any other politically-based explanation or account of judicial behaviour and decision-making. However, their proposed answers and solutions only have any theoretical bite if their defence of the fundamental question to be answered is convincing. But it is not. A fruitful space can be located and inhabited that is not reducible to either so-called principled judicial decision-making or the *ad hoc* political posturing. As such, there is not only a rich territory to be mined between the two, but there is also a significant and important difference between those who are thoughtful politicians and upright commentators and those who are political flunkies and media-savvy hacks. Politics can be a more than a dishonourable battle of opposing and intolerant ideologues, even if it is not the detached, neutral and disinterested enterprise that some idealist philosophers depict it to be.

To put all this in the chosen vernacular of juristic thought, I am suggesting that judicial decision-making in constitutional law can be a good faith exercise in principled reasoning. However, even if it does meet such a standard, there is no reason or justification for defending such reasoning as being thereby able to resist the charge that it is thoroughly political in nature and application. Of course, this assessment that principled reasoning is unavoidably political does not mean that it is unruly, manipulative, *ad hoc* and disingenuous. There is a way that judges can be both principled and professional as well as political and opinionated at the same time. This means that, as Dworkin insisted, while law 'is deeply and thoroughly political', it does not mean that, as he also insisted, 'law is not a matter of personal or partisan politics'.[16] Yet, in being personal and partisan, law and adjudication are neither unprincipled nor unprofessional. Although there is no objective and impartial status to the kind of principled and professional practice that constitutional law and adjudication can be, it can still be done in a way that distinguishes it from an open-ended and unreasoned political practice. In short, in law and adjudication, it is not that 'anything goes', but that 'anything might go' if it manages to persuade others in a principled, good faith and sincere manner.[17]

Of course, it might be riposted by some traditional judges and jurists that these abstract arguments are speculative and tendentious; there is no practical or proven bite to them. There is a kernel of plausibility to this response. Accordingly, it behooves me to play out these more general remarks in a more detailed and doctrinal setting within constitutional law. However, instead of doing so in a blatantly moral and contested area (eg, abortion, sexuality or racial discrimination), I will explore and defend the ramifications of this critical and informalist stand in a more opaque area of constitutional law that is often understood as being technical in scope and substance – the federal division of powers and environmental regulation. By showing how the treatment and resolution of this kind of pressing and contested issue is equally and inescapably political in nature and operation, I

---

[16] Ronald Dworkin, above n 13 at 146.

[17] I will be pursuing more fully both the jurisprudential and institutional implications of these critical insights for both the theory and practice of constitutional law and decision-making going forward. See chs 7–10.

will be better able to respond directly and forcibly to formalists and neo-formalists (and perhaps anti-formalists) in regard to the politics of constitutional law and adjudication.

Walking the Line

For most countries, one of the most pressing concerns on the contemporary political agenda is how to deal with the many challenges and serious ramifications of climate change. A major part of that is about what to do about greenhouse gas emissions. There is, of course, much heated and polarising disagreement about the best way to proceed; many interests and issues need to be balanced. However, in a quintessentially Canadian twist, the debate in Canada is as much about who should be able to decide what should be done as it is about what should be done – the federal government or the provincial governments? This federalism question raises constitutional matters of the most intense and most contested kind. Building on a troubled and fractured history that has stretched across over 150 years of Canada's existence, the courts and legislatures have gone head-to-head on how legislative powers and political priorities should be distributed. The recent dispute over the regulation of greenhouse gas emissions has brought the contemporary dispute to a head. In the process, it has thrown the accompanying debate around the relative legitimacies of courts and governments into sharp focus.

In 2015, Canada signed the Paris Agreement that requires state signatories to reduce substantially the amounts of greenhouse gases as a way to respond to the devastating effects of climate change. Although only the federal government has the constitutional authority to enter such international treaties, the power to implement its terms was a matter of constitutional nicety as to whether it could be done exclusively by the federal government without provincial approval and participation. As a result and after much political consultation between the federal and provincial governments, the Canadian Parliament assumed jurisdiction and passed the Greenhouse Gas Pollution Pricing Act (GGPPA) in 2018 that introduced a carbon-pricing scheme. Sensitive to constitutional concerns about the division of powers, the federal plan allowed provinces to devise and implement their own schemes. However, any provincial scheme that failed to meet a pan-Canadian benchmark for minimal pricing arrangements would be superseded by the federal scheme. Needless to say, after much back-and-forth manoeuvring, four provinces – Saskatchewan, Alberta, Ontario and Manitoba – objected to this approach; they either did nothing or introduced their own and less stringent schemes for curbing greenhouse gas emissions.

By way of objection, three provinces brought constitutional challenges to the federal legislation through the reference process. While the Ontario and Saskatchewan Courts of Appeal found the GGPPA constitutional, the Alberta Court of Appeal did not. The stage was set, therefore, for a combined hearing before the Supreme Court of Canada. The question at issue was whether the provinces had exclusive authority to enact carbon-pricing schemes under their Constitution Act 1867, s 92 authority over 'property and civil rights' powers or whether the federal government could rely on its general 'peace, order and good government' powers under that Act to validate its policies and legislation as matter of national concern. While the focus was on the public and political struggle to combat the immediate and devastating polluting effects of climate change, the broader engagement was about the continuing contestation over the relationship between federal and provincial constitutional powers in today's social and political circumstances.

Although the political disagreements ran deep and divided, there seemed to be a general agreement that resort to the Supreme Court would and should effectively resolve the matter. While there was understood to be underlying and sharp ideological differences between different governments about climate change and the best response to be made, there was a deeper and more unifying commitment to the idea that the Canadian Constitution stood apart from day-to-day politics. Properly interpreted by the Supreme Court, constitutional law was accepted to be a principled and reasoned refuge from the opportunistic hustle-and-bustle of the political arena. While Prime Minister Justin Trudeau and his provincial colleagues played politics and got stuck in the political mud, Chief Justice Richard Wagner and his puisne associates were expected to take a more detached stance and stay well clear of that cloying mud.

On both sides, therefore, the operating assumption was that the courts could fulfil their constitutional role by bringing a measured, rational and non-ideological level-headedness to political contestation. As regards the *GGPPA* case,[18] federalism was presented as some kind of technical, objective and neutral concept that could be identified and applied to federalism disputes in an impartial and apolitical manner. As put by Chief Justice Wagner (and implicitly accepted by all his colleagues), 'courts, as impartial arbiters, are charged with resolving jurisdictional disputes over the boundaries of federal and provincial powers on the basis of the principle of federalism.'[19] Notwithstanding the considerable challenge of demonstrating how and why constitutional law changes and re-changes over time,[20] this notion of the Supreme Court as a Dworkinian 'forum of principle', not another mud-bath of political haggling, was accepted by both the warring politicians and the opposing judges.

In contrast, I will insist that, while courts may well be impartial between the competing claims of the present federal and provincial governments in terms of party politics (where the federal government is liberal and the provincial ones are not), they are not and cannot be impartial as between competing visions and versions of federalism. Although not about party politics, the federalism debate

---

[18] *References re Greenhouse Gas Pollution Pricing Act* (2021) 2021 SCC 11.
[19] ibid at [50] (Wagner CJ).
[20] See Peter Hogg, *Constitutional Law of Canada*, 5th edn (Toronto, Thomson Reuters, 2017).

is as political as it can be; it involves, among others, deep-seated and contested accounts of governmental arrangements, social values, institutional power and democratic accountability. Courts and legislatures may have different discourses, different styles and different legitimacies when talking about a fair allocation of governmental powers between the federal and provincial governments, but they are no less political for that. In other words, judges cannot avoid making political choices; there are no lines to follow that can be drawn, followed or understood that do not derive from the contested imagery and ideas of federalism politics. After all, the basic schema contained in the text of the British North American Act of 1867 was a vague, makeshift and imperfect effort to balance federal and provincial powers. Indeed, any serious historical account of constitutional federalism must allow for the striking shifts and periodic turns in constitutional doctrine that defy traditional explanation and justification.[21]

From my perspective, the appropriate and pressing questions are not about whether judges can walk the law's lines, but whether they can draw and walk lines that lead in more, not less politically attractive or acceptable directions. As the Man in Black phrased it, 'because you're mine, I walk the line.'[22] By this, I mean that the judges who claim to be walking the constitutional lines are also those who draw those lines: the lines are theirs. It is not that they are not bound by the lines, but that they draw and re-draw the lines as they walk along and are bound by them. As I will show by way of the *GGPPA* decision, the Supreme Court makes it up (and then remakes it again) as it goes along; the lines in the (oil) sands of constitutional law are paths of its own making. Of course, none of this is to suggest that the judges act in bad faith or are decidedly manipulative in fulfilling their judicial duties. It is that there is no way to engage with and resolve federalism issues that can claim to be acting in the neutral and detached way that the judges and their traditional academic allies suppose.[23]

Into the Constitutional Haze

The Supreme Court decided by a 6 to 3 ruling that the federal government has the constitutional authority to impose a carbon-pricing scheme on those provinces that resist what they claim to be an unwarranted incursion on their provincial turf. Although both majority and minority judgments claim to be applying and remaining faithful to existing constitutional doctrine, they share little in their understanding about what that legal doctrine is and how it speaks to the environmental issue at hand. They have very different starting points and, therefore, very different end points. Whereas the majority leans towards a constitutional approach

---

[21] For a strong and early account of this, see Patrick Monahan, 'At Doctrine's Twilight: The Structure of Canadian Federalism' (1984) 34 *University of Toronto Law Journal* 47.

[22] Johnny Cash, 'Walk The Line' (1956).

[23] For a fuller account of bad faith, see ch 5.

that is flexible and interactive, the minority draws upon a classical approach that is much more contained and fixed. Indeed, on reading their respective judgments, those uninitiated in the complexities of Canadian constitutional law might think that they were dealing with very different constitutional texts, constitutional histories and very different legal doctrines. In interpretive terms, whereas the majority relies on a 'living tree' attitude à la Lord Sankey, the minority takes a more originalist line à la Lord Atkin.[24] However, although their separate and motivating interpretive assumptions are not unimportant in orienting the judgments, it is their political underpinnings that better explain and drive their decisions.

Although there are constant references in *GGPPA* to the Constitution Act 1867 (originally the British North America Act) and its informing legal doctrines in this beast of a judgment (its 405 pages is in record-breaking territory with a headnote alone of 73 pages), the constitutional text offers no real assistance because there is little textual direction in defining the federal Parliament's general 'peace, order and good government' (POGG) power or the provinces' authority over 'property and civil rights'. Sometimes, provincial powers have prevailed, and, at other times, federal authority has been favoured. However, although this is a pervasive problem throughout constitutional law, it is particularly acute in matters like 'environmental regulation' because such a notion was not at all part of the 1867 mentality or outlook. That said, both the majority and minority recognise that such a relatively novel matter should be dealt with in a way that respects and is faithful to the basic structure and overall dynamics of the Constitution. The problem is that judges have starkly different appreciations of what those basic features of the Constitution are and how they are to be negotiated. This is not helped by the fact that both the majority and the minority insist that their interpretation is not only preferable, but also is required by existing constitutional doctrine.

Writing for the majority, Chief Justice Wagner seeks to strike a delicate balance between 'a modern cooperative federalism, that accommodates and encourages intergovernmental cooperative efforts' and a recognition 'that flexibility and cooperation, while important, cannot override or modify federalism and the constitutional division of powers'.[25] In striving to achieve this, he draws upon the ideas of overlapping jurisdiction. For him, the doctrinal tool to operationalise that sense of federalism is the judicially crafted 'national concern' doctrine under the POGG power. This is interpreted as having three components – the matter must be of sufficient concern to the whole country; have a singleness, distinctiveness and indivisibility; and have an impact on provincial jurisdiction that is reconcilable

---

[24] See *Edwards v Canada (AG)* [1929] AC 124 and *Canada (AG) v Ontario (AG)* [1937] AC 326. See also Bruce Ryder, 'Equal Autonomy in Canadian Federalism: The Continuing Search for Balance in the Interpretation of the Division of Powers' (2011) 54 *Supreme Court Law Review* 565 and Jean-Francois Gaudreault-Desbiens and Johanne Poirier, 'From Dualism to Cooperative Federalism and Back?: Evolving and Competing Conceptions of Canadian Federalism' in P Oliver (ed), *The Oxford Handbook of the Canadian Constitution* (New York, Oxford University Press, 2017) 319.

[25] *GGPPA*, above n 18 at [6] (Wagner CJ). See, eg, *Reference re Employment Insurance Act* (2005) 2005 SCC 56, [77] (Deschamps J).

with the division of powers.[26] Accordingly, while the exercise of such a federal power will affect provincial authority on 'property and civil rights', this is acceptable as long as the effect is 'qualified and limited'.[27] Ironically, the thrust of the Chief Justice's opinion is that he upholds the federal law as constitutional under the rubric of 'cooperative federalism' over the objections of the provinces and with the effect of trenching on what might be considered traditional areas of provincial jurisdiction and authority.

The minority opinions of the Albertan Justice Brown and the Newfoundlander Justice Rowe (both from provinces with an oil-based economy) take a very different tack on what the constitutional doctrines of Canadian federalism demand.[28] For them, the Constitution parcels out certain powers exclusively and permanently to either the federal government or the provincial governments: reliance on the idea of overlapping jurisdictions is almost anathema to them. As such, the 'national concern' doctrine is considered not to be available if the matter falls within an enumerated head of provincial power, like 'property and civil rights'. In such matters, the POGG power of the federal government is 'a residual power of last resort'.[29] Consequently, Justices Brown and Rowe strike down the challenged legislation because the fact that the provinces could enact the same legislation, as the federal government allowed and conceded, was fatal in a constitutional scheme that granted the provinces 'exclusive and permanent' authority over the matters in hand; 'it is not possible for a matter formerly under provincial jurisdiction to be transformed, when minimum national standards are invoked, into a matter of national concern.'[30] In short, for the minority, the federal government's POGG power could not trespass on matters that are of a recognised provincial nature. To do otherwise, according to the minority, would undermine fundamentally the structure and dynamic of the Canadian Constitution.

Both sets of judges make it plain that they maintain that the other has rode roughshod over those rules and that their own position is more in tune with the underlying structure and substance of constitutional law. Indeed, Justice Rowe goes so far as to say that the majority 'departs in a marked and unjustified way from the jurisprudence of [the] Court'.[31] These are strong and pertinent claims that give expression to the institutional forces that divide and consume the Supreme Court – the proper and most legitimate way to resolve a heated ideological dispute between the federal and provincial governments that does not itself become simply a more stylised, but profoundly ideologically-driven way of proceeding. In short, whereas the federal and provincial governments can be unabashed in recognising

---

[26] ibid at [163]–[65].

[27] ibid at [198].

[28] Justice Côté would go along with the Chief Justice as regards the nature of modern federalism, but invalidates the challenged law as it confers too broad a discretion on the federal executive. ibid at [222]–[295].

[29] ibid at [457] (Rowe J). See, eg, *Reference re Securities Act* (2011) 2011 SCC 66.

[30] *GGPPA*, above n 18 at [15] (Brown J).

[31] ibid at [576].

that their arguments and positions are the stuff of political disputation, the courts need to be able to demonstrate that they are doing law that is capable of differentiation in some non-trivial way from politics. It is not enough to point up differences in style and presentation by courts, but their contributions must be fundamentally and substantively different from what governments and politicians do. The Supreme Court's judgments in *GGPPA* do not and cannot live up to that requirement and challenge.

The real issue, therefore, that divides the judges of the Supreme Court in *GGPPA* is not whether one side or the other has somehow got the law right; they both can make credible and plausible arguments that they have. Instead, it is about the persuasiveness and appeal of their different and principled visions of what Canadian federalism should be from a constitutional perspective – is a model of 'cooperative federalism' or a more compartmentalised and exclusivity-based template better suited to the demands of twenty-first century Canadian politics and its immediate challenges? While the majority and minority can come up with sufficient legal arguments to bolster their different opinions, it is the political resonance of their respective visions that both drives their judgments and, as importantly, will determine the acceptance of those judgments by judges and commentators within the Canadian polity and society at large.

Visions of Federal Order

The tension in *GGPPA* is between the majority's version of 'cooperative federalism' and the minority's more classical account of 'exclusive dualism'. Both these different visions of federalism have strong pro and con arguments to recommend them. For the majority, the need to be flexible in order to avoid 'irreversible consequences for the environment, for human health and safety and for the economy' is paramount and warrants generous federal powers.[32] This, of course, is no bad thing in the global challenges facing twenty-first century Canada. However, as a matter of general policy, the minority disagrees. For them, co-operation demands a basic equivalence, not a means by which to give the federal government a trump card. For the minority, such a balance can only be maintained by respecting the Constitution's dualist division of governmental powers; the provincial government has sovereign authority in some areas as does the federal government in others. As a result, they contend that, if the 'national concern' doctrine is not reined in, 'the federal nature of the Constitution would disappear not gradually but rapidly'.[33]

---

[32] ibid at [206] (Wagner CJ).

[33] ibid at [575] (Rowe J). I would likely align with the majority's modern account of Canadian federalism. This, of course, is an entirely non-professional and political preference on my part. However, this does not imply that the choice is arbitrary or capricious; I can back it up with a range of political reasons. But it does not lend itself to any final or objective resolution.

Understood in these terms, there might be a distinct temptation to represent these two models of federalism being offered as polar opposites. But this would be a mistake. While the majority and minority positions begin from contrasting ends of the federalism spectrum (and frame their basic measures and allegiances in line with those defining characteristics), they each edge closer to the middle ground. But this does not undermine or underestimate their conflicting positions. Although the majority prioritise federal power, they recognise that it must be contained so that it 'cannot be used in a manner that effectively eviscerates provincial power'.[34] On the other hand, although the minority give much greater weight to provincial powers, they accept that the federal power is significant and, 'once a matter is qualified as of national concern, Parliament has exclusive jurisdiction over the matter, including its intra-provincial aspects'.[35] As such, the question for all the judges is not whether they should attempt to reconcile federal and provincial powers – they all do. The pressing matter is how and where they can find any suitable and defensible equilibrium.

Most importantly, the majority come from the middle of the federal pole and the minority do so from the provincial end of the federalism spectrum. The most telling consequence of this is that, in discrete and controversial cases like *GGPPA*, the different lines of approach will prove decisive. The motivating preference for either a modern or classical approach to federalism issues will take control, even if, on many run-of-the-mill cases, the two models will offer similar and compatible recommendations. Although the differences between the two accounts are often nuanced and subtle, they can on occasion prove to be stark and irreconcilable. This is the case in *GGPPA*. However, from a more general theoretical perspective, while both accounts offer what they consider to be a defensible and persuasive justification for their chosen balance, it remains the case that there is no equilibrium that can be identified or reached in any professional, neutral or technical way; it necessarily involves taking a political stance, whether hidden or presumed, between the different models of federalism and the broader values that underpin and animate them. This is not a choice for the judges, but a necessary corollary of the judicial function in constitutional law.

In defending this critical stance, it must be emphasised that neither the majority's nor the minority's vision of federalism is necessarily better or more progressive than the other. Although there is a definite tendency within constitutional law scholarship and politics to think that the modern approach's flexibility and collaborative import is more progressive than the classical one, this is also mistaken. The political impact of either account will depend on a variety of contextual and contingent considerations that are in play. The most important of these is, of course, the political lie of the land at any point in time. So, as regards the *GGPPA* case, the fact that the federal government is Liberal in its politics

---

[34] ibid at [49] (Wagner CJ).
[35] ibid at [531] (Rowe J).

(and, therefore, more disposed to more aggressive responses to climate change) and the provincial governments of Alberta, Saskatchewan, Ontario and Manitoba are Conservative in their politics (and, therefore, less disposed to such aggressive interventions) is far from incidental. Although this existing state of electoral affairs is not necessarily a determining factor for the judges of the Supreme Court, even if it is very much part of the judicial mix, it is influential in ascribing a political orientation to each of the informing accounts of federalism.

The analysis that I have offered suggests that an application of the modern approach to federalism as favoured by the majority will grant greater power to the federal government and result in more aggressive policies and legislation on climate change. On the other hand, a more traditional approach would have granted greater authority to the provincial governments and, at least in those four provinces,[36] resulted in less aggressive policies and legislation. Of course, with the next spin of the electoral wheel, this could all change. For instance, if a Conservative party gains control of federal politics and more of the provinces were controlled by Liberal or NDP (more left-leaning) parties, the substantive political effects of modern or traditional understandings of federalism may well be very different. Thus, any effort to ascribe particular and partial political effects to any one account of federalism is wrong-headed. Like the judicial doctrines of federalism, the political implications of adopting one account of federalism over another have shifted back and forth across the political spectrum and over the decades. As such, the lines in the sands of constitutional law and politics have changed both in their precise location and in directions to which they lead. As such, the upshot is that law, like politics, is always on the move in terms of its origins, its practices and its effects; there is no one tried-and-true approach that can deliver consistent outcomes over time and across varying contexts.

When the constitutional scene is appreciated in this critical way, it is not simply, as former Chief Justice Dickson famously phrased it, that 'the history of Canadian constitutional law has been to allow for a fair amount of interplay and indeed overlap between federal and provincial powers'.[37] Instead, it is the doctrines of constitutional law themselves that have always been characterised by 'a fair amount of interplay and indeed overlap'. The ruling doctrines have permitted and possibly encouraged a large degree of diversity and indeterminacy in the shape and substance of constitutional law as it applies in specific and contested situations and circumstances. The judgments in *GGPPA* offer rich and ample testimony to that critical understanding of constitutional law and its internal dynamics. Moreover, mindful that the history of constitutional law is replete with U-turns and upheavals when the Supreme Court has simply rejected extant constitutional lines and put in place a new set of lines, any claim that there are

---

[36] The other provincial governments run from Liberal to Conservative. It is ill-advised to draw any firm or particular conclusions about any collective provincial approach to responding to the effects of climate change. Even allowing for different party politics, policy and legislated actions might differ.

[37] *Ontario (AG) v OPSEU* [1987] 2 SCR 2, [27] (Dickson CJ).

lines in the sand that stand apart from judicial and juristic claims to the contrary are unpersuasive.

Conclusion

At bottom, the *GGPPA* decision of the Canadian Supreme Court speaks to the fragile assumptions of institutional legitimacy that operate in both political and judicial circles – elected politicians and legislators are free to act in ideologically and often unprincipled ways, but unelected judges should and, as importantly, can operate in reasoned and principled ways. As I have sought to show, both of them represent unnecessarily extreme and unconvincing depictions of politics and law. Although judges have no place to stand that allows them to be unpolitical in their reasoning and opinions, it does not mean that, in being political, they must be unprincipled or crudely ideological. It is a cruel caricature to suggest that judges directly and deliberately, if secretly, indulge their political preferences; this is a crude and unconvincing explanation that casts all judges as acting in bad faith. Once it is conceded that judges are as much political as their governmental and elected counterparts (ie, they cannot avoid taking a stand on contestable and ungroundable matters, like what counts as the better or more compelling version of federalism), the pressing question becomes of a very different order – what is at stake is not the settled or objective quality of constitutional law, but how the different branches of government can be better organised and constructed so that they can perform better in fulfilling government's overall democratic responsibilities. That involves both drawing and walking the lines. And, as importantly, it entails a recognition that both judges and politicians are making it up as they go along. In short, that constitutional law is politics.

7

Rethinking Legitimacy:
A Jurisprudential View

There is an important difference between traditional and critical theorists. Traditional theorists are content to work within the established paradigms, to identify with their general interests and ambitions, and to make the existing set-up a better version of its basic self. In contrast, the critical theorist is much less committed to the status quo, seeks to question the benefits gained and the interests served by those established values and ideas, and recommends that change, radical or otherwise, is required. Consequently, whereas the former see themselves as part of the same professional community as lawyers and judges, the latter align themselves with a broader and often different social context of socio-political allegiances. In short, traditional jurists are members of the legal profession first and foremost; critical theorists see their involvement with the legal community only as a necessary corollary to their more general identity as members of the professoriate. This presents an obvious and significant intellectual and institutional tension between the work and apologist assumptions of traditional jurists and the broadly emancipatory project of critical theorists.

In law and legal theory, critics of mainstream and accepted views face a variety of responses. The first is that they are simply ignored – why would traditional theorists take them seriously if they can simply be disregarded? A second reaction is often ridicule – there is no need to give their ideas serious consideration if they can be laughed off or made fun of. A third response is demonisation – by challenging their *bona fides*, critics' work can be undercut by showing that they are wilfully and even maliciously mischaracterising the arguments and intentions of traditional jurists and judges. If none of these does the job of effectively sidelining the critics and their ideas, a fourth response is to patronise them – to concede that they make some good points, but that they overstate their case. This fourth phase is where we are today in regard to critical theorising about constitutional law and its legitimacy.[1] Traditionalists respond to critics by remonstrating that, whatever the negligible force of their criticisms, they have little to offer by way of constructive

---

[1] It might also be said that another response is co-optation – that a watered-down version of the critic's arguments is incorporated into the traditional account of law and adjudication. In this way, the critical edge is blunted and the vigour of the criticism is dissipated. See Allan Hutchinson, *Law, Life and Lore: It's Too Late to Stop Now* (New York, Cambridge University Press, 2018) 18–39.

suggestions for change or improvement. In short, it is protested that, even if the traditionalist project is flawed and incomplete, 'it is not possible to replace something with nothing'.

In this and the remaining chapters, therefore, I will make some proposals and recommendations about what the jurisprudential and institutional implications are for the central critical claim that 'law is politics' for the practice and legitimacy of constitutional law and adjudication. In the first section, I examine what is the connection between the content and development of constitutional law and the broader politics of society at large. The next section unpacks claims about the supposed authority of Supreme Courts to interpret the Constitution and undercuts the idea that there is some true or final meaning to be attributed to a Constitution. The fourth section rejects the semi-traditional response to the law-is-politics critique that candour and transparency will be enough to save the day. In the fourth section, I explore what constitutional law and judicial decision-making might become if there is a real acceptance that law-is-politics. Finally, I begin to hint at what a new sense of legitimacy might comprise if there are open, transparent and transformed political courts. Throughout the chapter, the challenge is to make some practical and attitudinal proposals and still remain true to the critical mind-set. I do not intend to allow the prime critical insight – constitutional law is politics throughout and always – to be co-opted or integrated into the traditional approach to constitutional law and adjudication. In short, if law is politics, then legitimacy must itself be practical and political, not theoretical and legal.

The Politics of Law's Politics

The first point to make (and perhaps the most important) is that the law-is-politics critique is not simply one more contribution to the plethora of offerings made about how constitutional law and politics does and should work as something different from political debate. A law-is-politics approach is not a preference, but is the social and political reality in contemporary North American society. No thinking to the contrary is either feasible or possible; there is not an available theory of constitutional law-making and judicial decision-making that can fix or finesse that conclusion. While the hope of the traditionalists that judicial review can be objective, neutral and impartial is entirely understandable, it is no more than that – a forlorn hope. There does not exist a juristic method or means of proceeding that can sidestep or evade political choice and thereby relieve judges of charges that they are infusing their political values into the performance of their professional role and responsibilities. Judicial review is inescapably political, and no theory or practice can sidestep that – judges are obliged to rely on contested values in reaching their decisions. This is not a policy choice or structural impediment, but it is a social actuality that cannot be ignored either by theoretical ingenuity or practical intransigence.

That said, it remains a matter of dispute and disagreement about what the consequences of that central critical claim are. In a manner of speaking, it is fair and appropriate for traditionalists to offer a riposte to the critic of 'so what?'. Accordingly, it is incumbent upon critics to be clearer and more sustained about the implications, both jurisprudential and institutional, of their critical charge. So, as an introductory riposte, there are some obvious corollaries of the claim that law-is-politics:

- Any effort to revive or resurrect any mode of legal formalism is destined to fail: all accounts of constitutional law must address and incorporate the political complexities and social context of legal issues and their resolution.

- Any claim by judges and jurists to be acting neutrally and apolitically must be rejected; such an evasion, no matter how sincere, is always and inevitably itself part of a political stance that favours one set of interests over another grouping.

- Any inference that constitutional law can be understood as a self-contained field of activity that does not implicate other external considerations – sociology, economic theory, and political philosophy – is neither helpful nor possible.

- Any preoccupation with an exclusively court-based focus on the development of constitutional law is to be disregarded; there are multiple sites and sources through which constitutional law is applied and advanced.

- Any attempt to square judicial review with a forceful and uncompromising commitment to democratic governance must be met with a healthy scepticism; the democratic legitimacy of courts as the final arbiters of constitutional propriety is suspect at best.

Although these consequences of a law-is-politics critique are wide-ranging and of variable effects,[2] there is one particular question that has to be confronted directly and conscientiously – what are the political ramifications of understanding constitutional law and decision-making as a thoroughly political enterprise? In particular, the connection between the content and development of constitutional law and the broader politics of society at large must be explained. This, of course, is an issue that has probably received less attention among traditional jurists and critical scholars themselves than ought to be the case. For traditional jurists, although they make some necessary concessions, the prevailing view remains that constitutional law is and should be largely, if not exclusively, autonomous from society's politics. Indeed, this is the major *raison d'être* for the traditional view that law must be appreciated as an objective and neutral process and practice that is not reducible to partisan or ideological dispute. For critical scholars though, the relation between the critical claim that law-is-politics and the political composition of social values and views is more complicated and more contestable.

---

[2] It is, of course, the main onus of this and the next chapter to explore and detail these consequences. See this chapter and ch 8.

There are two preliminary observations to be made. First, law and political society are not separate fields of activity; they are both intimately and mutually constitutive zones. It is not possible to think about political society without recognising and appreciating its legal forms and structures. For example, any talk about there being a market-based structure of economic and social relations must accept that this is dependent upon a particular scheme of property and contractual rules. Similarly, it is not also possible to think about law without noting and granting that it is serving the particular society of which it is part and, therefore, must remain aligned in at least general terms with its various demands and interests Secondly, despite the operating assumptions of many jurists on both the left (eg, socialists) and right (eg, law and economists), there is no one abiding and enduring connection between law and its informing political society. Indeed, the force of a critical standpoint is that any claim to offer a scientific and almost mono-causal account of how law instantiates and promotes a particular mode of social arrangements is not only unnecessary, but is to be studiously avoided.[3]

That said, it is possible and worthwhile to offer some more informative and less evasive response to the question of what is the politics of 'the politics of law' – if law is politics, what are the kinds of relations that exist between that politicised law and its political context in the present era of North American society? As a general preface, it is important to set up a general, if not universal metaphor for grasping that relation. I want to suggest that the relation between law and social politics is like that between sheep (politics) and woollen sweaters (law) – law is constrained by the politics of society, but it is not fully determined by them. There is some considerable leeway for courts to fashion and fabricate all kinds of products from the sheep, but they cannot make garments or anything else from other non-ovine sources of raw materials; their hands are loosely tied, but they still can use ingenuity and craft to manufacture a range of such goods. As long as the social relations are sheep-like, courts cannot and will not be able to reach outcomes that are more horse-like or even mineral-like in their nature and character.

In order to develop this notion more jurisprudentially, I will concentrate on the role of looseness (or, more usually, indeterminacy) as a feature of both constitutional law and constitutional politics. This can best be done by thinking about the indeterminacy of law from a legal and political perspective; they both operate dynamically and constitutively, but in slightly different ways. Whereas law is radically indeterminate when understood in exclusively legal terms, it is much more constricted, but still under-determined, when it is looked at from a political perspective. In short, while law is thoroughly indeterminate as a freer-standing body of rules and principles, there is much less unpredictability in regard to the outcomes reached and orientations taken. As such, constitutional law is largely indeterminate on its own terms, but is far more predictable in political terms.

---

[3] Allan Hutchinson, *It's All in the Game: A Non-Foundationalist Account of Law and Adjudication* (Durham, Duke University Press, 2000) 216–51.

So, from a purely legal stance, law is deeply indeterminate; there is nothing about legal argument or its doctrinal sources that constrains the possibilities of creating an argument that could meet a threshold of plausibility. In almost all cases, a decision and its justificatory reasoning can be cobbled together from the extant legal materials; there are too many options and pathways that guide the judge in opposing directions. Indeed, the fact that many decisions comprise a dissent that is defensible in legal terms shows that that there is no implicit or exclusive logic to the legal materials on offer. The competing judgments in *Dobbs* are strong evidence of this.[4] Furthermore, when it is remembered that Supreme Courts are entitled to overrule their previous decisions, again as in *Dobbs*, it is very difficult to insist that the law speaks with any distinct, uniform or settled voice. The best example of this are the great cases of constitutional law, like *Brown* and *Roncarelli*.[5] These landmark cases possess the rare quality of reversing received understandings and setting constitutional law off on a new path. In metaphorical terms, the judges have all kinds of designs and formats at hand that allow them to produce sweaters of many different colours, sizes and shapes.

From a political perspective, the internal looseness and prolificity of law's rules and principles are what gives law its political character. Because there are choices to be made and those choices are under-determined by the legal materials, judges must resort to their own or society's sense of values in order to decide what decisions they should make and what justificatory reasoning they should rely on. However, they are not out on their own so that 'anything goes'; judicial choice does not necessarily collapse into arbitrariness or perversity, even if it occasionally does so. Judges do not stand outside of society. As social creatures who, even if endowed with elite power (and perhaps especially because of that), draw their own sense of self and their formative values from that same society, judges' choices are reflective of and beholden to the general cut and thrust of prevailing social and political views. In metaphorical terms, the judges can treat society and its values as whatever kind of sheep they choose, but they cannot treat it as any kind of animal that they prefer. As society might evolve and transform itself, then judges will be presented with different choices and different possibilities.

All of this can be phrased in a more technical or scholarly vocabulary. Constitutional law has 'relative autonomy' from the prevailing forms of socio-political life. The substance of what judges decide and their overall doctrinal output are structurally determined, albeit significantly under-determined by those prevailing forms. The law never stands still because it is part of a dynamic process and activity that constantly changes its details, designs and personnel. As such, constitutional law is neither a vehicle for radical transformation nor a forum for intransigent conservation. Of course, those forms are themselves not fixed or

---

[4] See ch 5.

[5] See *Brown v Board of Education* (1954) 347 US 483 and *Roncarelli v Duplessis* [1959] SCR 121. See also Allan Hutchinson, *Evolution and the Common Law* (Cambridge, Cambridge University Press, 2005).

inflexible; the forms of socio-political life are contingent and dynamic over time and place. As described by Samuel Moyn:

> [law's] meaningfulness is not autonomous from social relations in the broadest sense …. Law does not simply arrange and rearrange by creating and sustaining institutions or dictating legal outcomes; it is also a meaningful practice that works in and through the self- conception of the agents who produce and reproduce society.[6]

This means that constitutional law is oppressive or exploitative to much the same extent as the society that it helps constitute and maintain. However, there is considerable wiggle-room for judges to manoeuvre within that generalised context, but they are not free to do as they might otherwise wish to craft law in their own image; it is a matter of numbers as much as persuasion. Indeed, it may be that critical legal scholars, like myself, have not done enough to tackle and chart in sufficient detail the dynamics of this connection between the existing elite orientation of society and its legal structures. There has been a tendency to concentrate too much on undermining the hold that formalism has on the jurisprudential mind-set and imagination.[7] Although not a justification or an excuse, this focus by jurists, both critical and traditional, is not surprising as their bailiwick is law, not politics. Nevertheless, the effort to pay more attention not simply to developing and driving home the idea that 'law is politics', but to the politics of law's politics, remains pressing and pertinent.

Constitutional Authority

My critical approach draws upon a Rortyian-influenced pragmatic approach to philosophical or theoretical analysis.[8] It is thoroughly anti-authoritarian in the sense that it flatly denies the possibility that there is some overriding method that can deliver and warrant a fixed notion of truth or correctness that is beyond dispute or revision. In other words, there is no authoritative process or set of answers that can provide a solid and universal basis that transcends its own context; all views

---

[6] Samuel Moyn, 'Reconstructing Critical Legal Studies' (2024) 134 *Yale Law Journal* 77, 87.

[7] Umut Özsu, 'The Necessity of Contingency: Method and Marxism in International Law' in Ingo Ventzke and Jon Heller (eds), *Contingency in International Law: On the Possibility of Different Legal Histories* (Oxford, Oxford University Press, 2021) 62 and Rob Hunter, 'Critical Legal Studies and Marx's Critique: A Reappraisal' (2021) 31 *Yale Journal of Law & the Humanities* 389, 392.

[8] For a strong account of the pragmatic approach, see Douglas McDermid, *The Varieties of Pragmatism: Truth, Realism, and Knowledge from James to Rorty* (London, Continuum, 2006). For my own elaboration and defence of this style and substance of theorising, see Allan Hutchinson, *The Province of Jurisprudence Democratized* (New York, Oxford University Press, 2008). As a pragmatic sceptic, I reject, like Posner, 'academic moralism; the effort to deduce practical recommendations from abstract moral principles is wasteful and unconvincing.' See Richard Posner, *The Problematics of Moral and Legal Theory* (Cambridge, Harvard University Press, 1999) 38–42, 85–90. However, I do not maintain, like Posner, that a rejection of such theorising entails a necessary turn to social science as an alternative and preferable mode of analysis. ibid at 206–11. Both – moral theory and social science – succumb to a pragmatic critique.

and proposals are unstable and contestable. Beyond the socially-based practices of theorists, there is nothing to underwrite the veracity or validity of their conclusions. The only authority that can be developed or relied upon is generated within those practices and their capacity to persuade others that what is defended is worth defending and that it can contribute to a better society (which, of course, is itself a contestable and contextual idea). As such, the test of any set of ideas is not their recommended correctness or truthfulness, but their usefulness and worth in helping to resolve significant issues in the prevailing context. The search for lasting, final or objective solutions is to be abandoned; there is no source that can relieve us from the opportunity and responsibility to create and live by our own preferred standards and resulting solutions.

Another way to put it is to say that notions of truth and authority must themselves be understood in a pragmatic sense. As Richard Rorty insists, there is no difference nor is anything added by contending that something that is a good justification for us can become something that is a good justification, *period*: 'philosophers have long wanted to understand concepts, but the point is to change them so as to make them serve our purposes better.'[9] While the temptation to make such objectivist and ahistoricist claims is understandable, it cannot help but be hubristic in design and realisation. Inquiry and analysis should be about justification, not about truth-seeking – the search for universality and transcendence is a sleeveless errand as it will always be context-dependent and will never attain the contextless status that its defenders claim or strive to achieve. Of course, because social practices are themselves not a seamless or uniform web, there will be disagreement and division; justification will be contestable and varied. But the temptation to maintain that there is some meta-realm that can be sought that will overcome or get beyond such disagreement or division is illusory: any reputed higher ground will itself be only one more socially bounded and often partial social practice that reflects some interests over others.

So, what does this all imply for traditional theorising and judicial decision-making in regard to constitutional law? I maintain that there are enormous implications for both the theory and practice of constitutional law.[10] The most general thing to note is that, if (as I have insisted) law is politics, then so is legal theorising. The insights offered by jurists are valuable and helpful (or not), but only in regard to their own context and situations. Whatever claims are made for them, these ideas only hold weight insofar as they garner support and approval by society; they do so in virtue of their helpfulness, not by dint of their correctness. In relying upon the short-hand phrase 'legal theory is politics', I am not suggesting that legal theory is reducible to a theorist's own agenda and ideals, although it might well be. I am using 'politics' in a much more ample and less confined sense – politics refers to all the contextual forces at play and includes

---

[9] Richard Rorty, *Pragmatism as Anti-Authoritarianism* (Cambridge, Harvard University Press, 2021) 83, 65. See also Stanley Fish, *The Trouble with Principle* (Cambridge, Harvard University Press, 1999).
[10] I will be pursuing these implications throughout this and the remaining chapters.

social dynamics, moral commitments, pervasive ideologies, power relations, and the like. Although a theorist's own preferences will have enormous leverage, those values will themselves be situated within and motivated by a broader and more complicated context of values and ideals. And, of course, there is no Context of contexts available to bring closure to the jurisprudential and judicial struggle to do what is best.

Further, any effort to overcome the counter-majoritarian dilemma by way of an overarching reliance on so-called neutral principles or by any way to supersede the supposed failings of the democratic process represents an authoritarian impulse: it is a high-handed, not high-minded act that seeks to impose one set of values over another.[11] Although claimed to be warranted and underwritten by some method that transcends its informing and limiting context, it is little more than an elite manoeuvre by jurists and judges to impose their favoured values over those of others. Legal and political debate is no more (and no less) than a human practice; it is situated, fragmentary, organic and flawed. It is a way of coping that is more or less successful in direct proportion to its capacity to achieve substantive justice in the contextual circumstances. People (and judges particularly) make 'bad' decisions because of their substantive leanings, not because of a weakness in the philosophical or legal method that they employ. As such, judgment is a substantive instinct whose application is always contextual. And, because there is no defining or exclusive context, there is no easy, pat, uncontroversial, neutral or exclusively principled way to decide what to do. Importantly, a pragmatic rejection of the operative assumption by traditionalists that politics is a realm of arbitrary and idiosyncratic values does not lead to the converse assumption that politics can provide the stability and grounding that traditional scholars seek. Political and, therefore, legal debate can be principled, but not authoritative or stable in the sense of being final, definitive and beyond reproach.

As a pragmatist, I take the view that any valid or worthwhile scrutiny of constitutional law and politics can only be understood within its social and political context. Being less concerned with coherence and analysis, it looks to the consequences and effects of legal theorising; claims of timeless truths and enduring certainties are replaced by standards of usefulness and efficacy. By replacing a dogmatic tendency with a more fallibilistic perspective, pragmatic criticism eschews the recognition of a special method that is considered outside contingent practice and that can validate its results in addressing that practice; it concerns itself less with truth or essential insights, but more with what works in particular situations and contexts. Indeed, there is much pragmatic wisdom in Justice Jackson's assertion about the authority of Supreme Courts – 'we are not final because we are infallible, but we are infallible only because we are final.'[12] Supreme Courts have the last say and they are authoritative because of that, not because it

---

[11] See chs 2 and 3.
[12] *Brown v Allen* (1953) 344 US 443.

is final in some grand or enduring sense. Moreover, the very idea of infallibility is something to be jettisoned entirely; there is no stance that is not open to revision and reappraisal.

Judges and jurists must, therefore, abandon the notion that they are tasked with finding constitutional truths and principles that are considered theoretically correct and that authorise the legitimacy of their opinions. At the heart of the traditional project is the grandiose belief that it is possible to generate a grand theory of constitutional law that can distinguish the necessary from the contingent, the universal from the particular, and the conceptual from the concrete. Although often expressed in less extravagant terms, this stance is very much part of the traditional jurisprudential canon. After all, Dworkin enlisted the support and assistance of his super-human judge and alter-ego, *Hercules*, to underwrite the fact that 'particular propositions of law should be taken to be sound or true'.[13] For Dworkinian-influenced jurists, constitutional law could and should be read rationally and objectively: their constitution was not only their preferred constitution, but was passed off as *the* constitution. This is a both a methodological and political arrogance that should not be indulged.

Similarly, judges adopt an equally high-flying posture. For example, the *Dobbs* majority's approach to originalism is framed as having an objective and clinical method that keeps the judges detached from political influences or personal predilections. They believe there is an objective interpretation of the Constitution and that only originalists have access to its truths.[14] This sense of entitlement leads to disregarding other judges' interpretations and can come across as condescending. However, the *Dobbs* minority are not much better at this. While they recognise that the Constitution is neither fixed nor static, they do insist that it is objective and does not give Justices *carte blanche* to do whatever they wish. In particular, they find that there is a firm constitutional ground that gives authority and meaning to constitutional law: 'applications of liberty and equality can evolve while remaining grounded in constitutional principles, constitutional history, and constitutional precedents'.[15] As such, both sides of the jurisprudential spectrum – originalist and organicist – remain committed to claims about constitutional law being more found than made and about the role of judges being more about constitutional law as something different from constitutional politics.

Of course, a pragmatic demonstration that some judges' and jurists' conclusions are not as universal or absolute as they claim does not mean that they can simply be ignored without more. While it robs them of their claimed authority as objective truths, their proposals must still be judged as contingent tenders for making sense of constitutional law and its transformative possibilities. The loss of transcendental authority is no loss at all because there never were any such

---

[13] Ronald Dworkin, *Law's Empire* (Cambridge, Belknap Press, 1986) 110.
[14] See *Dobbs v Jackson Women's Health Organization* (2022) 142 S Ct 2228.
[15] ibid at 2326.

constraints in the first place. Rather than waste valuable energy in such intellectual grandstanding, these jurists and judges should come down from their mountain tops and deal with more down-to-earth problems, such as unemployment, racism, poverty, and the like; they should stop looking for justificatory height in order to attain moral depth. Most importantly, future renditions of constitutional law must cease to speak in the discourse of correctness and truth; any legitimacy must be earned through their usefulness and acceptability to society. Whether those proposals rely on new values or old ideas, they must be pertinent to today's citizens and relevant to their problems and their resolution.

Beyond Candour

One particular response to these critical challenges by those who are persuaded that 'law is politics' is noteworthy. It is suggested that moving beyond the traditional project and its shaping of the challenges to be met and the kind of responses recommended will itself reap important benefits. In particular, it places great weight on the virtues of judicial candour, institutional transparency and a reasonable sense of political engagement. Yet, while candour is a significant and necessary step forward in advancing any kind of scheme of democratic govern-ance, candour alone will not be sufficient to handle effectively or persuasively the institutional and jurisprudential challenge presented by an acknowledge-ment that 'law is politics'. The reliance on candour both promises too much (ie, that candour will resolve the problems and failings of the present constitutional set-up) and promises too little (ie, that candour will not need to be supplemented by other initiatives if it is to have any success). In short, the virtue of candour cannot carry the kind of institutional and jurisprudential weight that its propo-nents recommend.

For instance, Erwin Chemerinsky holds the firm belief that the greater the candour shown by judges and scholars about what they do and why they do it will have a proportionately positive and almost decisive effect on constitutional law and decision-making. Indeed, concentrating on the failings of originalism, he seems to think that, once its false allure has been exposed and its real political thrust and dynamics are revealed, judges and jurists will have to be more forthright and open about the political nature of their legal reasoning. Moreover, so liberated and emboldened, they will engage more directly and honestly in the debate about what values are truly fundamental and worthy of judicial protection as a matter of constitutional imperative. Consequently, if there is more candour, judges and scholars will be obliged to come clean about their political values and to defend them, not as constitutional entailments, but as political preferences:

> Thus, rejecting the premises that have controlled constitutional law for decades would be liberating. It would provide the opportunity for the development of meaningful constitutional theories; it would encourage greater judicial candour; and it might

stimulate more independent constitutional protection by the other branches of government.[16]

There is much in this that is praiseworthy. Unfortunately, Chemerinsky's optimism and confidence in candour is a tad naïve. The fact is that, by Chemerinsky's own account and critique, originalist judges are easily revealed to be more devious than deluded. The problem with the candour argument, therefore, is that it suggests that originalist judges are somehow unaware that originalism is a shell-game and that they are not deliberately hiding that fact. But, as Chemerinsky himself insists, this posture defies any genuine or serious credibility. It is not that originalists do not understand that originalism is as much a political manoeuvre as a legal argument. On the contrary, it is that they recognise that their obfuscation of this fact is the best way to hide and advance their ideological agenda. As another commentator puts it, 'today's judges are not conservatives because they are originalists; they are originalists because [originalism] is conservative.'[17] If originalism has any genius, it is that, by positioning itself as a mode of legal interpretation, it finesses the 'law is politics' critique at the same time that it implements a particular ideology. As such, the claim that the Constitution and its doctrines can be applied in a principled, correct and politically neutral way is itself thoroughly ideological.

However, Chemerinsky is on the right track when he recommends that critics develop a reading of constitutional law that is more conducive to a progressive liberalism. Emphasising that 'we are not living in the world of 1787 and should not pretend that the choices for that time can guide ours today',[18] he puts equality, democratic process and individual empowerment to the fore in his version of constitutional law. As part of this progressive agenda, he advocates for 'better theories for when to distrust decisions of the other branches of government and when courts should become involved due to their institutional strengths.'[19] With enviable clarity and common sense, Chemerinsky offer an alternative version that blends the principled and the sensible, the ideal and the institutional, and the progressive and the pragmatic. But, in making this effort, Chemerinsky is not dissimilar in his jurisprudential efforts to naturalists, like Ronald Dworkin. He recommends that the task of judges is to identify and work with the law's overall purposive enterprise that we 'inevitably help to create as we strive (in accordance with our obligation of fidelity to law) to make the [law] a coherent,

---

[16] Erwin Chemerinsky, 'The Vanishing Constitution' (1989) 103 *Harvard Law Review* 43, 99.

[17] Michael Waldman, *The Supermajority: How the Supreme Court Divided America* (New York, Simon & Schuster, 2023) 257. For a critique of originalism, see ch 4.

[18] Erwin Chemerinsky, *Worse than Nothing: The Dangerous Fallacy of Originalism* (New Haven, Yale University Press, 2022) 24. See also Joseph Fishkin and William Forbath, *The Anti-Oligarchy Constitution: Reconstructing the Economic Foundations of American Democracy* (Cambridge, Harvard University Press, 2022); Mark Tushnet, 'Progressive Constitutionalism: What Is "It?"' (2011) 72 *Ohio State Law Journal* 1073; and Robin West, *Progressive Constitutionalism: Reconstructing the Fourteenth Amendment* (Durham, Duke University Press, 1994).

[19] Chemerinsky, *Vanishing Constitution*, above n 16.

workable whole'.[20] Of course, like them, Chemerinsky has no way of insisting that this rendition is more valid or self-evidently better than anyone else's, including that of the originalists. However, he insists that his account of constitutional law, although based on obvious and contestable political values, can be defended as something more than his own favored ideological vision of a just society; it is a defensible account of the Constitution itself.

Nevertheless, Chemerinsky and like-minded critics will have to do more than assert that their alternative egalitarian account of constitutional law is 'desirable'.[21] Indeed, Chemerinsky seems to assume that, once informed about the unescapable politics involved in constitutional law and decision-making, people will work together more reasonably and produce more reasonable results. If this was ever true, it is no longer the case: modern American society is fractured and deeply divided, especially over what might count as reasonable, let alone desirable. While it is important to elaborate an alternative vision of constitutional law, little will be achieved by assuming that its reasonableness, by being apparent and obvious to all, will convert others to its cause. Moreover, Chemerinsky remains firmly within the traditionalist church when he bases his efforts on showing that it is possible to anchor that alternative 'reasonable' vision in the constitutional text itself; he still is wedded to the idea that the task of judges is to derive their constitutional authority from the text itself. He might be a non-originalist, but he takes the Constitution's text very seriously. Chemerinsky will have to do much more to bring the originalists even half-over to his own ideological refuge. In blunt terms, Scalia's latter-day devotees are unlikely to capitulate or be converted from their conservative views by a simple plea for candour.

In offering his account of what a progressive rendition of the Constitution would look like, Chemerinsky seems to be content to preach to the choir – that is, he writes for fellow-progressives and has little persuasive to say to non- or anti-progressives, like originalists. As such, his efforts might well be welcomed and embraced by similar-minded liberals or progressives, but they might further galvanise his conservative and even reactionary adversaries in their opposition. In short, work like Chemerinsky's will do little to convert, convince or placate his judicial and scholarly antagonists. While he does demonstrate that originalism is 'worse than nothing', he will struggle to persuade those sympathetic to him, let alone those that are antagonistic to him, that his own progressive something is itself more than nothing as a matter of constitutional law and interpretation. Chemerinsky seems to want his cake and to eat it too. In contrast, I maintain that it is best to move entirely beyond the idea that constitutional law has some immanent, if flexible, meaning that can confer authority on its adherents.

---

[20] Lon Fuller, 'Positivism and Fidelity to Law: A Reply to Professor Hart' (1958) 71 *Harvard Law Review* 630, 667 and Ronald Dworkin, *Freedom's Law: The Moral Reading of the American Constitution* (Cambridge, Harvard University Press, 1996).

[21] Chemerinsky, *Worse than Nothing*, above n 18 at 168.

At root, the problem for Chemerinskian-aligned jurists is that they are not prepared to follow through on some of the more unsettling implications of his central assertion that 'the content of the law and how it is applied, especially by the Supreme Court, is largely a function of who is on the bench and their values'.[22] They seem unwilling to accept that they are offering a much more subversive and destabilising challenge to constitutionalism generally. Indeed, not only does the 'law is politics' critique sweep away the jurisprudential ground from under both originalist and organicist opponents in the battle-royal over constitutional interpretation, but it also threatens the whole institutional structure and decision-making process within which constitutional law is presently understood and developed. In short, it is hard to see how it will be business as usual once Chemerinski's particular ideological cat is let out of the constitutional bag.

From my critical perspective, it is equally naïve to maintain that a demonstration of the inescapable politicality of legal principles would lead to any necessarily progressive or ameliorating consequence. The fact is that, although candour will encourage constitutional judges and scholars to talk about political values in a more informed and direct way, candour alone is unlikely to affect any substantial progress in bridging the rift between political left and right. It will also, of course, show that the emperors really do have no legitimate clothes on; they will stand naked in their political affiliations. Further, it seems optimistic, at best, to pretend that, once judges accept the inescapable politics of law and judicial decision-making, judges will work together more reasonably and produce more reasonable results. If this was ever true, it is no longer the case. While this is certainly the case in modern American, where society is deeply fractured and divided, it is also true of Canada (and the United Kingdom), albeit in a slightly less polarised and more understated way. After all, the middle-of-the-road is as political as any other part of the road. The major reason that Canadian and British judges are less overt and less diverse in their politics is that, apart from significant cultural and institutional constraints in place, they are drawn from a much narrower and more establishment-oriented stratum of society. The cloak of institutional legitimacy is still considered an imperial and protective garment that can cover their political (and establishment-oriented) nakedness.

Toward a New Legitimacy

If judicial decision-making is primarily a political enterprise, it places the continuing role and power of courts in serious jeopardy. An insulated and privileged assembly that functions in a directly political way is antithetical to most accounts of democratic governance. Concerns about accountability are pressing and significant. As a result, the primary and traditional rationale for Supreme Courts'

---

[22] ibid at 24.

democratic legitimacy is largely dependent on its operation as a distinctly legal forum. If politics are accepted to be as much a part of judicial decision-making as legal reasoning, the authority of the courts will be compromised – how can judges as unelected officials be seen to be acting as politicians and, in the process, countermand the decisions of elected legislators? At the very least, it would seem that, if Supreme Courts are not to be done away with entirely, their influence and involvement should at least be severely reduced.[23] This challenge about how to retain courts as the makers and appliers of constitutional law and grant them some form of democratic legitimacy is at the heart of any critical challenge to be more constructive.

If the content of law is largely reducible to the ideological make-up of its sitting judicial custodians, it would seem that there is little reason for the courts to receive any particular or special deference in making policy or defending their decisions; what the law is and what it should be becomes nothing more (and nothing less) than whatever the judiciary determine it to be. This does not mean that the choices made will thereby be substantively bad or suspect *per se*, but it does recommend that there is no escaping the conclusion that judicial decisions will be neither simply neutral (in the traditional jurisprudential sense) nor impartial in origin or effect. Both the common law and constitutional law are straight-out politics in judicial garb; they have no greater claim to democratic authority than the executive or legislative branches of government whose actions they evaluate against constitutional law and, on occasion, strike down. As John Hart Ely famously put it, 'we may grant until we're blue in the face that legislatures aren't wholly democratic but that isn't going to make courts more democratic than legislatures.'[24]

Moreover, so long as a commitment to democratic values and processes are thought to be a mainstay of a society (as they are claimed to be in the United States and Canada), then the already-fragile legitimacy of the courts and their constitutional output is further reduced. Indeed, this fear helps to explain the persistence and intransigence of traditional scholars in their desire to strike upon a way of proceeding that can persuasively distinguish judicial work from political work when they resolve matters of constitutional law. As a corollary, therefore, of the critical insistence that 'constitutional law is politics', the need for a substantial jurisprudential rethink is paramount. Moreover, there is a constructive obligation to propose a significant set of accompanying institutional reforms that can complement this jurisprudential renovation.

Looked at from an avowedly critical perspective, the appropriate and pressing questions for jurists and commentators will no longer be about whether constitutional judges act judicially and, therefore, legitimately by adopting a principled

---

[23] See Allan Hutchinson, *Democracy and Constitutions: Putting Citizens First* (Toronto, University of Toronto Press, 2021).

[24] John Ely, *Democracy and Distrust: A Theory of Judicial Review* (Cambridge, Harvard University Press, 1980) 67.

approach or not to the duties. Instead, the challenge becomes about whether what it means to act judicially can be understood in more openly political terms. In saying this, I am not suggesting that there is no difference between judges and politicians. However, I am suggesting that the difference is not as large or as significant as most scholars recommend. Moreover, no matter how desirable it might be thought to maintain the traditional distinction between judges and politicians, it is simply not achievable or realisable as a practical matter – judges cannot fulfil their roles in deciding legal issues without resort to or reliance on controversial and disputed political values. In particular, Supreme Courts are inevitably and unavoidably political. In other words, if acting judicially is one more way of acting politically, what is the democratic basis for continuing with the judicial practice of making and applying constitutional law?

One of the rare authors both to accept the law-is-politics critique and to make proposals about how a 'political' court might be defended in democratic terms is Terri Peretti. In a broad-ranging and neglected inquiry, she flips the traditional dilemma about the non-democratic character of courts. Instead, she contends that, far from being a threat to democracy, a political court will enhance democratic values and processes; it is traditional scholars with their perversely persistent efforts to locate the holy jurisprudential grail of 'principled appraisal' who offer much more of a risk to the viability of any democratic project and its practical realisation. So Peretti not only defends a political court, but also feels that it serves better the pluralist idea of American democracy that depends upon and encourages the dispersal of political power among multiple locations and forums. In short, she defends a political court as a vehicle for enhancing popular participation and consensus-building: 'democratic ends – political representation and responsiveness – are served by [a political court].'[25]

There is much in Peretti's analysis and approach that is praiseworthy; she refuses to retreat from the unavoidable political character of constitutional law and decision-making. However, she overstates her case. The idea and practice of a political court is, at best, capable of being accommodated within democracy, but it does not thereby improve or enhance the democratic process. Indeed, Peretti's assertion that popular representation and consensus-building are promoted by the present scheme of constitutional law adjudication is, at best, wishful thinking; some might consider it almost delusional. Those cases that do reach the courts are more often driven by well-funded interest groups whose agenda more often than not does not align with popular interests. Furthermore, while it might be 'noble' to portray political courts as consensus-builders,[26] this is more the exception than the norm; the reception accorded to *Dobbs* is good evidence of this. In a society

---

[25] Terri Peretti, *In Defense of a Political Court* (Princeton, Princeton University Press, 1999) 131.

[26] ibid at 231. For a similar optimistic line about judicial review as a vehicle for popular participation, see Tom Hickey, 'Legitimacy – not Justice – and the Case for Judicial Review' (2022) 42 *Oxford Journal of Legal Studies* 893.

that is divided along social and political lines, there is no reason or evidence to suggest that political courts can act as healing vehicles for greater social cohesion and harmony.

Nevertheless, Peretti is on to something when she notes that American democracy is not simply about legislative supremacy; it has a more pluralistic dynamic that distributes the responsibility to advance democracy and constitutional values to multiple sites and settings. Moreover, she astutely points out, in real as opposed to theoretical terms, that the other branches of government are no less counter-majoritarian than courts. Lacking full democratic authority, the executive and legislative branches struggle to retain genuine democratic legitimacy; periodic electoral voting and oppositional politics cannot provide the kind of reliable democratic mandate that will confer a plausible degree of legitimacy on the executive or legislative handling of any particular and contested issue. In this regard, therefore, it must be emphasised that courts are not deviant institutions because they fail to receive full democratic backing in all things that they do; majoritarian politics and existing executive and legislative practices are not synonymous with a robust democracy.[27]

In contrast to Peretti's stance, I want to recommend that the law-is-politics approach merely makes plain and up-front what is already true – that judges vote with their values or chosen understanding of the Constitution. While this need not be their own personal values, it can simply be their sense of what best serves the public interests on particular issues at particular times. If political courts are to assert and receive any kind of popular legitimacy, it must be done by looking at democracy in a system-wide way by asking whether the overall governmental arrangements are in practice, not only in theory, more democratic than not. The most important benefit in democratic terms of putting politics front-and-centre in the judicial work of constitutional law is that it will make courts more, not less accountable for their decisions and their reasons for making them. By being more open and more honest, judges will not be able to hide behind a vast library of legal arguments and initiatives. Instead, they will have to be up-front and direct in defending the political grounds on which they decided and justified such decisions in the way that they did. In this way, candour and transparency are the first steps.

In all this, it must be remembered that, despite the protestations of traditional jurists and judges, the legitimacy and success of the courts is based more on the instrumental impact of their decisions than on their perceived jurisprudential and institutional legitimacy.[28] Mindful that court opinions are not read by persons outside the legal establishment, the courts' prestige and status are more dependent upon the results achieved in individual cases than anything else; their process of legal reasoning is of much lesser significance in the popular and public eye than it is among lawyers and jurists. Indeed, the public are not as gullible or as impressed

[27] See ch 8.
[28] See ch 1.

by Supreme Courts as conventional scholars and pundits think. For most citizens, the bottom line is not whether the judges acted in accordance with the prevailing (and shifting) touchstones of legal argumentation; it is whether the individual decisions made are agreeable to or, at least, fall within the broad parameters of substantive reasonableness. Substance eclipses form.

Once it is conceded that courts are political institutions where the prevailing ideological views of judges reign, it becomes necessary to propose some different and more democratically-compatible ways of proceeding. This is no small undertaking. However, there are, at least, two general initiatives that seem to flow from the law-is-politics critique and that might be congruent with a more progressive approach to democratic politics. The first is to multiply and diversify the institutional sites at which legal authority can be exercised; the judiciary might become only one player in a much more diffuse and decentralised scheme of constitutional lawyering and decision-making. The second is to rethink what counts as legitimacy in Supreme Courts and other alternative forums that are charged with interpreting and developing constitutional law. Both strategies can and should be pursued simultaneously because each will have a beneficial impact on the achievement of the other.[29]

As regards legitimacy, it will be imperative to develop and defend a revised understanding of what counts as legitimacy in judicial decision-making in constitutional law. Of course, to follow through on the claim that law-is-politics would make constitutional law into a very different exercise and undertaking than it presently is. Any such re-think will have profound implications for what standards and expectations ought to be in play to evaluate the performance and acceptability of constitutional decisions made by courts. There are already strong concerns expressed about the fragile legitimacy of such courts if its judges are perceived to be following their own political agenda rather than an impersonal legal mandate. However, if the political character of constitutional review is acknowledged and acted upon, the concern would no longer be that a constitutional agency, whether it is the final court of appeal alone or some other combination of bodies, would have no credibility or authority. Instead, a new set of arrangements would have to be complemented by a fresh frame of critical reference that understood good and bad constitutional decisions in quite different terms than the present doctrinal and professional ones. Rather than pretend that they have no responsibility for the social and political effects of their decisions (as most judges tend to do), decision-makers would have to accept and defend the political consequences of those decisions made.

In short, the phony war over whether law can and should be treated as something separate and different from politics could be abandoned. Engagement should shift from an increasingly sterile exchange about what courts can and should do to meet the standards of 'principled appraisal' as the traditionalists like to phrase it.[30]

---

[29] I will pursue the institutional dimensions of this critical strategy in the next chapter. See ch 8.
[30] See ch 3.

Instead, both juristic and political attention and energies might be directed towards the much more productive and important task of evaluating whether the decisions of the Supreme Court contribute to a more democratic or better society. This entails worrying less about the argumentative form of decisions being made and more about the substantive kind of decisions that are made. If it is conceded that constitutional law is politics, then legitimacy must itself be thought of in political, not legal terms. By getting beyond the reasoned principles/raw power dichotomy, jurisprudential and constitutional theorising can cease trying to salvage the judicial process through futile efforts to demonstrate that it is more professional than ideological in its reasoning and result. At a minimum, judges would be obliged to take personal responsibility for the decisions they make; they will have to defend their substantive merit directly rather than hide behind the pseudo-constitutional truths that their judicial methodologies claim to disclose.

Crucially, I am not suggesting that such an evaluative standard of criticism will increase the likelihood of an elusive consensus among competing judicial antagonists or that it would even be conducive to temporary agreement among these decision-makers. But what it does recommend is that, rather than there being a bogus trade in so-called constitutional verities or neutral principles, the worth of constitutional law would be measured in terms of its capacity to protect and enhance the democratic society that it is supposed to serve. There will, of course, be different versions of what counts as democracy and what best advances or protects it. But such a debate would become part of the justificatory process that judges would need to develop and explain in their opinions. In this way, it might become possible to combine the institutional form and the ideological substance of constitutional law – what are the most democratic locations at which to engage in political debate about those values and commitments that can best advance a democratic society?

Conclusion

The main thrust of any acceptance that law-is-politics is to re-orientate both legal theory and legal practice. To paraphrase space pioneer Neil Armstrong, what I am recommending would be 'a small step for judges, but a giant leap for democracy'. In theoretical terms, this stance strongly urges that jurists abandon their existing preoccupation with offering an account of law and adjudication that is analytically sound in the sense of being universal and necessary. While the tendency to generalise is not to be ignored or jettisoned, juristic efforts must be more directed towards how law, politics and morality can be appreciated in contingent, local and practical contexts. In particular, this judicial work should be informed by a keener and more focussed sensibility that looks to make better (and worse) insights in particular contexts about the law's capacity to achieve justice – what is it about law that can facilitate the move towards it being more just than less just? In practical terms, there is an urgent need to get beyond the reasoned-principles/raw-power dichotomy. Lawyers and scholars should stop trying to salvage the judicial process as a semi-technical enterprise and to show that it is professional, not ideological in its reasoning and result. Instead, and at a minimum, judges would be obliged to take personal and professional responsibility for the decisions they make; they will have to defend their judgments' substantive merit directly rather than hide behind the jurisprudential pseudo-truths that their judicial methodologies supposedly disclose and rely on. In short, while the terrain is contested and perilous, the alleviation and, where possible, the eradication of injustice must be the guiding ambition of judges, jurists and lawyers.

8

Rethinking Legitimacy: A Judicial View

The hope of the traditionalists that judicial review can be objective and impartial is entirely understandable. In a society that claims to be committed to democracy (no matter how watered-down that commitment might be in practice), there is a strong desire to locate and rely on a juristic and/or judicial method that can side-step or finesse political choice: such choices are to be left to more democratically grounded institutions and actors (eg, politicians and executives). However, it is simply a hope and a misleading one that does more harm than good. The ines-capable truth is that this hope cannot be fulfilled or achieved – judicial review is inescapably political, and no theory or practice can redeem that. The only choice for judges is not whether to rely on contested values or not, but whether they should concede this and avoid pretending otherwise. Relying on contested values in reaching their decisions is neither a policy choice nor a structural impediment: it is a social reality that cannot be denied either by theoretical ingenuity or practi-cal intransigence. The myth of 'principled appraisal'[1] as a preferred and defensible mode of judicial-making is as far-fetched as the existence of Father Christmas is for teenagers (or ingenuous jurists).

To ignore or fail to give sufficient weight to the political dimension in grasp-ing the dynamics of judicial reasoning and legal theorising is, as I have insisted, unconvincing. Indeed, it is like staging Shakespeare's *Hamlet* without the Prince: it elides the main explanatory factor (ie, political values and choices) for the play, its performance, and its meaning. The same is true for constitutional decision-making and theory: the political and moral preferences of the judges and jurists are at work to a greater and lesser extent. In saying this, I am not suggesting, as some apologists claim that critics do, that 'the justices simply vote political prefer-ences … without regard to law'.[2] The rejection of the idea that there are objective legal standards or principles that vouchsafe distinct forms of judicial reasoning and results does not lead to a cynical or opportunistic perspective. On the contrary, it recognises that, although judicial decision-making is inevitably ideological, it can still be thought about in terms of being principled, reasoned in good faith, and not done in an *ad hoc* way. A badly reasoned opinion is as unlikely to garner the support and approval of the legal community as a respected precedent whatever its

---

[1] Herbert Wechsler, 'Toward Neutral Principles of Constitutional Law' (1959) 73 *Harvard Law Review* 1, 16.

[2] Richard Fallon, *Law and Legitimacy in the Supreme Court* (Cambridge, Belknap Press, 2018) 2.

political leaning or ideological appeal. But legal craft alone cannot carry the day: it will be a significant piece in a much larger and intricate puzzle about constitutional justice.

In this chapter, therefore, I will undertake the crucial task of exploring and recommending the kind of impact that a law-is-politics approach could have upon the performance of the judicial role in matters of constitutional law – what might judicial opinions look like in a politicised account of constitutional law? In the first section, I will reinforce the case for why a more transparent fulfilment of judicial duties will advance the case for a politicised court that abandons the traditional-ist mind-set. The second section looks at how judges might grasp the politicised nettle and become more pragmatic in their approach to constitutional law and constitutional politics. Rather than persist with the stilted discourse of the tradi-tional project, they can be both more expansive and more legitimate. In the third section, I will explore how this transformed *modus operandi* might affect dealing with the vexed problem of abortion rights in the early twenty-first century. Finally, the fourth section will undertake similar explorations in regard to the challenges of resolving federalism disputes in a modern world of climate change and envi-ronmental despoilation. Throughout the chapter, the ambition is to be suggestive rather than conclusory about what a law-is-politics critique will mean for a revi-sion of judicial roles and responsibilities in contemporary constitutional societies.

An Open Court

Despite the range and reach of criticisms of the art of judicial opinion-writing, there is still one strain of traditional justification for allowing a Supreme Court-like body to determine the substance and style of constitutional law. It is often said that, because judges are removed from the day-to-day pressures of standard party politics, they are better able to reflect upon the deeper and longer-term implica-tions of one particular stance on contested constitutional values over another. This idea has some pertinence and explanatory power, even from a critical perspective. But this is not because it will somehow facilitate and underwrite the search for constitutional truths or anything like them. On the contrary, it will allow judges to construct political arguments and ideas that contribute directly to useful and efficacious ways to think about society's pressing problems and what might be the most suggestive way to resolve them. Consequently, they will need to vacate the imagined high ground of constitutional law and become policy advisers to politi-cians and citizens. As such, as pragmatically inclined officials, judges will inhabit the realms of practical politics as much as abstract theorising; they might begin to act as 'justices' in both name and purpose.

Within such a revised mandate, judges would forgo the shadow boxing that presently comprises constitutional decision-making. It will no longer be thought sensible, let alone persuasive or useful, to maintain that judicial decision-making can be done in a way that is meaningfully distinct from more open-ended political debates about what makes a just and fair democratic polity. Having given up on the idea that they should be in the obfuscating business of identifying the true, proper or correct account of what the Constitution really means, judges will be able to devote their considerable talents to making and defending proposals on what today's society can and should be. So, rather than perpetuate the increasingly desperate and ineffective efforts to maintain the traditionally construed legitimacy of the courts in constitutional law, judges might begin to develop and express their constitutional judgments in more honest and transparent terms in both form and substance. In doing so, they will enhance, not sully, the reputation of the courts as privileged and accountable contributors to the demanding task of improving constitutional law and its democratic legitimacy.

One contemporary jurist who goes a long way to doing this is Mary Anne Franks. In a powerful and almost jeremiadic survey of American constitutional law's history and its fundamentalist tendencies, she rightly condemns both liberals and conservatives for their predilection for reading the Constitution 'selectively, self-servingly, and in bad faith'.[3] For her, constitutional scholarship and judgment writing is too often a thinly disguised exercise in ideological cherry-picking. Indeed, Franks offers a devastating critique of how constitutional law has been utilised to advance very particular and partisan projects (ie, the agendas of white, male and vested interests). She dismisses two centuries of constitutional law and jurisprudence as being cultish in that they amount to a misplaced and excessive elevation of particular and contested interpretive preferences to the reverential status of constitutional truths. All this is compelling as far as it goes. However, it does not go far enough. Unfortunately, she loses her critical nerve at the moment when she needs it most and succumbs to a more traditionalist expectation – to offer a proposal for the right or proper way to do things.

Implicit in Franks' critique is the underlying idea that constitutional lawyering and judging can, if suitably revised, be done in good faith by adhering to the correct meaning of the Constitution. She maintains that it is still possible to 'have faith in the Constitution'.[4] But this means that, like many of those fundamentalists that she severely chastises, her overall goal is to implement her own form of constitutional fundamentalism by espousing 'an unflinching commitment to the principle of reciprocity expressed in the Fourteenth Amendment's equal protection clause'.[5] This is the epitome of the cultish behaviour that she is at pains to condemn – there is one meaning to the Constitution and she knows what it is. While she is less doctrinaire and dogmatic than some traditional fundamentalists, she remains part of the same jurisprudential project as those fundamentalists she condemns; 'the Constitution is worth defending' and 'one can only honour the

---

[3] Mary Anne Franks, *The Cult of the Constitution* (Stanford, Stanford University Press, 2020) xii. See also ch 4.

[4] ibid at 21.

[5] ibid.

Constitution by honoring equality.'[6] While some (including me) might find her proposals to 'reorient our constitutional attention to those whose rights have been excluded, ignored, and subordinated', attractive,[7] it is not so much a jurisprudential ambition as a political aspiration. Or, as I have insisted throughout, that this jurisprudential goal is itself as political as any other on offer. As Franks insists upon, but only half-heartedly so, there is no neutral, objective way to read the constitution that can trump all others.

Accordingly, contrary to Franks' conclusions, it is entirely defensible that any alternative to constitutional law's search for 'neutral principles' or 'constitutional truths' need not be arbitrary, crass or unprincipled. Political judges will strive to be scrupulous, principled and just in their work.[8] Indeed, all the skills and talents that are attributed by traditional jurists to today's ideal judge will also be extremely important to an avowedly and unapologetically court of political judges – being balanced, acting with integrity, possessing strength of character, exhibiting intellectual capacity and, perhaps most significantly, proposing an informing vision of what makes the good democratic society. By demonstrating that politics can be all those things rather than a mud-slinging bun fight, a court of political judges will help to enrich and intensify political debate and, therefore, democracy. They will be part of civic politics as opposed to, as they presently pretend to be, apart from or above the political fray of democratic politics. Accordingly, rather than make unconvincing claims that they have hit upon the true meaning of the constitutional project, judges and jurists will simply strive to do the best that they can do in the service of contemporary society and its democratic commitments.

Of course, even when they fulfil their tasks conscientiously and convincingly, these political judges will not perform democratic or political miracles. In particular, they will not dissolve deep social and political conflict and bring people together in a harmonious unity. Indeed, it would be naïve and dangerous to conclude otherwise. However, what these revitalised judges and jurists might do is at least frame the disagreements in less divisive terms and offer a deeper appreciation of what those differences of opinion entail. The ambition is to help political antagonists to find some middle grounds of compromise, if not reconciliation. While this will not occur in each and every situation, a political court might be able to build some bridges and lower some barriers that prevent civil and engaged dialogue about what road to follow. This is presently lacking. Indeed, Supreme Courts have an unfortunate tendency to entrench unconsidered opinions and increase polarisation, not mollify it. By addressing the political issues directly rather than indirectly and through the disarming professional discourse of law, political judges might do a much better job of becoming more relevant to public debate around contentious

---

[6] ibid at 202.

[7] ibid at 204.

[8] It is likely a stretch to suggest that such an alternative can or should be 'utopian speculation' as Duncan Kennedy once (mischievously?) recommended. See Duncan Kennedy, 'Cost Reduction Theory As Legitimation' (1981) 90 *Yale Law Journal* 1275, 1283.

social and moral issues. As things stand, Supreme Courts seem to be more in the game of end-running the real issues that divide citizens than confronting them and contributing to their resolution. However, as is often the case, when decision-makers back into a problem rather approach it head on, the chances of falling down and missing the point are much greater.

A Public Stance

If the courts are openly political, the judgments published by the judges will need to be quite different in both form and style from their present incarnations. While courts will likely look to earlier cases, they will do so on an advisory and persuasive basis; this is much the same as any situated and informed debate about political values and justifications. In particular, judges will not treat earlier pronouncements as 'precedents'. Although this might appear to be a radical proposal, this would be much the same as presently occurs. At the level of Supreme Courts, it is simply inaccurate to claim that there is any serious or compelling doctrine of *stare decisis* in effect. If cases like *Dobbs* are anything to go by, Supreme Court judges follow earlier constitutional doctrines when it suits them and ignore them when it does not. Some argue that there is a structured doctrine of precedent, derived from respect for the Rule of Law, that limits overruling landmark cases to the most limited of circumstances.[9] But this seems to be too formalistic by far; it is a mistake (that is entailed by the traditional model of neutral judging) to pretend that *stare decisis* outweighs the Justices' personal or collective commitments about constitutional justice. Indeed, if *Dobbs* is anything to go by, it is entirely reasonable to conclude that the majority's overruling of *Roe* had everything to do with political substance and little to do with legal form. As always, politics trumps most other legal considerations.

Within a more politicised understanding of constitutional law and adjudication, the force and cogency of earlier judgments will ebb and flow in relation to changing social dynamics and views; what was once considered influential, settled and accepted might become inconsistent, unpersuasive and out-of-line with prevailing values. But, contrary to traditional understandings, this will be a matter of political calculation, not precedential authority: there is no doctrinal opinion or judicial decision that is simply and always part of the constitutional furniture. Furthermore, an added advantage of a politicised account will be that both popular and academic evaluations of the judges' performance will not be based on an exclusively legal line of criticism (eg, doctrinal consistency, precedential respect, and formal integrity), but will instead be guided by reference to the political values

---

[9] See, eg, Nina Varsava, 'Precedent, Reliance, And *Dobbs*' (2023) 136 *Harvard Law Review* 1845. The same applies in Canada. Although the Supreme Court has outlined a detailed doctrine for determining if and when established precedent should be overruled, its Justices are driven more by political substance than legal form. See *Carter v Canada (AG)* (2015) 2015 *SCC* 5.

and concerns that underpin judgments. Mindful of Holmes's quip that 'historic continuity with the past is not a duty, it is only a necessity,'[10] it is pragmatic wisdom to suggest that today's values take priority over the past's standards if the only reason for observing the past's values is their pastness.

Moreover, a recognition of constitutional law's inevitably political nature might encourage judges to write in a way that is directed less to an exclusively professional audience. It is perplexing, at best, that the resolution of some of society's most pressing challenges should be framed, phrased and reasoned through in a discourse that is largely alien and inaccessible to most non-lawyers and typical citizens. By adopting a more comprehensible and less obscure mode of discursive explanation, courts will become sites at which popular participation and public involvement will be more easily facilitated. Also, this effort to cultivate a more straightforward way of proceeding will complement and enrich political debate, not seek to put an end to it. Indeed, judges might strive to help shape and substantiate such political debate rather than dominate it and hive it off from such general political discussion. In this regard, the fallibility of the courts might become a strength, not a weakness, if they replace the false allure of constitutional truths with the pertinent usefulness of constitutional argument. Democracy would be much better served by such curial humility.

One judge whose work and approach hint at how such a mode of judicial discourse might pan out is William O Douglas in the mid-twentieth century. Although something of a maverick (and early environmentalist) by both design and inclination, some of his judgments do capture the themes and attitudes that a more pragmatic, principled and politicised style of opinion writing might incorporate. He abandoned certain legal niceties and sought to develop a style of writing that was less professional and sterile, but more vibrant and engaging. Never afraid to dissent or move constitutional law forward, he treated constitutional law as a living tableau that should serve the interests of contemporary society, not act as an unvarying and restrictive relic from society's past. In taking such an inventive and flexible approach to his judicial duties, he took into account the practical effects of the Court's decisions on everyday people in their ordinary lives. An example of this is his lead judgment in *Griswold* in 1965.[11] Striking down a statute that banned the use of contraceptives, Douglas was clear and concise in his willingness to read the Constitution as relevant to a changing society and to having a democratic dynamic at its heart. For him, enumerated rights were to be supplemented by unenumerated rights that caught the spirit, if not the letter of the Constitution. In short, even though his judicial philosophy was not uniformly adopted or universally admired, it does chime much better with the critical idea of constitutional-law-as-politics.

---

[10] Oliver Wendel Holmes, Jr, 'Learning and Science' in *Speeches* (Boston, Brown Little, 1896) 68.

[11] *Griswold v Connecticut* (1965) 381 US 479. Of course, Douglas's politics were not to everyone's taste. He managed to bring together elements of both socialism, libertarianism, environmentalism and social justice. See Bruce Murphy, *Wild Bill: The Legend and Life of William O. Douglas* (New York, Random House, 2003).

Finally, by way of introduction, it should be noted that it is condescending to think that the general public will not accept or agree with the stance that courts are and should be political in performance and result. They are much more savvy and worldly than many judges and jurists are prepared to concede. Available surveys and polling data strongly indicate that citizens are primarily interested in substantive outcomes and results: they are more than content to subscribe to almost any posited constitutional theory or institutional process that will produce the kind and range of decisions that will advance the values and interests that they most cherish.[12] This, of course, is as true for liberals as it is for conservatives. Because there is no available escape from politics, the appropriate response is to become better at political argument and to extend its reach and expectations across and through society.

For instance, while liberals tend to reject originalism in favour of a more organic approach, they do so for decidedly political reasons, not purely hermeneutical or jurisprudential ones. Liberals are very happy to sign on to an originalist theory that leads generally to the kind of decisions that promote values and interests that they politically approve of. Ironically, it is academics, if anybody, who seem gullible or arrogant enough to think that constitutional law is or can be insulated from out-and-out ideological deliberations and political sensitivities. As Ronald Dworkin was fond of arguing, within much the same epistemological parameters as originalists, law 'is deeply and thoroughly political ..., but law is not a matter of personal or partisan politics.'[13] He shared much the same philosophical ambitions as his conservative antagonists – to demonstrate that constitutional law had a necessary and proper political orientation. Of course, this presumed objective politics of constitutional law turned out to be very much the same as Dworkin's own liberal and partisan preferences. In this, he was no different from his originalist counterparts.

On Abortion

It is, of course, almost impossible to predict precisely what might happen if the idea and practice of a politicised court was taken seriously. What will persuade people about a preference for one political position over another is itself a matter of continual and contextual disputation. All argumentative threads and their relative prioritisation emphasise some values and issues over others; it is not possible to put together an opinion that does not instantiate a leaning one way over another, especially in contested and controversial matters. A political argument that will work in one case or at one time might not be so successful in other cases

---

[12] See chs 1 and 5.

[13] Ronald Dworkin, *A Matter of Principle* (Cambridge, Harvard University Press, 1985) 146. Others who run a similar line include Richard Fallon, above n 2 and Lawrence Lessig, *How the Supreme Court Has Read the American Constitution* (Oxford, Oxford University Press, 2019).

and at a different time; there will be a judicial need to be less dogmatic and doctrinaire in both arguments made and positions taken.[14] Understood from this kind of pragmatic perspective, this rhetorical dynamic can be appreciated not as an inherent weakness of legal argument, but as an abiding strength: constitutional law and decision-making can be treated as a flexible and responsive practice that allows judges to ensure that their decisions are appropriately and substantively attuned to changing values and commitments. In short, constitutional argumentation and opinions can be one of the sites for making good on the political character of constitutional law.

In doing this, although it will still be essential to take constitutional law and doctrinal materials seriously, it will also be as essential not to take them *too seriously*. By this, I mean that constitutional doctrine must be addressed and dealt with in a respectful and attentive manner; it cannot simply be ignored or treated as so much excess argumentation or padding. However, it also must be recognised that, within a politicised practice of decision-making, there is more to constitutional law than its own self-contained and professional universe; there are other terms and perspectives through which to apprehend and tackle the challenges of constitutional law than on law's own insular and professional terms. While a keen appreciation of constitutional law's traditions and resources can be helpful and illuminative in approaching and deciding contemporary problems that come before the courts, they alone cannot carry the constitutional project forward. Once constitutional law and decision-making are accepted to be political and inescapably so, exclusive reliance on law's own self-generated resources and inward-looking forms will not be sufficient. There must be a greater pragmatic and politicised awareness of law's effects on society and its formative interests – achieving justice, not following law, is the governing ambition.

However, all that said, it is worth looking at how these revised considerations of a politicised constitutional law and decision-making could play out in the two cases that I have focussed some of my critical arguments around – the *Dobbs* decision on abortion rights and the *GGPPA* decision on federalism and environmental pollution. While this analysis can only be speculative and suggestive, it can help to point up both the benefits and, of course, the limitations of how a political court might go about its constitutional work and decision-making. The beauty of this possibility is that there are no built-in standards of performance or criticism that will constrict the court in how it proceeds; judges will be both empowered and contained in fulfilling their constitutional responsibilities and re-working those standards for critical appraisal. The emphasis will rightly be on achieving a result that maximises the important democratic qualities of social usefulness, informed opinion, civic connection and political persuasion. This does not recommend or lean toward any particular outcome. However, by proceeding

---

[14] See, eg, Robin Reames, *The Ancient Art of Thinking for Yourself: The Power of Rhetoric in Polarized Times* (New York, Basic Books, 2024).

in this way, constitutional law might become both more relevant and thereby more justice-oriented.

In *Dobbs*, the majority would not be able to hide behind 'the true Constitution'. Instead, they would need to present more cogent and pertinent arguments about why their substantive views on abortion and governmental responsibility should prevail in a contemporary rendition of constitutional law. Those judges would not be obliged to abandon their substantive stance, but they would have to show why the *Roe* approach taken over the last 50 years should be set aside as a matter of constitutional politics. This established precedent would carry weight that could only be dislodged by reference to evolved social and moral values. In short, the majority would have to argue why their political view should be adopted, not as a process of historical truth-telling or established authority, but as a matter of pragmatic and supported contemporary justice. This would demand a much richer and subtle account of many issues and interests – women's social role; reproductive fairness; bodily security; and the like. None of this, of course, would dictate that a woman's right to abortion must prevail at all times and in all circumstances, although it might. After all, the majority would likely still uphold the same position and reach the same outcome. The crux of any proposed politicisation of constitutional law and decision-making is in defending and making explicit the substantive values that are and should be advanced and protected as a matter of constitutional justice.

On the other hand, the minority would not be able to hide behind the assumed authority of established precedent. While *Roe*'s identity as a long-standing feature of the constitutional terrain would count for something, that alone would not recommend its continued acceptance as a matter of contemporary justice. After all, the settled existence of some precedents, as in *Brown*, for example, might actually work against their persuasiveness depending on contemporary conditions. As such, there would need to be a more substantive defence of the *Roe* ruling than a reliance on its historical longevity. Like the judges in the majority, these judges would have to put forward a positive and affirming account of why women should be able to exercise their reproductive freedom without state interference (and perhaps with state-supported resources). This would demand a more expansive and encompassing justification of the same issues as those that had to be addressed by the majority – women's social role; reproductive fairness; bodily security; and the like. By engaging with each other on substantive merits rather than jousting over more formal arguments, the members of the Supreme Court might (but only might) be able to contest and argue about the real values and interests that divide them.

Beyond Pollution

In *GGPPA*, all the Supreme Court judges sought to validate their stances by claiming that Canadian federalism was a technical, objective and neutral concept that could independently and on its own justify their opinions and decision on the substantive matter at hand. From a critical perspective, this is a formalist manoeuvre that only works as a convenient screen and substitute for more deeply-based political disagreements. Indeed, there is ample juristic commentary and even court judgments that recognise that federalism disputes and their legal resolution involve irreducible and essential efforts to make functional and contestable decisions about how to distribute and re-distribute power 'to the government thought to be most suited to achieving … particular societal objective[s]'.[15] This exercise cannot be carried out in a technical, objective and neutral fashion. Instead, it demands that judges and courts must take a stand on how this can be done in modern society with diverse political and regional interests. As one prescient and respected constitutional scholar concluded around the time of Canada's patriation of its Constitution in 1982, 'in making these relative-value decisions, all that can be rightly required of judges is straight thinking, industry, good faith, and a capacity to discount their own prejudices.'[16] In both federalism and other constitutional matters, this is no bad standard for judges to measure their performances against and up to.

To do this in the *GGPPA* case would require the Justices to forgo the traditional refuge of constitutional law's supposedly neutral analysis and its pretence that it is possible 'to identify the true subject matter of the challenged statute or provision'.[17] Instead, the Court's majority would have to make substantive arguments about why 'cooperative federalism' is worth upholding and why it redounds to the federal government's jurisdictional benefit on the facts of the case before them. Rather than simply assume that it held sway because it has become the increasingly dominant judicial preference in recent decades, the judges would need to explain why it represents a better approach to governmental arrangements, social values, institutional power and democratic accountability in the twenty-first century; there would have to be an informed preference for this over a more compartmentalised and exclusive-leaning account of the division of powers. In other words, the judges would have to put their political cards on the table, make a candid and proactive defence of them, and play them with deliberate skill and craft. The ambition would be to put political values and commitments front-and-centre because they are what actually divide the Supreme Court's justices, not their internalised reading of existing constitutional jurisprudence.

In contrast, the Court's minority in *GGPPA* would not be able to claim that they are to be excused of personal responsibility for their opinions and decision by their reliance on textual or doctrinal truths within the constitutional canon of federalism. The fact that those views might well be in line with a pseudo-originalist

---

[15] Reference re Secession of Quebec [1998] 2 SCR 217, [58].

[16] William Lederman, 'Classification of Laws in The British North America Act' in *Continuing Canadian Constitutional Dilemmas: Essays on the Constitutional History, Public Law and Federal System of Canada* (Toronto, Butterworths, 1981) 239.

[17] References re Greenhouse Gas Pollution Pricing Act (2021) 2021 SCC 11, [53] (Wagner CJ).

understanding of Canadian federalism over more than a century and a half ago is not a convincing or persuasive argument in itself: 'the exclusivity of provincial jurisdiction over [designated] matters ... is fundamental to the Canadian brand of federalism, and was a unique and deliberate choice by the makers of the Constitution who were concerned about federal overreach.'[18] Such originalistic thinking has no special authority in constitutional law or politics: the decision to render the federal legislation unconstitutional is not unpersuasive or unacceptable in itself. But such an outcome must be bolstered and supported by both political and legal arguments that defend the substantive merits of such a position in the contemporary context; the assumed and contestable vision of politicians over 150 years ago (who had no concept or awareness of 'the environment', let alone climate change) is not sufficient in itself to do that. If this account of federalism is to prevail, it must do so by virtue of its contemporary relevance, cogency and efficacy.

Instead, those dissenting judges would have to engage in a similar style of argumentative justification to the majority, albeit with a different goals and different purposes. The judges would have to defend more amply the traditional vision of federalism and judicial role that informs their decision. Indeed, as part of that task, they would have to engage with the majority's preference for a cooperative vision of federalism (as the majority would have to do with the dissenting judges' account). In so doing, all the judges might join substantive issue over, at least, the underlying substantive matters that divide them rather than the pseudo-formalistic arguments about the jurisprudential and doctrinal past. The focus should be on contemporary discussions about 'the government thought to be most suited to achieving particular societal objectives'.[19] Of course, this would not lead to any necessary agreement over how to move forward in some unified or consensual manner; political differences will still remain and still be decisive. However, valuable energy and insights will be directed toward the fundamental and underlying visions of federalism in dispute and not be wasted on the kind of distracting legal posturing that presently constitutes constitutional argument and legal doctrines.

Again, as with the *Dobbs* debacle, there is a lasting lesson to all this – the kind of political court and decision-making that I am advocating would embrace, not seek to evade, the demands and dynamics of constitutional politics. In particular, federalism disagreements would become not dissimilar to other modes of constitutional law that centre around rights and freedoms; the political quality of the issues at hand would be more keenly conceded and confronted. Moreover, in taking such a perspective, constitutional law would move towards becoming part of, not apart from, the broader political and social debate about the more effective role of different levels of government in handling contemporary challenges, like climate change. If properly understood and appreciated in the way that I am recommending, acting in this way would at least allow constitutional judges to

---

[18] ibid at [348] (Brown J).
[19] Dworkin, above n 13.

claim a degree of political honesty and integrity that can only add to a Supreme Court's prestige and legitimacy.

Conclusion

So, the law-is-politics take on legal theory and constitutional law encourages, not discourages, jurists and judges facing reality and coming out from behind the Ozian curtain of traditional thinking. As in the Baum book, judges, like the Wizard himself, must disabuse themselves of the notion that their power and legitimacy somehow depend on people suspending their disbelief and toeing the traditionalist line. Instead, judges must stop imagining that they will be exposed and vulnerable if the formal curtain and their wizard-like trappings are swept away and they are revealed as mere mortals. This need not be the case. Although, as I have forcefully insisted, although judicial decision-making is inevitably ideological, it can still be thought about and done in ways that are principled, reasoned, in good faith, and not simply *ad hoc*. Indeed, by putting their humanness on display (and not pretending to be like Dworkin's Herculean super-heroes), people might become more respecting of judges and their demanding role in a democratic polity. Indeed, although perhaps it might be too optimistic a hope, people might begin to be more, not less, appreciative of the deep-rooted challenges of constitutional law and politics.

9

Rethinking Legitimacy: A Political View

As with most things, the proof of the jurisprudential pudding is in the judicial eating. Abstract reflection and theorising have their place and undergird, expressly or tacitly, the practical and prosaic routines of good governance. This applies acutely to constitutional law and decision-making. It will be important, therefore, to explore the political as well as the jurisprudential, institutional and democratic dimensions of that task. However, mindful of the prevailing self-image of constitutional jurists and judges as trading in authoritative truths, it is vital in developing a more pragmatic approach to hold fast to the informing idea that there is no one sanctioned or superior way to participate in constitutional decision-making. Instead, it will be for judges and jurists to nurture the kind of arguments and opinions that they think will best persuade citizens of the wisdom and legitimacy of their judgments and decisions. Reliance on purported truths and authoritative platitudes will not do the job. I cannot, therefore, put forward any kind of script or menu that can be relied on to fulfil judges' institutional responsibilities. It is very much a catch-as-catch-can style of engagement: what works for one society at one time might not work for another society (or even the same society) at another time.

However, what I can do is to be suggestive and offer illustrative examples of what those arguments might look like. I will do this by responding to a hypothetical set of facts that might come before the American or Canadian Supreme Court in the near future. Again, there is nothing canonical or controlling about the examples that I offer or the doctrinal reasoning that I utilise. It will be for judges and jurists to work with different approaches over time and across disputes. In so doing, they must be alert to the notion that flexibility and experimentation is the hallmark of the politicised and pragmatic judge: a faux-dogmatism or absolutism is not at all the route to go. However, this does not imply that judges or jurists should not take a principled stand and pursue it with energy, commitment and good faith; they are obliged as both judicial officers and democratic citizens to give their best efforts at proposing and crafting reasoned and reasonable responses to pressing and recurring social and political occurrences. As such, a pragmatic approach to constitutional law and decision-making is the most fitting complement to the demands and challenges of providing desirable answers to taxing ideological questions in any society that is committed to principled and democratic governance: sophistry and second-order rationalisations have no place.

In this chapter, therefore, I will take a risky stab at what and how court judgments might develop and be formulated if there is a rigorous and unapologetic acceptance of the fact that constitutional law and decision-making is a political undertaking. In the first section, I will sketch out a practical constitutional issue about student protest that might come before the courts and unpack its various components from a legal and political perspective. The second section explores the constitutional terrain and emphasises the contested relation between constitutional rights and private property. In the third section, I examine in more detail the nature of protected expression and any justifiable political limits that might be placed upon this important constitutional and democratic freedom. The fourth gets to grips with whether and how freedom of speech might be affected by other constitutional norms, especially claims to equality. In the fifth section, I explain what it means to take a political reckoning of these matters in terms of constitutional politics. Throughout the chapter, I will recommend the kind of operative implications that a law-is-politics approach will have on the practical fulfilment of the judicial dimension of constitutional law and decision-making.

Making a Fresh Start

There are so many simmering and inflamed problems that modern society faces. Any number of contested issues might be explored. However, one set of circumstances that is of considerable topical interest and is likely to come before the courts in both Canada and the United States is one that involves recent political protests on university campuses. This is a highly charged and divisive issue – whether and how pro-Palestinian/anti-Israeli or pro-Israeli/anti-Palestinian student groups should be able to act and express their conflicting views about the embattled conflict in Gaza. Imagine the following facts:

> *A prestigious university has two campuses in the city. There are several squares and park-like areas on each campus that are normally used by students for a variety of activities. In the recent past, there have been protests and demonstrations, but they have been on a relatively small scale; these included some flag-waving, leaflet distribution and chanting by small groups. The university has a set of regulations about campus use by students. Highlighting generally the need for fairness and respect, the regulations prohibit any activity that disturbs or runs afoul of the educational mission of the university. In particular, the regulations forbid students from living in or on these areas and from preventing other students having equal access to those common spaces.*
>
> *Over the past few weeks, competing student groups have engaged in protests about the Israeli-Palestinian conflict in Gaza. Most of the protesters are students, but there are a handful who are not. Although these events began modestly in size and volume, they have now become more acrimonious and extreme. One Palestinian group has taken over a large area on one campus and established an encampment there with about 20 inhabitants; it flies Palestinian flags and there are many signs that contain anti-Israeli messages. On the other campus, a pro-Israeli group has assembled and demanded that the university*

administration act to banish the pro-Palestinian group whom they accuse of being antise-mitic in its actions. Dissatisfied by the administration's response, a number of this group have occupied the administration office. As an effect of both the encampment and the sit-in, many non-protesting students have complained that all this is interfering with their efforts to study and get on with their lives.

The university has gone to court to have both groups removed from campus. A range of varying constitutional arguments were raised about political expression, equality, property status, and time-and-place restrictions. The university has been unsuccessful in obtaining an appropriate court order and the earlier status quo prevails. The case has now gone on appeal to the Supreme Court.

This is not a novel issue that the courts have not faced before. There is ample legal doctrine that deals with the general problem of student protests.[1] Indeed, if anything, there is too much legal doctrine on the problem; there are more legit-imate paths to follow than might seem reasonable. However, the constitutional issues that this hypothetical set of facts raises are far from settled or definitive in all their aspects. As one mainstream scholar frames it, judges must fulfil their 'core mission' by providing 'reasoned justice under law' that is supported with 'argu-ments that they advance in good faith'.[2] But this is not the disciplinary constraint or caution that it is intended to be. Indeed, almost any reasonable outcome can be bolstered and supported by the available case law and, as importantly, can be presented in a principled way. Available and accredited legal stances are too numerous and too diverse to underwrite one outcome that will garner support across and within political lines. As such, the demand to 'be principled' offers no genuine constraint on what should or should not be decided. Moreover, not only might there be a range of defensible arguments, but there is also no one account from the political left or right that establishes a left or right position that is decisive or conclusive. Multiple perspectives disagree over the basics and their practical application in these specific circumstances of student protest. Accordingly, the constitutional resolution of this hypothetical set of facts lends itself to the kind of political analysis and legal rulings that a law-is-politics stance is recommending.

One of the most important insights about law and legal reasoning that is often overlooked is that the questions selected to be asked often contribute to the kind of answers to be given. Indeed, heeding the poetic advice of (law professor) Archibald McLeish that 'we have learned the answers, all the answers; it is the questions we do not know,'[3] more attention needs to be paid to the questions asked; they can be as politically loaded as the analysis offered or answers given. Accordingly, in

---

[1] My references to extant legal doctrine are not meant to be exhaustive, but only illustrative of the paths and patterns of both American and Canadian jurisprudence. I intend to canvas the main argu-ments and do not intend to explore all possible approaches. For a straightforward and contextualised survey, see Stephen Newman, 'The Politics of Campus Free Speech in Canada and the United States' (2020) 29 *Constitutional Forum* 19, 23.

[2] Richard Fallon, *Law and Legitimacy in the Supreme Court* (Cambridge, Harvard University Press, 2018) 130.

[3] Archibald MacLeish, *The Hamlet of A. MacLeish* (Boston, Houghton Mifflin, 1928).

approaching the hypotheticals set of facts, it will be appropriate, at a minimum, to remain sensitive to how different questions might prompt or suggest different kinds of answers. That said (and with a keen awareness of this caution), I want to go with three questions that might garner approval from most constitutional judges and lawyers:

- Does the Constitution extend to the regulation or scrutiny of activities that occur on university campuses?

- If so, do the protests and/or encampments constitute a form of constitutionally protected expression?

- If so, are there constitutionally accepted limits that can be imposed by universities on such student protests?[4]

In answering these questions, it is important to appreciate the position that courts have traditionally taken on such matters. This is not to ensure that precedential priority is given to those earlier cases and the arguments relied on, but to ensure that they are taken seriously as a matter of intellectual integrity. The constitutional tradition that has evolved and its popular acceptance will be an important, but not necessarily pivotal, consideration in deciding what a judge maintains is the preferable approach to contested matters of free expression and student protest in a modern society that is as globalised as it is localised. The objective is not to prioritise the legal duty to let the past dictate the future, but the political responsibility to achieve results that best advance the cause of justice in today's democratic society. Again, there is no one accepted approach or standpoint that can do this. But, with an acceptance that constitutional law is, always was and always will be a political affair, the judicial task is to present and apply the most compelling principled arguments as to why a particular outcome is more or less conducive to a society today that values the virtues of democratic processes and substantive rights.

Constitutional Territory

Almost all serious accounts begin from the starting point that the Constitution does not apply evenly or at all across society to all subjects, sites and situations. The problems and disagreement have been over where a line should be drawn between those subjects, sites and situations that are subject to constitutional scrutiny and those that are not – when, where and to whom does constitutional law apply? Although there is a tendency to divide the constitutional universe into public spheres (where constitutional norms generally apply) and private spheres (where they do not), this simple bifurcated framework has proved unsuited to

---

[4] I recognise that there might well be a fourth question added to these three – if not, are there any legal obligations that the university has to the student protesters? This raises interesting issues, but they are more to do with private and administrative law than constitutional law.

and incapable of working easily and fairly. Even though both the American and Canadian constitutional texts talk about prohibitions on 'government' (especially on matters of free speech/expression), judicial answers to this constitutional conundrum have shifted and changed over time. In modern society where the multiplicity of actors and institutions – corporations, religious bodies, hospitals, unions, student bodies, media groups, municipalities, shopping malls, non-citizens, etc – refuse to fit easily into a sharp and decisive division between the public and the private, the courts have laboured to maintain distinctions that are convincing or consistent in regard to the application of constitutional norms and values. This is particularly so with educational institutions – if they are not governmental, that hardly makes them entirely private.

In regard to universities, the Canadian and American courts have reached different resolutions about the reach of constitutional law. Generally, the constitutional domain is broader in the United States than in Canada. In regard to speech and expression, the present American position is that state universities do fall under First Amendment jurisdiction, but private universities do not; government has a stake in the creation and control of public universities. So, students in public universities can generally claim constitutional protection, but private students cannot.[5] However, American doctrine is more nuanced in that private students can on occasion claim a para-constitutional protection if the university has a relevant code of conduct and it is failing to follow it.[6] In contrast, Canadian jurisprudence has been less expansive. Public universities (and that means almost all universities) are not considered to be vulnerable to a Charter of Rights scrutiny because, although created and partially funded by government, they are considered to be autonomously controlled. The upshot is that students cannot claim constitutional protections against incursions by university administrators on their rights to free expression and protest.[7]

Despite these differences in approach and application, both American and Canadian courts claim to be guided both by their constitutional texts and by society's own social and legal traditions on the regulation of speech and expression. But these arguments only have limited traction. After all, the word 'government' is hardly self-defining and the different definitions relied on by American and Canadian courts are plausible, if not conclusive. Although both approaches can be criticised as going too far or not far enough, it is significant that neither offers a proper or full analysis of the larger task and rationale for drawing territorial lines between government and private property. In order to

---

[5] *Healy v James* (1971) 408 US 169, 180. See, eg, *Matter of Doe v Cornell University* (2017) 59 Misc 3d 915.

[6] *Peck v Baldwinsville Central School District* (2005) 436 F.3d 617.

[7] *McKinney v University of Guelph* [1990] 3 SCR 229, 275. See, eg, *Lobo v Carleton University* (2012) 2012 ONCA 498; *Canadian Federation of Students v Ontario (Colleges and Universities)* (2021) 2021 ONCA 553; and *University of Toronto (Governing Council) v Doe et al* (2024) 2024 ONSC 3755. It must be added that there might well be federally or provincially legislated human rights codes that apply to such activity.

offer a more convincing account of why constitutional norms should not apply to private or, at least, non-public subjects, sites or situations, it is essential to confront the partial and political assumptions that underlie these demarcation efforts. In short, the courts must provide a substantive and persuasive explanation of why private property should trump constitutional values (ie, important constitutional norms do not affect private property owners). In doing so, legal formalism must be replaced by political engagement. There will, of course, be no settled or shared response to why or whether this is so. Nonetheless, such a re-focussing will put this disputed relation between constitutional law and private property as well as the normative justifications around it firmly on the constitutional and, therefore, political table.

'Private property' is not simply an item or idea that is separate and immune from governmental control; there are government hands all over its recognition, protection and regulation. Within the two main theories of private property, there is one (a Lockean approach) that defends the claim that right to private property is a pre-social and natural entitlement; any governmental involvement depends on the property owner's consent. The other understanding (a Benthamite approach) supports the understanding that there is no natural right to property and that the right to private property is a positive entitlement that is created by and within a particular state.[8] Although these appear to be starkly different in thrust and slant, both approaches rely upon government to protect any right to private property: a Benthamite view is obviously anchored in the state, but the Lockean account also depends upon government to incorporate such a view into a state-backed and state-designed scheme of property law. Accordingly, it seems a little far-fetched to base constitutional law upon the normative assumption that government plays no role in the maintenance of private property and, therefore, by virtue of that fact alone, private property and its quasi-private parallels are necessarily outside the constitutional realm.[9]

Outside the regimen of theoretical supposition, it is clear that society allows and imposes all manner of restrictions on the ownership, use and enjoyment of so-called private property. In a complex and wide set of government laws at different

---

[8] The Lockean view is also adopted by Hugo Grotius, Samual von Pufendorf, John Locke, Immanuel Kant and George WF Hegel, and the Benthamite view is supported by Thomas Hobbes, David Hume, Adam Smith, Jeremy Bentham, Emile Durkheim and Max Weber. For a straightforward introduction, see Sukhninder Panesar, 'Theories of Private Property in Modern Property Law' (2000) 15 *Denning Law Journal* 113. For a more instrumental critique, see Michael Heller and James Salzman, *Mine! How the Hidden Rules of Ownership Control Our Lives* (New York, Doubleday, 2021).

[9] Of course, the flip side of this problem that tends to complicate further the debate over constitutional territory is the question of who receives entitlements and rights under the Constitution. So, a full analysis of this area would require a similar level of critical scrutiny and defence of the status of those who possess constitutional benefits – individuals, corporations, fetuses, animals, non-citizens, prisoners, natural entities, etc. For instance, if some of the protesters in the set of hypothetical facts were not students at all or even if they were temporary foreign students, this might raise some potential issues about whether, even if universities were located in constitutional territory, they could make constitutional claims about their protest activities. See pp 138–40.

levels, ownership and use of private property is heavily regulated and restricted – tax, criminal, zoning, conveyancing, building, torts, rights codes, etc. Indeed, private property is nowhere near as 'private' as many suppose. Perhaps most tellingly, many who object to this level of regulation as being somehow invalid or unwarranted are quick to demand government protection when their property rights are infringed by other private or semi-private individuals. This raises the pressing question of why, if private property is already subject to a range of public norms and values, it is not also brought within the constitutional reach and its celebrated and fundamental public values. Of course, there are several possible arguments and retorts to this query about private property, but they need to be argued for, not assumed, as a constitutional metric for such matters. As things stand, it might appear that private property has been elevated to a formal status that has greater significance than constitutional law and its supposed fundamental and prioritised social values.

As regards the hypothetical set of facts, it is not at all obvious or axiomatic as to why any universities should be immune from constitutional purview. Or, to put it differently and specifically, it is unpersuasive why the public or private status of universities should be the only and conclusive measure of whether a student's constitutional norms are in play. Hardly anyone thinks that universities are governmental. But nor do they think that they are entirely private. Like many sites and situations, they are a mix of both public and private. Although they retain a degree of administrative autonomy, they almost always receive some public funding and are subject to varying standards of government control. Insofar as universities, both public and private, 'are dedicated to the use of the public',[10] it seems highly unconvincing to determine the rights of students and others by reference to a formalistic distinction that requires one kind of public university to be treated as outside the constitutional realm and another kind to be inside it. Moreover, this distinction's reliance on the fact that government has a hands-off role to universities is undercut by those universities' willingness to call in government, by way of the courts and police, to regulate or remove protesters. This smacks of hypocrisy at best.

So, what is the purpose of all this? What does it say about how a political court would perform? As a matter of constitutional law (and, therefore, as a matter of politics), it has to be conceded that rights to property are neither self-defining, non-political nor uncontroversial. There are many reasons to delineate and protect a private zone that is to be treated as outside the reach of constitutional norms. As such, a political court will have to get beyond the weak and one-dimensional formalism of the public/private distinction. Instead, they will have to dig deeper and get their hands dirty by coming to grips with the political soil in which such a constitutional and legal idea is rooted and sustained. Judges will need to identify the different values in play, their normative force, and their relative prioritisation

---

[10] *Committee for the Commonwealth of Canada v Canada* [1991] 1 SCR 139, 165 (La Forest J).

in different contexts. Indeed, the same piece of property might be understood as private for some purposes and public for others. This seems to be exactly the case for universities – they stand on the shifting terrain in which constitutional norms might apply on some occasions and for some activities, but not for all occasions and for all activities.

An Expressive Function

Few would disagree that protecting 'free speech' or 'freedom of expression' is a vital aspect of a just society and a reliable symptom of its political and democratic health. In many situations, theorists and commentators maintain a united front about its importance as a fundamental bulwark against oppressive or autocratic government. Without free speech or freedom of expression, it is considered that society and its members cannot live full or fulfilled lives. However, beyond this general commitment, there is considerable and broad disagreement. Indeed, although many refuse to concede the tensions that lie at its heart, there are many points of conflict that are neither openly accepted nor easily resolved. As such, the challenges of mapping the contours of free speech and freedom of expression are so severe that it seems misguided and almost perverse to think that there is some neutral, principled, objective or impartial basis for confronting them, let alone meeting them, that will trump other proffered resolutions.

Those challenges cover a wide range of issues and problems. The history of jurisprudence and constitutional law evidences the different and changing questions and answers that have been thought to be essential to any convincing and credible account of free speech or freedom of expression. The most persistent are – the purpose for protecting expression (eg, truth-seeking; democratic governance; and self-actualisation); the nature of protected speech (eg, political; commercial; pornographic; and violent); the kind of acceptable limits, if any, on protected expression (eg, time and place); the relationship of free expression to other constitutional protections (eg, equality; criminal rights; and electoral participation); and the role of government in protecting expression (eg, hands-off; protection of vulnerable individuals; and control of disinformation). Importantly, it must be remembered that the extent and reach of the constitutional territory will have a significant impact on where and if a person's expression rights can be exercised. So, although corporations might be granted expressive freedom, individuals are unlikely to be able to claim their speech rights have been infringed by corporations. Consequently, debate around the nature and limits of free speech and freedom of expression is as heated and as divisive as it can get; it strikes at and shapes the heart of political debate and democratic contestation.

In dealing with the hypothetical set of facts, I will confine my attention to three matters – what counts as expression for constitutional purposes; are there any permissible limits that might be placed on a person's expressive freedom; and how, if at all, might other constitutional norms and entitlements be related to free speech or freedom of expression? It is not that the other matters are unimportant, but they are likely not centrally at issue as regards student protests. In particular, it seems that, whichever purposive basis is given priority in framing and responding to the issues at stake, it is not clear that this will affect significantly the situation. Indeed, whichever purposive basis is favoured, the competing rights and responsibilities of the university and the protesters on the Gaza question are unlikely to be treated with any significant practical difference.

The first issue to be dealt with by a political court is what is to count as expressive conduct. The judicial and social traditions of both Canada and the United States have made heavy weather of this. The different responses by the American and Canadian courts say much about the contested identity of expressive conduct that is found to be worthy of constitutional protection. While there is agreement around political protest as worthy of protection (even if what amounts to 'political' is far from settled), there is considerable divergence around electoral financing, labour picketing, defamation and obscenity. Moreover, both jurisdictions tend to recognise a hierarchy that gives more protection to some forms of expressive conduct (eg, political) than others (eg, commercial).[11] So, not all forms of speech or expression are created or treated equally. In summary, this means that there are choices to be made and justified all over this particular corner of the constitutional map. So, not only is there no simple fact of the matter, but there is no technical or methodical way to draw such distinctions or consider such particularities.

As regards the university protests, a specific issue will be to what extent encampments and/or sit-ins can be considered to be part of protected speech. For some, encampments will cross the line between protected speech and unprotected conduct; it is argued that it is not an exercise of speech to take possession of a 'public space' and inhabit it when they could use other campus venues to protest vigorously. For others, encampments will be an integral part of the message intended to be conveyed; the fact that students are inhibiting the use of certain spaces day and night is taken to reinforce the seriousness and strength of their political views. As for students occupying parts of the administration buildings, this goes further than the encampments. Again, some might view such conduct as an integral part of the students' message and the resulting inconvenience to the university administration as defensible; others might conclude that this has crossed a line and cannot be justified because it is occurring in a traditionally non-public area.[12] In all this disagreement and engagement, the fact that protests are

---

[11] For example, in Canada, compare and contrast *RWDSU v Dolphin Delivery* [1986] 2 SCR 573 and *R v Butler* [1992] 1 SCR 452 with *Irwin Toy Ltd. v Quebec (Attorney General)* [1989] 1 SCR 927 and *Ford v Quebec* [1988] 2 SCR 712.

[12] For example, the Canadian Supreme Court has indicated that some occupations can be a protected act of expression of a political message. See *Committee for the Commonwealth of Canada*, above n 10 at 165.

taking place at a university rather than another venue (eg, a shopping mall) may or may not be pivotal in determining the limits of protected political speech.[13]

This constitutional tension becomes even more fraught when it is accepted that there are a series of limits and restrictions that can be judicially imposed. There are two kinds that seem pertinent to student protests. First, both American and Canadian jurisprudence acknowledge that government can rely on reasonable conditions about when, where, and how expressive conduct can happen. So, it might be defensible for universities to regulate the noise levels of protesters, to confine them to specific areas of campus, and to take steps to ensure that public safety is not threatened; the inconvenience or discomfort of other students is insufficient. These, of course, are very context-specific and will require subtle and good faith exercises of judgment by the authorities. Secondly, it has been considered of great importance that any restrictions that are imposed on different groups of student protesters must be politically neutral. So, universities cannot make decisions about the if, when, where, and how of protests and treat groups differently based upon the substantive content of their viewpoints.[14] This, of course, becomes a volatile issue when different sides are denigrating the overall religious or cultural identity of the other. Again, there is no simple fact of the matter and there is no uncontroversial or detached way to make such contested judgments.

Take it to the Limits

Apart from legitimate limits that might be placed on protected speech or expression that are time-and-place based and are content-neutral, it is a point of fierce contention whether respect for other constitutional rights can be a basis for placing limits on what would otherwise be protected speech or expression. For instance, views differ widely on so-called hate speech. Some argue for an absolutist defence of free speech that elevates speech above other constitutional claims, whereas others insist that freedom of expression is one constitutional right among others and must be understood in relation to those others. American and Canadian jurisprudence also tend to diverge on this matter. American First Amendment jurisprudence leans towards treating hate speech as protected speech so long as the expression does not entail a credible threat of violence.[15] In contrast, the Canadian Charter of Rights has been interpreted to determine that the criminalisation of the wilful promotion of hatred can be a reasonable limit on the right to free expression.[16] This divergence strikes to the heart of much democratic debate around student protest on university campuses.

---

[13] See, eg, *Brewer v City of Albuquerque* (2021) 18 F.4th 1205, 1219–20.

[14] See, eg, *Corry v Leland Stanford Junior University* (1995) County of Santa Clara Superior Court, Case No 740309, 27 February. For a consideration of how hate speech might be a limit on the exercise of expressive freedoms, see pp 141–42.

[15] See *RAV v City of St Paul* (1992) 505 US 377.

[16] *R v Keegstra* [1990] 3 SCR 697.

That said, these differing jurisprudential viewpoints cut to the heart of an even deeper divide in contemporary political theory and action – the relation between individual freedom and social equality. Indeed, how and when one of these primary political norms is prioritised against others is a major marker for the generalised difference between political left and right views. On one side, the traditional view is that the offensive quality of any expression or message is insufficient to place it outside the sphere of constitutional protection; curbing speech is much more socially dangerous and injurious than allowing it.[17] On the other side, the more progressive view is that hateful or racist speech causes real harm to those who are its subordinated targets in modern society; the imbalance of power between groups can fundamentally change offensive expression into violent hurt.[18] However, these pat positions do not work easily in complex and nuanced settings, like university protests. It is less about always preferring one value over the other, but more about the weighting given to one against the other: traditionalists recognise that equality can be an occasional check on untrammelled freedom, and progressives maintain that the social drive for equality cannot ride roughshod over all the freedoms of individuals.

On university campuses, this tension between protecting expressive freedom and combatting discrimination has proved to be divisive and difficult. Not surprisingly, the conservative response has been to double-down and argue that free expression and debate are primary values of the higher educational experience; if content-neutrality and uninhibited debate are not encouraged at universities, they stand little chance of being valorised elsewhere.[19] However, the less traditional line is that free expression cannot be used as a cover for outright hate by way of racism, sexism and other forms of discrimination; there are values and commitments that can and should stand on at least an equal footing with the right to spew hatred towards others.[20] These positions are not easily reconcilable; they are the stuff of long-standing and deep ideological conflict. When applied to the protests over and around the Gaza confrontations and excesses, the challenge is very demanding and is exacerbated by its religious dimension. Each political side has no obvious or straightforward argument about how the protesting stand-off, like the Palestinian-Israeli conflict itself, can be resolved by reference to the ideals of freedom or equality – antisemitism, anti-Zionism and Islamophobia are undoubtedly offensive, but are they motivated by or productive of hate?

---

[17] Jonathan Turley, *The Indispensable Right: Free Speech in an Age of Rage* (New York, Simon and Schuster, 2024). Although he offers much absolutist posturing, Turley is obliged to concede that some speech – defamation, violent threats, criminal conspiracies, fraudulent inducements, etc – is not entitled to the constitutional protection of no-limit status.

[18] Mari Matsuda, 'Public Response to Racist Speech: Considering the Victim's Story' in Mari Matsuda et al (eds), *Words that Wound: Critical Race Theory, Assaultive Speech, and the First Amendment* (Boulder, Westview Press, 1993) 17.

[19] See *Healy*, above n 5 and *Corry*, above n 14.

[20] See, for example, Erwin Chemerinsky and Howard Gillman, *Free Speech on Campus* (New Haven, Yale University Press, 2017) and Helen Norton, *Advanced Introduction to US First Amendment Law* (Northampton, Edward Elgar Publishing, 2024).

Canadian jurisprudence has made a stab at trying to chart the disputed borderline between freedom and equality. It considers that there is a significant distinction between speech that is merely rude or discourteous and that which expresses offensive views toward an historically disadvantaged group. In *Whatcott*, the Canadian Supreme Court sought to identify and determine those circumstances in which expression or protest crosses the threshold that separates protected speech from criminal hate speech.[21] It offered a three-part test:

(1)   Whether a reasonable person, aware of the relevant context and circumstances, would view the expression as exposing the protected group to hatred?
(2)   Does the expression incite the level of abhorrence, delegitimisation, detestation and vilification that runs the real risk of causing discrimination or other harmful effects?
(3)   Is the expression likely to expose the targeted person or group to hatred by others?

Of course, such a proposed and balance-seeking schema will not be acceptable to the arch-conservative defender of free speech. Nor might it find favour with those uncompromising progressives who would want to see a more robust and definitive defence of equality and non-discrimination than one that defers to the mythical behaviour and faux-neutral views of the reasonable person. Efforts to deploy that strategy have not worked well in other settings, so there is no reason to think that it will work in the constitutional realm.[22]

That being said, it is clear that there is no elusive Archimedean point of technical accuracy that can be identified or discovered that will miraculously affect a bargain between the freedom-preserving conservatives and the equality-advancing progressives. While the balancing of interests seems to be an attractive and inevitable compromise to both the legal and political mind, it has no inherent or objective merit. Indeed, it is hardly likely to satisfy those who do not gravitate to the middle-of-the-road: those with an unbending commitment to a self-identified principle will not be persuaded by such an arrangement. Furthermore, there is no unified or common position within either the left or the right poles of politics; even those people who might share a general political orientation might also disagree strongly about the value or validity of allowing students protests and encampments on university campuses. In short, free speech and expression is truly a contestable and intellectual minefield: it is politics at every turn and in every direction. It is naïve to think that traditional constitutional analysis can resolve these matters in a reasoned and apolitical manner.

---

[21] *Saskatchewan Human Rights Commission v Whatcott* (2013) 2013 SCC 11, [56]–[68].
[22] See, for example, judicial efforts at regulating pornography in *R v Sharpe* (2001) 2001 SCC 2 and *Miller v California* (1973) 413 US 15.

A Political Reckoning

So, where does all this leave us; how would a political court deal with the constitutionality of student protests; and what arguments and reasons might fare better than others? These are significant and difficult inquiries. From a pragmatic standpoint, there is no definitive or conclusive answer that can be given. Indeed, the array of variable positions both politically and doctrinally attests to the controversial nature and perhaps irresolvability of the challenge; there are no easy or pat answers about whether protesters have constitutional rights and what, if any, the nature and extent of those rights are. This is more of a problem for traditionalists who insist upon a distinction between law and politics; too much choice does little to reassure citizens or sceptics about the objective thereness of constitutional law. However, the fact that both political and legal decision-making is indeterminate and unpredictable is less challenging for the law-is-politics pragmatist who does not profess to trade in constitutional truths and political objectivities. In short, the politics of constitutional law can be partially hidden, but it cannot be done away with entirely.

Moreover, this state of affairs is even more debilitating when another fact is thrown in – that, even under extant modes of legitimate judicial decision-making, constitutional law can do doctrinal U-turns, abandon established paths of reasoning and set off in new or, at least, different directions as and when recalcitrant and heated issues present themselves for resolution. So-called hard cases, like *Brown* and *Dobbs* in the United States and *Carter* and *Saskatchewan Federation of Labour* in Canada,[23] are strong evidence of this. These are occasions on which the predictability of constitutional law is seriously challenged. Insofar as such decisions are treated as landmarks on the constitutional terrain, they render constitutional law even more unstable and volatile because they can and often will be thrown aside by the next landmark case.[24] There is no better example of this phenomenon than the *Dobbs* decision itself which overturned *Roe* and asserted itself as the new normal both in its result and its adjudicative methodology.[25] Of course, the fate of *Dobbs* is itself far from settled or predictable; time will only tell whether it will last 50 years or more.

The main difference between a traditional account of constitutional law and its political alternative is not that it will lead to different results. Those who presently decide one way will not necessarily change their political colours and take

---

[23] *Brown v Board of Education* (1952) 344 US 1; *Dobbs v Jackson Women's Health Organization* (2022) 597 US 215; *Carter v Canada (AG)* (2015) 2015 SCC 5 and *Saskatchewan Federation of Labour v Saskatchewan* (2015) 2015 SCC 4.

[24] There is obviously a vast literature on the importance and effect of 'great cases'. A leading example is Ronald Dworkin's mainstream attempt to defend law's progress as being based on continuity as much as ingenuity. See Ronald Dworkin, 'Hard Cases' (1975) 88 *Harvard Law Review* 1057. For my different take on this, see Allan Hutchinson, *Evolution and the Common Law* (Cambridge, Cambridge University Press, 2005) ch 5.

[25] See ch 5.

a different position. They might, but that does not in any way follow from the law-is-politics stance. The main difference will be that, as compared with the alternative political approach, the reasoning offered and built upon by the traditional account will be an internal and boot-strapping professional exercise that does as much to avoid the political underpinnings of the reasons used and the positions taken as to identify and defend them. As such, reliance upon earlier decisions and precedents offers apparent foundations for such judicial work. But, on closer inspection, these foundations are shaky, shallow and more in the mind of the judicial beholder: they are pseudo-footings that depend on a take-our-word-for-it mentality rather than on a genuine effort to defend and justify basic understandings Too often, legal arguments amount to little more than convenient shorthand for another judge's or a court's earlier take on a controversial issue or principle; they are more insubstantial than fundamental, more ramshackle than robust, and more fleeting than fixed.

With law, the main work is done within a technical bubble (or, at least, this is the impression given and projected by its traditional proponents). Established rules and principles are applied to the issue at hand and decisions are made and rationalised on the basis of them; reference to the political values that drive and sustain those rules and principles are elided. Indeed, the heavy ideological lifting occurs decidedly off-stage and implicitly on the basis of political assumptions made and normative stances taken. These postulations that undergird and ground appeal to the received legal wisdom of constitutional doctrine are not defended directly, but are hidden within and supposed by existing constitutional doctrine and cases. Much is assumed and, therefore, much is missed. As such, traditional accounts of constitutional law tend to omit or take for granted the very ideas and arguments that give political bite and normative substance to the rules and principles that are relied upon. This is especially so with modes of interpretation, like originalism,[26] that claim to sidestep and obviate such matters.

The political alternative model operates very differently. Rather than submerge or push to the margins those underlying political values and ideological assumptions that animate and shape constitutional doctrine, it addresses them directly and openly: there is no reliance on rules and principles embedded in constitutional for their own sake. Staying honest to its central claim that constitutional law is politics all the way down, it takes seriously the obligation to go beyond rules and principles and to unearth their political indicators and indices. Indeed, rather than deal with these important ideological footings 'under the table', as it were, there is a willingness to put them out 'on the table' and grapple with them first-hand. With a pragmatic sensibility and sense of ideological purpose, the political jurist and judge will not shy away from this task. In a manner of speaking, they will recognise and embrace the idea that, if you are making political decisions, it will not be helpful to maintain or pretend that you are not. It is by confronting politics that the

---

[26] See ch 4.

constitutional adherent will have any chance of regenerating the kind of broader legitimacy that the traditional approach to constitutional law has undermined.

In light of this, it would be naïve and foolish to recommend, therefore, that a pragmatic approach can cut a clear and decisive path through the dense forest of doctrinal trees and arrive at an objectively just and neutrally fair destination. Whatever path is chosen, judges will have to draw limiting lines in different places and erect guiding signposts to different directions; this is the case under both existing models of principled adjudication and a critical version of constitutional law as politics. Although the options are numerous and varied, some of the more obvious and possible paths to be taken in both law and politics in determining if protesters' constitutional rights have been infringed are:

Getting to No –

(1) Universities are not public spaces and, therefore, constitutional rights are not in play.
(2) Universities are public spaces, but there are strict limits on the kind of activities that can be pursued to exercise freedom of expression.
(3) Universities are public spaces, but there are restrictions that flow from other constitutional norms being considered.

Getting to Yes –

(4) Universities are public spaces and, therefore, an unconditional constitutional right to expression is protected, even where invasive activities are involved.
(5) Universities are public spaces, and even though limits can be placed on the constitutional right to expression, those are not present in regard to political speech.
(6) Universities are public spaces, but although the constitutional right to freedom of expression has to be balanced against other constitutional norms, those are not decisive in regard to political speech.

Although it by no means follows in any direct or necessary way, a pragmatic approach does lean (but no more than that) towards a proposed decision and supporting set of arguments that favours 'getting to maybe': paths (3) and (6) are more conducive to such an approach. Indeed, in today's diverse and antagonistic society, there is much to be said for plumping for a resolution that might draw in a range of persons with conflicting political commitments. Compromise has much to offer over dogmatism and fundamentalism on both sides of the ideological spectrum. However, this is not to suggest that compromise is the same thing as a 'splitting the difference' strategy or locating the middle of the road for its own sake. Instead, the pragmatist will seek to offer a principled, political and open approach as to why a specific compromise is preferable both generally and in the particular context of student protests. This is not at all an easy way out, but demands of itself the same extent of rigour and reasoning as any other approach. The beauty of pragmatism is that it is willing to be flexible, inventive and experimentalist in order to get the political job done.

At its theoretical and political heart, therefore, a pragmatic perspective on constitutional law and politics appreciates that the strength of any reasoned approach to freedom of expression (and other contentious matters) can be found not only in its core idea and approach, but also in the limits that it places upon them. Of course, this pragmatic mind-set and plan of action will be done with an awareness of and engagement with politics, not as an effort to somehow end-run or evade ideological considerations: pragmatists are open to the fact that all and any intervention in constitutional law and politics will be revisable and self-critical. As such, for the pragmatist, law and adjudication, whether done by way of compromise or conviction, is done better when it is understood as an unconcealed exercise in political persuasion, not a faux-project of technical retrieval or calculated demonstration.

Conclusion

The upshot of all this is that there is no ground that jurists or judges can stand on that will allow them to be untouched (and occasionally be submerged) by the powerful whirls and eddies of constitutional politics. And principled reasoning with a claim to be impartial and neutral is certainly not such a ground. It will be for each jurist and judge to stake out the political territory that they are prepared to defend. Almost all positions that can be taken are capable of being supported by cases and doctrinal materials; there is a plethora of principles that can inform and guide judges in reaching very different conclusions on similar matters. Constitutional law highlights the issues, but it does not offer an obvious or persuasive basis for how to resolve them. Even if judges wish to adopt the various stances taken within extant constitutional doctrine, they must defend that choice and outcome with reference to both political principles and pragmatic arguments that go beyond the familiar boot-strapping manoeuvres of constitutional law and decision-making. Simply 'following the rules' is not an option. Or, to put it differently, judges are constantly making and re-making those rules as they claim to be following them.[27]

---

[27] See Allan Hutchinson, *It's All in the Game: Toward a Non Foundationalist Account of Adjudication* (Durham, Duke University Press, 2000).

10

Rethinking Legitimacy:
A Democratic View

Traditional theorists are wrong about many things, but they are right about one thing – the law-is-politics critique offers a subversive and destabilising challenge to constitutional law, democratic politics and judicial decision-making generally. Indeed, this radicality is one of the main reasons why many astute traditional judges and savvy jurists resist its jurisprudential and institutional force so keenly and so determinedly. If the law-is-politics critique is taken in complete seriousness, it can no longer be a case of business-as-usual in regard to constitutional law and democratic governance generally. Not only does the law-is-politics assault sweep away the jurisprudential ground from under the feet of most judges and jurists in the battle-royal over legal interpretation and decision-making,[1] but it also threatens the whole institutional structure and decision-making process within which law and adjudication is presently understood, developed and justified. This critical upshot presents both a deep challenge to the existing jurisprudential status quo as well as offering a genuine opportunity for introducing changes within and around the existing structures and arrangement of democratic governance.

Confronted with this choice between a radical overhaul of the whole scheme of democratic governance and some more piecemeal reforms to it, traditionalists will obviously be in favour of a series of more modest reforms and less structural alterations. This is understandable. Although I maintain that it is important to explore what a more substantial reworking of the overall system might look like, my more practical side believes that a more modest and less disruptive slate of changes might have much greater chance of acceptance and implementation. Of course, such a less radical and more piecemeal approach will run the risk of making the best of a bad job. The traditional mind-set might still prevail, and any real changes would be more cosmetic than deep-rooted; the appearance would belie the reality. Nevertheless, on the basis that it is imprudent and counter-productive to allow the best to always be the enemy of the good, I will make a serious and sincere effort to recommend a range of proposals that will remain true to the law-is-politics critique. For good and bad, it will also be constrained by the general outlines of the present scheme of democratic governance, even if the ambitions of democracy are as likely to be observed as much in their breach as in their fulfilment.

---

[1] See ch 7.

In this chapter, therefore, I will make some proposals about how constitutional law and decision-making might proceed if the law-is-politics insight is pursued, followed and institutionalised. In the first part, I will make a reasoned rejection of the so-called counter-majoritarian dilemma as the central pivot of the jurisprudential and constitutional project. Secondly, I will reframe the democratic challenge by demonstrating that modern constitutional law and its judicial development are confronted with a participation predicament, not a majoritarian quandary. In the third section, I explore ways that it might be possible to de-centre Supreme Courts by making them a less supreme and less authoritatively final judicial body. Fourthly, I look at the balances and checks that might be utilised to bring about this de-centring and de-finalising of Supreme Courts. In the final section, I will look at how this transformed understanding of constitutional law might work to advance more sincerely the self-confessed goals of democracy in a contemporary society. Throughout the chapter, my focus will be on how to rejig constitutional law and judicial practice to function in line with the law-is-politics approach so that they can be better in the service of democratic justice.

Democracy and Majorities

While 'democracy' is a vital idea and practice for understanding the organisation and performance of the present arrangements for constitutional governance, it is also one of the most contested and divisive concepts in political theory and jurisprudence. In particular, what is considered to be the best or even the most acceptable version of democracy is centrally important for any appreciation of what legitimacy means; differing models of democracy will suggest different standards for determining the legitimacy of various arrangements and actions by governmental actors. Indeed, this goes to the heart of the legitimacy debate in constitutional law – those who are entrusted with power are expected and required to perform their tasks and responsibilities in certain pre-established ways if their contribution to governance is to be treated as being justifiable and valid.

There are numerous kinds of democracy, and 'constitutional democracy' is only one of them – direct democracy; representative democracy; deliberative democracy; democratic socialism; and many more. Questions about how governments are supposed to function and be held accountable will very much depend on the kind of democracy that is being considered. For instance, in regard to a constitutional democracy (as in the United States and Canada), it is considered imperative that there will be both an institution and a method to determine what the constitution requires or allows and how those decisions can be enforced against both citizens and other governmental actors. If that responsibility falls to an unelected and unrepresentative agency (eg, courts), it will be expected that its personnel should act in a professional and expert-like way that is very different from that of those who can claim an elected and more representative basis for their exercise of power over others. This is doubly the case when courts are granted (or have assumed for themselves) the authority to contradict and override the actions of the other legislative and executive branches of government. As I have been at pains to point out, this is a central and often perplexing challenge of constitutional law.

Apart from examining and determining whether what is supposed to happen has a sufficient connection to what is actually happening, it is necessary to dig a little deeper and look to the version of democracy that is relied upon tradition-ally in setting up the standards and performance of legitimate decision-making in constitutional matters. Because there is a wide range of possible meanings and imperatives that can be attributed to democracy, it is essential to be clear about what particular idea and practice of democracy is traditionally being relied upon before it is feasible and worthwhile to examine the compliance of courts as government actors with their democratic duties and responsibilities. One impor-tant aspect of that general requirement is to inquire into whether the so-called counter-majoritarian dilemma that is invoked by traditional jurists is an adequate or persuasive account of the democratic problem that courts present in modern schemes of democratic governance and constitutional decision-making: judicial review runs so fundamentally against the basic precepts of democratic governance that it might actually 'weaken the democratic process'.[2] If there is not an adequate or persuasive account available, then it will be necessary to develop a more attrac-tive and authentic account of democracy and explore its intimations for the judicial development of constitutional law.

For most traditionalists, the standard by which courts are to be judged in fulfill-ing their constitutional role and responsibilities is their compatibility with and observance of a mode of professional conduct that can be explained and warranted through the idea of democracy as an exercise in majority rule.[3] I disagree. While the counter-majoritarian dilemma is one dimension of the challenge for explain-ing and justifying the role of courts in the performance of their constitutional role, it is not the most pressing or one that represents the better way of thinking about democratic governance in the twenty-first century. Accordingly, I will seek not only to show the inadequacy of thinking about democracy as primarily or even exclusively about being synonymous with majoritarian rule, but also to endorse a theory and practice of democratic governance that does a better job of understand-ing democratic practices as well as charting the institutional implications of such an understanding for the constitutional work of courts and judges in the future.

Democracy comes in different shapes and sizes. Its various kinds are a varia-tion of the idea that people should govern themselves. Indeed, in their different ways, each variant makes a trade-off about how the ambition of government by the people, for the people and of the people might be achieved. In its strong incarnation, therefore, democracy stakes out its turf by demonstrating faith in the

---

[2] Alexander Bickel, *The Least Dangerous Branch: The Supreme Court at the Bar of Politics* (Indianapolis, Bobbs-Merril, 1962) 21–23.
[3] For more on this, see chs 2 and 3.

responsibility and capacity of political participants, widely assembled and deeply acknowledged, to do 'the right thing'. In its weakest form, it puts some participatory icing on the governmental cake and allows popular involvement in occasional and limited circumstances. Understood in terms of constitutional law, the balance is between democracy and judicial review. Although a strong commitment to democracy would recommend that a subservient, if important role should be extended to judicial review, a weaker commitment to democracy would treat democracy as a secondary source of governmental authority to a judicially construed constitutional compact. In other words, there is a tension between the reliance on popular views and the authority of professional experts. The origins and continuing history of both the American and Canadian system of constitutional governance lean very much towards the priority of professional insights over popular opinions.

Accordingly, while there is much talk about the importance of democracy and popular sovereignty, the constitutional scales are very much weighted in favour of professional expertise. It is the opinions of judges that will carry the day in deciding upon the parameters of popular choice and participation. Indeed, not only are some contentious issues taken out of the hands of the populace (eg, health care and gun control) but the courts have begun to determine what counts as valid and acceptable democratic processes for engaging and incorporating popular participation (eg, free expression and campaign financing). Of course, these very different approaches to democracy are as contested and heated as the resolution of specific issues within democracy. Nevertheless, a full appreciation of what it means for a society and political culture to think of itself as democratic must be taken into account when considering the role and responsibilities of governmental institutions and their practices. It is against this larger backdrop that the juristic debate over the proper role of Supreme Courts takes place – how should and must judges act in order not to fall foul of the counter-majoritarian dilemma that confronts them; and does that formulation of the challenge make theoretical or practical sense?

A look at the recent events surrounding the election of the leaders in both the United States and Canada is revealing. For instance, in 2016, Donald Trump was elected President even though he received less (46%) of the popular vote than his opponent, Hilary Clinton (48%); the United States has an electoral college system for a final decision. Moreover, only 60% of eligible voters cast a ballot. This meant that Trump became President with less than 30% of the electorate voting for him. In 2020, Joe Biden became President with about 51% of the popular vote. On this occasion, 66% of eligible voters cast a ballot; this was the highest turnout since 1900. This meant that Biden became President with about 34% of the electorate voting for him.[4] Also, Canada was no better in this regard. In fact, its situation was slightly more troublesome. In 2021, Justin Trudeau's Liberal Party received 33% of the

---

[4] Hannah Hartig et al, 'Voter turnout, 2018–2022' (*Pew Research Center*, 12 July 2023) www.pewresearch.org/politics/2023/07/12/voter-turnout-2018-2022/.

popular vote and that was less than the 34% of the Conservative Party; Canada's parliamentary-based system allows for minority governments as long as they can obtain the continuing support of smaller parties (which the Liberals did). Out of a turnout of 62% of eligible voters, Trudeau became Prime Minister, therefore, with what amounted to 21% of the electorate voting for him.

Although this is only a narrow and crude snapshot of contemporary democratic politics, there are important observations that can be made about its practice and foundations as it affects an understanding of the counter-majoritarian dilemma in constitutional law and scholarship. First, it is apparent that perhaps the most powerful person or office in both Canadian and American politics is not elected or supported by a majority of their citizens. Indeed, a majority of citizens either voted against them or simply could not bring themselves to support them and so failed to vote. As such, it seems unrealistic and optimistic at best to suggest that majoritarianism lies at the heart of the American and Canadian systems of governance. Whatever the overall historical situation, contemporary democratic politics cannot be described or justified as being based upon democratic legitimacy by way of majority support. There must be some other significant dynamic at work. If the political leader lacks majoritarian support, then it is not surprising that a society's legal leaders will also do so.

Secondly, it is clear that there is a serious problem with democratic politics when one in three people do not participate regularly in the electoral process. If there is any winner in presidential elections, it is as likely to be the apathetic and disaffected citizenry as anybody else. This problem is compounded by the fact that the electoral opportunities for people to participate and vote are quite limited. Indeed, in Canada, there can be and has been a change of Prime Minister without any electoral participation; political parties can have internal votes to change leaders and thereby, on occasion, the Prime Minister. Also, as regard the election of the very powerful positions of President and Prime Minister, the only occasion to have an effective say occurs once every four years or so. Moreover, reducing and confining participation to a solitary vote at that time is hardly a reassuring indication of a vigorous democracy at work; citizens spend most of the time on the outside looking in.[5] As such, it is mistaken and perhaps misleading to conclude that the central dilemma for judges and juries is based upon an account of democracy that gives pride of place to its majoritarian tendencies. Instead, I maintain that the central problem is a startling lack of participatory involvement in government by rank-and-file citizens. This is a pervasive and disabling problem that afflicts all areas and dimensions of democratic governance.

When this participatory deficit is combined with the pseudo-professionalism of judges (ie, constitutional law is as much politics as law), the legitimate basis of democratic governance becomes even more fragile. The authoritative control of courts in constitutional matters (ie, Supreme Courts get the last word) and the

---

[5] Benjamin Barber, 'Voting is Not Enough' (1984) 253[6] *The Atlantic Monthly* 45.

general prioritisation of constitutional truths over democratic politics further helps to undermine the relevance and reliance on the 'counter-majoritarian dilemma' as at the heart of the legitimacy challenge. Indeed, it comes close to being wrong-headed and perhaps perverse. Taken together, this seems very much a case of where, if you ask the wrong question, you will vastly increase the chances of getting the wrong answer. By framing the jurisprudential challenge to be about dealing with the non-majoritarian character of courts, it sends jurists and judges off in the wrong direction. As such, it is well past time for a change of dilemma and direction.

A Different Dilemma

Before deciding how best to reframe the challenge for judges and jurists in offering a legitimate account of constitutional law and decision-making, there is an important preliminary matter that needs to be addressed – how much or how little reform is possible or likely in the effort to act upon a different democratic and legitimating imperative? By this, I intend to ask how blue the skies are in theorising about institutional and fundamental changes. In other words, is it worthwhile to suggest a root-and-branch range of reforms and reorganisations, or is a more modest set of initiatives the better way to go? I have already offered a more radical number of structural and transformative alterations that will be better able to respond to the democratic shortcomings of present governmental arrangements as it affects both the electoral process and courts.[6] However, in this project, I will propose a much more moderate and restrained collection of reform projects that might be undertaken in order to meet any democratic challenge about the legitimacy of courts in handling constitutional issues.

Having chosen that more modest and realistic course, I need to offer a number of cautions and riders in regard to my overall plan of action and, in particular, what its built-in limitations are. The most important thing to make clear is that this response to the constitutional dilemma is distinctly second-best. For it to have any bite or justification, it has to be understood that it is a response that accepts that only small and incremental changes are practically feasible within the institutional status quo. While more radical alterations would be preferable, they are simply not possible at the present time. Indeed, my proposals will be treated as half-hearted and weak, if not downright unconvincing, unless they are appreciated within the transformative confines of existing governmental and administrative arrangements – the continued existence of Supreme Courts; their staffing by judicial professionals; an executive-driven appointment process for such personnel; and present unlikelihood of constitutional amendments. That said, there is no

---

[6] See Allan Hutchinson, *Democracy and Constitutions: Putting Citizens First* (Toronto, University of Toronto Press, 2021).

need to accept that there is a complete inertia and sclerosis in place that prevents any changes at all; this would be an entirely defeatist and pessimistic stance. Consequently, I will try to work the fraying edges of the institutional envelope of democratic politics in order to ameliorate things, but I will accept the general contours and limits of that envelope. In short, I will be reformist, not programmatic; I will be strategic, not revolutionary; and I will be pragmatic, not idealistic (as befits a critical pragmatist).[7]

The main thrust of my reframing of the constitutional dilemma is that judges and jurists are confronted with a participation predicament, not a majoritarian quandary. In this, courts are not so different to other governmental bodies and agencies; they are less an outlier, but more a part of the pervasive failings of governmental institutions generally. The glaring deficiencies of democratic politics' dynamics and designs are on display throughout the overall scheme of governance. Democracy is an idea and a practice that is defended everywhere, but is also flouted everywhere. The participation of citizens in their own self-government – the beating heart of democracy – is woefully limited and sporadic. The majoritarian deficit is simply one symptom of that broader participatory malaise. Indeed, as de Tocqueville warned over 175 years ago, democracy has managed to fulfil its tendency, if left unguarded and taken for granted, to degenerate into a 'soft despotism'.[8] Although there is a formal appearance of democratic vigour, the lived reality belies and often contradicts such a prognosis. So, if extensive and continuing participation is a measure of a democracy's vitality and strength, both the United States and Canada are in a frail and sickly condition.

Within this contemporary scenario, it is apparent that it is not only courts that lack sufficient democratic legitimacy as a result of a marked shortage in civil participation; it is a scarcity that characterises most government offices and officials, including those of the President and Prime Minister. The exercise of enormous power and authority is entrusted to a handful of politicians who can claim only a very thin and insubstantial degree of democratic justification for their office and actions. The result of this is that, while the existence of decidedly non-democratic public institutions, like courts, within a supposedly democratically governed society are problematic, there is no compelling reason to suggest that their status and legitimacy are entirely illegitimate when compared to or contrasted with other branches of government. Most controlling institutions and actors who wield substantial power – administrative agencies; police chiefs and local authorities – are also short on democratic legitimacy if the issue is whether they can be justified in terms of majoritarian rule alone. As such, a small and sporadic amount of

---

[7] See ch 7.

[8] Alexis de Tocqueville, *Democracy in America*, vol 2, book 4 (Stephen Grant (ed), Indianapolis, Hackett Publishing, 2000) ch 6. He was also prescient in fearing that democratic rule might not be up to the task of resisting the powerful inegalitarian tendencies that are present in the development of capitalism; a new aristocracy of manufacturers and entrepreneurs might replace the old landed aristocracy. In the new and second Trump presidency, this will become a very real possibility, if not a reality already.

participation is the norm with constitutional and democratic governance. Indeed, it seems that this state of affairs is not so much an unfortunate occurrence, but a preferred and prized quality by those in positions of power and authority.

However, when it comes to courts and judges fulfilling their constitutional responsibilities, the stark (and repeated) warning of John Hart Ely cannot be ignored – 'we may grant until we're blue in the face that legislatures aren't wholly democratic, but that isn't going to make courts more democratic than legislatures.'[9] This is a pressing warning that all jurists, including myself, need to take seriously; it is an objection that should be met by anyone who wants to confer even a minimal degree of democratic legitimacy on an account of a judicially controlled constitutional law that disciplines the work of legislators and executives. Of course, this is why traditionalists stick so closely and doggedly to the claim that judicial work can and should be understood and practised in strictly professional, not political, terms. But, as tempting as this ambition and aspiration is, it simply cannot be met – constitutional law and decision-making are political and no amount of wishful thinking will make it otherwise. So, any cogent riposte to the jurisprudential gauntlet that Ely threw down has to be found elsewhere. In particular, it has to build on the operating premise that constitutional law is an unavoidable exercise in politics through and through. Moreover, legislative supremacy is not the be-all-and-end-all or gold standard in contemporary democratic governance; there are other possibilities that need to be explored.

The fact that the Supreme Court must be treated as a political institution, like many others, offers a democratic opportunity. As I have argued, the idea and practice of a political court is, at best, capable of being accommodated within democracy, but it does not in itself substantially improve or enhance the democratic process generally. What it will do is make the role of one particular and powerful institution – courts – less undemocratic. When judged against some ideal standard of democratic participation and legitimacy, my proposal will fall well short. However, when a more realistic and comparative evaluation is made, it will improve at least marginally the democratic standing and performance of the courts as constitutional practitioners. It will not confound Ely's scepticism: legislatures would still have a slight edge in terms of democratic legitimacy. But the gap between the two will have been reduced and some democratic progress will have been made. Although this recognition of courts as political actors may seem a small gain, it will be preferable to the status quo. Any increase in popular participation in decision-making will be better than none. Most importantly, it will serve to make the courts both more transparent and also more open to greater popular participation. These are not mean achievements in societies, like the United States and Canada, in which the current trend is away from, not towards, greater democratic accountability.

---

[9] John Ely, *Democracy and Distrust: A Theory of Judicial Review* (Cambridge, Harvard University Press, 1980) 67.

The acceptance of a political court can open the way to Supreme Courts being at least less undemocratic on several fronts. The two main possibilities work along two axes and tend to reinforce each – greater popular participation and more extensive decentralisation. The first set of innovations can be achieved by the courts themselves as they come to terms with becoming an open and unapologetic forum of political deliberation and decision-making; these might engender a more vibrant and responsive mode of democratic engagement. The second group of initiatives might work to disperse and distribute constitutional law-making and political power across a broader and more diverse range of locations and agencies. While direct participation might be the most preferable mode of democratic governance, more indirect and secondary processes of participation are not to be dismissed out of hand. I will deal first with the possibilities for greater participation and then turn to ways in which constitutional authority can be brought about.

Efforts to open up courts and give greater access to litigants are not uncommon, even if their success is mixed.[10] It is still the case that lawyers, corporations and wealthy entities have too strong a presence in litigation and that ordinary citizens are pushed to the sidelines. This is as true in constitutional litigation as in any other area of law. However, simply allowing more citizens to be parties to constitutional litigation will not be an adequate solution in itself. Citizens do not necessarily possess the expertise that is required to engage in sustained debate and make informed decisions about constitutional matters. But this does not mean that so-called experts should dominate and marginalise those with less knowledge and experience. When it comes to government and governance matters, experts should be put in service to the citizenry, not vice versa. A bureaucracy should not usurp the citizenry's prerogative to be the final decision-makers. This is no more apparent than in the case of courts and judges: it is important that the legal tail does not wag the democratic dog.

Consequently, there are a number of changes that could be made that would help to democratise constitutional litigation. Individually, these initiatives are not particularly game-changing, but, taken together, they can make a significant contribution to that needed effort. These proposals are not only all within the competence and jurisdiction that courts already possess, but they are also not so far removed from existing reforms and procedural innovations:

- The hearings (and even the deliberations) of the Supreme Courts should be entirely open and available to the public; this might involve a designated viewing channel on public television.

- A much broader range and occurrence of non-party intervenors should be permitted; broad participation should be encouraged.

- Because the Supreme Courts will be more overtly political, there is no need for a professionalised and excluding constitutional discourse.

[10] See, eg, Jennifer Leitch, 'Having a Say: "Access to Justice" as Democratic Participation' (2015) 4 *UCL Journal of Law and Jurisprudence* 76.

- Presentations to the Courts can become less legalistic in content and thrust; briefs and arguments can be a suitable mix of the political and the legal.
- Courtroom settings should be made less intimidating and more informal; traditional requirements for dress and presentation should be abandoned.
- Involvement need not be restricted to lawyers; other advocates can be accredited and their participation should be facilitated.
- Funding must be made available to parties who cannot afford counsel or other professional advocates; wealth and resources should not be determinative of the quantity and quality of advocacy.

I am not suggesting that these changes will democratise the courts and constitutional law in a strong sense. But, taken together, they will help to move them more positively along a participatory spectrum that runs from very little through to extensive. Most importantly, I am proposing that Supreme Courts are not thought of in the way that they are presently understood today as legal agencies. Instead, they could be viewed as political second-look bodies. Their task will be to make detached and independent, if political, evaluations of how constitutional law can best serve a modern and diverse society. As such, it will be an engaged and principled task, not a reflective and recherché process for applying a pseudo-legal logic to disputes and issues; the focus will be on making substantively just decisions, not on following a supposedly objective and often inaccessible mode of constitutional interpretation. As such, courts would no longer be institutions that pretend that they are taking exclusively legal stances as opposed to political ones. When viewed and carried out in this way, their non-democratic character will be less dominating and more user-friendly.

Off Centre

It is a basic precept of democratic governance that concentrations of power are to be assiduously avoided. There is a centrifugal dynamic to democracy that seeks to disperse power as well as push it down to the citizenry. As such, concentrated power in one institution or person is considered anathema to a genuine democracy; forms of autocracy and dictatorship cannot meet even the most basic demands of a citizen-centred mode of government. Within such a model, Supreme Courts may be the highest and final level of courts, but they are not and should not be the highest and final institutions of democratic governance. So, once it is accepted that constitutional law and decision-making are thoroughly political in character and substance, it becomes imperative to de-finalise, as it were, and reduce the role and centrality of courts in the democratic scheme of things. The dispersion and diffusion of judicial authority will be essential if there is to be a shift to a more democratic and participatory mode of government that runs more deeply and broadly than it more presently does.

Achieving this objective is far from easy. As well as undermining the ideological underpinnings of the courts as the only legitimate venue for constitutional
politics, it will be necessary to recommend practical initiatives to multiply the sites
for interpreting the Constitution and acting in line with it. Although there are
serious obstacles to doing this, there is nothing within the American or Canadian
Constitution that prohibits such a pluralistic undertaking. Indeed, it is often forgotten or overlooked that the constitutional mandate of Supreme Courts is, at best, on
weak and unstable ground. Although Supreme Courts like to claim that they are
the final arbiters of constitutional law, there is no established authority or textual
anchor for that claim other than the courts' own self-serving say-so. While there
is general agreement that the Constitution is supreme and overrides other laws,
neither Canada nor the United States has a fixed or formal source that confirms
the power of Supreme Courts to resolve constitutional matters and render laws or
actions unconstitutional and inapplicable.

In the United States, its Supreme Court seized power to fulfil that authoritative
role in the (in)famous case of *Marbury* in 1903: 'it is emphatically the province and
duty of the judicial department to say what the law is.'[11] This power grab has come
to be accepted by judges and government since then as almost natural, inevitable
and unavoidable. In Canada, since 1949, the Supreme Court of Canada adopted
the authoritative role taken by the British Privy Council in earlier times. In doing
so, the Supreme Court simply asserted that 'the need for a final, independent judicial arbiter of disputes over federal-provincial jurisdiction is implicit in a federal
system'.[12] In both the American and Canadian settings, these curial moves can
be understood as themselves involving primarily political as much as exclusively
constitutional initiatives.

That said, there is no authoritative or clear source (other than the courts'
own pronouncements) to grant the final word to Supreme Courts in constitutional matters. It is a matter of tradition, convention and judicial opinion that has
become part of the constitutional furniture. For a judicial and juristic community
that places such strong importance on the need to be loyal and subservient to the
Constitution itself, this is a revealing and confusing stance. Indeed, it is one thing
for Supreme Courts to depend upon such a vague and ungrounded assumption
(ie, that someone must have the final word), but it is another thing entirely to
maintain such a position when it is self-serving – someone must have the final say,

---

[11] *Marbury v Madison* (1803) 5 US (1 Cranch) 137, 177 (Marshall CJ). See my 'The Politics of Law:
Cats, Pigeons and Old Chestnuts' in Allan Hutchinson, *Is Killing People Right? More Great Cases That
Shaped the Legal World* (New York, Cambridge University Press, 2016) 42–59.
[12] *Reference re Supreme Court Act, ss. 5 and 6* (2014) 2014 SCC 21, [83]. See Peter Hogg, *Constitutional
Law of Canada*, student edn (Toronto, Thomson Reuters, 2023) 159–62. While s 52 of the Constitution
Act 1982 makes the Constitution the supreme law in Canada, there is no explicit recognition of the
Supreme Court of Canada's power to monopolise interpretive authority. There is also s 52 of the
Supreme Court Act 1985 that states that 'the Court shall have and exercise exclusive ultimate appellate
civil and criminal jurisdiction within and for Canada, and the judgment of the Court is, in all cases,
final and conclusive.'

so let it be us. Mindful of the enormous power that this self-interested assumption gives to unrepresentative and unelected Supreme Courts, it is an exercise of authority that sits very uneasily with a sincere commitment to democratic governance. In many ways, this state of affairs underlines the central problem of courts in constitutional democracies.

Against this backdrop, it does not seem either radical or unattainable to recommend that, if so minded, what the courts can do, they can also undo. An appreciation of the role of Supreme Courts as final arbiters is ingrained in both the legal system and the civic culture. But it is not impossible to change, even if it would require courts to self-harm, as it were. It would require neither formal amendment nor electoral approval. However, ironically, it would likely not receive the immediate approval of politicians and executives; they have become comfortable with the existing arrangements. After all, their own power and prestige is itself on shaky democratic footings, so any change toward a more democratic set-up will be viewed with a practised suspicion and scepticism. Nevertheless, this is not a reason to resist a more experimentalist and innovative move towards an improvement in the development of constitutional law. It is not a zero-sum choice between legislatures and courts. As such, my proposal runs sharply against the contemporary trend over recent decades that sees Supreme Courts accumulating and centralising their already considerable constitutional and institutional power.[13]

Accordingly, jurists and judges must disabuse themselves and others of the idea that Supreme Courts are the only governmental venue that can resolve constitutional disputes in any decisive or principled way. It has become received wisdom among all stripes of constitutional theorists that only Supreme Courts can deduce constitutional truths in an authoritative way. Within the traditional canon, being for the Constitution means also being for the Supreme Court as its primary expositor and guardian of its values. In adopting this stance, jurists and judges have backed themselves (and also the citizenry) into a constitutional corner. The acceptance of Supreme Courts as the final and authoritative arbiters of constitutional disputes reverberates throughout the whole political and governmental world. Because Supreme Courts are treated not only as having the final word, but also speaking on behalf of constitutional truths, other branches of government have developed a see-what-we-can-get-away mentality. Rather than offer and act upon good faith efforts to bring their governmental work in line with what they consider to be a reasonable meaning of constitutional law's requirements, they act in a cavalier and often irresponsible way that is almost indifferent to constitutional law and its more generous reading.

In recommending a less supreme and less authoritatively final judicial body, it is less a matter of what Supreme Courts can and should do, and more about what they cannot and should not do – they should stop asserting the claim that

---

[13] See Mark Lemley, 'The Imperial Supreme Court' (2021) 136 *Harvard Law Review* 97.

they are the 'final, independent judicial arbiter of disputes' in constitutional law.[14] Replacing hubris with humility, this switch entails judges taking a large step back and granting space and authority to others to provide and apply other constitutional imperatives. If constitutional law is inherently political, then the political and democratic branches of government can take up some of the institutional slack of constitutional decision-making.[15] By so acting, the Constitution might reanimate citizens' authority and primacy in democratic politics. Indeed, more progress might be made if all those involved were to recognise that the main action and central bone of contention is not about abstract jurisprudential theory, but about constitutional politics – what are the political values and ideological commitments that drive judicial decision-making? And what are the most democratic locations at which to engage in debate about those values and commitments?

In fulfilling this critical responsibility, democratic institutions and instincts can assist by ensuring that people are emancipated as far as practicable from bondage of all kinds (ie, economic, social, cultural, and, especially in this context, intellectual oppression). This can be done by ensuring that participation is as wide and unconstrained as possible. The task is most definitely not to purge intellectual inquiry and debate of its politicalness as a traditional reliance on judicial review recommends. Instead, mindful that power can also be constitutive and enabling as well as restrictive and distorting, a democratic approach can meet power's challenge by organising democratic arrangements so as not only to maximise people's life choices and lifestyles, but also to provide a set of communal resources through which the intellectual bases for these choices and styles can be debated and criticised. This might entail a commitment to devolve and diffuse power as much as practically possible by fostering 'multiple-veto points' in constitutional law across the governmental landscape.

In line with this commitment, strong democrats will look to extend and proliferate the opportunities for participation in micro-communities rather than to narrow and accrete decision-making power to small and centralised elites in the name of political expertise and constitutional truth. This institutional transformation involves two important initiatives in regard to existing arrangements. First,

---

[14] For earlier arguments against leaving full constitutional authority with the Canadian courts, see Jacques-Yvan Morin, 'A Constitutional Court for Canada' (1965) 43 *Canadian Bar Review* 545 (1965) (recommending a different appointment process and including non-lawyers as members of such a Court); Paul Weiler, *In the Last Resort: A Critical Study of the Supreme Court of Canada* (Toronto, Carswell, 1974) ch 6; and Jennifer Smith, 'The Origins of Judicial Review in Canada' (1983) 16 *Canadian Journal of Political Science* 115. It should not be forgotten that there is a legislative override provision in the Canadian constitution. See p 15 [this chapter].

[15] See, for example, Mark Tushnet and Bojan Bugarič, *Power to the People: Constitutionalism in the Age of Populism* (New York, Oxford University Press, 2021). For Tushnet, to be pro-constitution is not to be anti-democratic: it is courts and judicial review that are the problem, not the Constitution. With a keen sensitivity to the demands of a democratic imperative, he explores how constitutional law might be wrested from the suffocating grip of the Supreme Court, distributed to other institutional venues, and handed back to the people: 'all constitutional provisions are up for grabs at all times.' Mark Tushnet, *Taking the Constitution Away from the Courts* (Princeton, Princeton University Press, 1999) 42.

it will be important to reinvigorate democratically those bodies and organs (eg, parliaments, legislatures, state agencies, etc) which presently claim to be the decisive seat of democratic government. Rather than function as remote entities that have tenuous claims to democratic legitimacy through occasional elections, they might begin to be less entrenched and more responsive in their designs, deliberations and decisions; local government would supplement and be partners with federal government at the heart of democratic involvement. Of course, nothing is guaranteed by way of outcome or result; the constitutional debate will be popular and broad, but it will not be fixed or conclusive.

Secondly, it will be important to ensure that, if there are to be diverse and second-look agencies that contribute to advancing citizens' rights and checking the constitutional merits of legislative enactments, such institutions will themselves be more representative and accountable to popular views. Of course, judicial review does not meet such a standard; appointed (and even elected) judges tend to operate in the same calcified and elitist ways as the legislatures that they are supposed to check. Accordingly, it will be necessary to engage citizens directly in more imaginative and participatory ways in such deliberative bodies, including special tenure protections, non-legal personnel, and the like. Moreover, as part of such a shift, it might be possible, in Jeffersonian fashion, to develop practices whereby every decade all fundamental laws and institutional arrangements might be allowed to lapse and periodic assemblies could be convened so that each generation had the 'right to choose for itself the form of government it believes most promotive of its own happiness'.[16] In this way, citizens might claim constitutional law as their own and take responsibility for the deep structure and substance of their political society.

Balances and Challenges

Democracy demands that power should be in the hands of citizens as much as possible. In large and complex societies, this demand has to be attenuated and understood realistically in light of existing social conditions and circumstances. Citizens are entitled to expect that, where power is granted to individuals and institutions, there will be accountability to a degree and extent that is feasible and enforceable. This means that, insofar as this is not possible or practical as a regular occurrence, it is imperative that a series of checks and balances be in place to guard against the accumulation and exercise of power by one branch of government relative to others. These strictures seem particularly pertinent to the operation and work of Supreme Courts. As the power of judges becomes more extensive and more centralised, it is even more pressing to examine and activate the checks

---

[16] Letter from Thomas Jefferson to Samuel Kercheval (12 July 1816) in *Thomas Jefferson: Writings* (Merrill Peterson (ed), New York, Library of America, 1984) 1402.

and balances that are and should be available. In short, a democratic critic, like myself, will want to know what possibilities exist within the existing constitutional arrangements and structures to ensure that the governmental power is controlled and becomes relatively open to more, not less, democratic accountability.

In pursuing this inquiry, I have emphasised that it is both important and neces-sary to grapple with this issue in regard to 'the existing constitutional arrangements'. It is relatively easy, but of no practical relevance to suggest a range of constitutional amendments that would more easily accomplish the kind of democratic achieve-ments and changes that I have recommended. However, in both the United States and Canada, while there are constitutional provisions that allow amendments to be made, the actual likelihood of that occurring in present circumstances is close to zero. As a practical and reasonable matter, constitutional amendments of any size or significance will not be happening in the foreseeable future. In the United States, as a result of a very restrictive approval-and-ratification process, there have been only 27 amendments in over 200 years, with only two in the last 50 years. In Canada, although the Constitution was repatriated in 1982 and a Charter of Rights and Freedoms incorporated at that time, the amendment process is so onerous that only minor and limited changes seem presently possible.[17] Accordingly, any substantial change in the distribution and accountability of government power will have to be done within the existing constitutional arrangements, not within a revised version of them.

That said, the options and possibilities for change within the existing consti-tutional arrangements are by no means as limited as many insist. Indeed, with a little imagination and resolve, there are procedures and initiatives that can be utilised to bring about substantial change to the institutional and constitu-tional status quo. The problem is as much cultural and political as it is legal and constitutional. Of course, the fact that the obstacles are cultural and political does not make the chances of change any more likely; engrained atti-tudes and social practices can and often are as difficult to shift. However, the excuses about the barriers to reform being formal and entrenched hold less water; politicians and jurists cannot claim that their hands are tied and that a response to democratic pressures for some institutional change is simply impossible and beyond attainment. It is possible and attainable. A deficit of political will is the real problem, not the presumed strait jacket of constitutional options.

Bearing this in mind, there are several avenues in the American and Canadian constitutions that can be identified and explored in order to tackle the central problem of democratic accountability in regard to Supreme Courts. Each of them has to be understood and appreciated in terms of their capacity to chal-lenge and disaggregate the contemporary tendency towards increasing, not decreasing, the authoritative power of Supreme Courts as the final constitutional

---

[17] For a fuller discussion, see Hutchinson, *Democracy and Constitutions*, above n 6 at 75–80.

arbiters. While it is entirely mistaken to report that these 'political checks on the Court are effective',[18] they do present strategic opening and unmined opportunities. These possibilities recommend ways in which the Supreme Courts' ultimate supremacy can be influenced, limited and even challenged:

- *The appointment of the judges* – there is ample room for Presidents and Prime Ministers to change this process and to introduce a scheme that is more open to professional participation and civic input. In doing so, while the formal appointment and approval would be by those executives (and, in the United States, with a legislative committee's approval),[19] the process and criteria for appointing judges could become both more inclusive and more transparent than is presently the case.

- *Legislative push-back* – history shows that there have been countless efforts by legislators and administrators to respond to judicial decisions in an effort to clarify, amend and rework some of the constitutional ground rules. This kind of exchange seems to represent the productive tensions that exist between different branches of government. Indeed, in a fully functioning polity, this give-and-take seems to be indicative of a healthy democracy.[20]

- *Change composition of court* – there is a plentiful historical record of government efforts to rethink changing the membership of courts and how they function. While the courts have traditionally resisted such efforts, such initiatives are anticipated by constitutional law and do not run afoul of any explicit constitutional bar.[21]

- *Failure to comply or enforce* – although this occurs in an arguably extra-constitutional manner (and some might argue in an unconstitutional manner), there is no formal process and direct powers that courts have to oblige other branches of government to respect and follow their judgments. The bite of judicial decisions is very much a function of the relative power and legitimacies of the different branches of government.[22]

---

[18] Terri Peretti, *In Defense of a Political Court* (Princeton, Princeton University Press, 2001) 5. Having said that, her account of some of these possibilities is extremely useful in this democratising project.

[19] See US Constitution 1787, art II, s 2 and Constitution Act (Canada) 1867, s 98.

[20] See, eg, Abner Mikva and Jeff Bleich, 'When Congress Overrules the Court' (1991) 79 *California Law Review* 729 and Peter Hogg and Allison Bushell, 'The Charter Dialogue between Courts and Legislatures (Or Perhaps the Charter of Rights Isn't Such a Bad Thing after All)' (1997) 35 *Osgoode Hall Law Journal* 75. Another powerful illustration of this is the continuing aftermath to the *Dobbs* saga: see ch 5.

[21] See, eg, the Judiciary Act (US) 1869 and the Supreme Court Act (Canada) 1875. The court-packing threats of Roosevelt's government in the 1930s succeeded, in part, because they were not constitutionally suspect. See Laura Kalman, *FDR's Gambit: The Court Packing Fight and the Rise of Legal Liberalism* (New York, Oxford University Press, 2022).

[22] See, eg, Eric Posner, *The Executive Unbound After the Madisonian Republic* (New York, Oxford University Press, 2010); Mark Tushnet, *Why the Constitution Matters* (New Haven, Yale University Press, 2010); and Peter Russell, *The Judiciary in Canada: The Third Branch of Government* (Toronto, McGraw-Hill Ryerson, 1987).

- *Create new constitutional bodies/agencies* – one of the signal features of the last 100 years has been the growth in tribunals and committees to adminis-ter a wide range of delegated executive powers and responsibilities. There is no constitutional prohibition against such developments, although there are questions about the reach and force of such delegations. That said, there is no constitutional reason that similar bodies might not be set up to offer opinions on discrete constitutional matters.

- *Take away some of Supreme Courts' jurisdiction* – although there have been a number of attempts to do this (and they have been met with judicial resist-ance), legislators and executives can make use of neglected constitutional provisions to chip away at the extended jurisdiction that Supreme Courts have assumed in settling constitutional disputes. This effort will at least oblige courts to defend the contemporary trend towards them becoming more centralised and final authorities in democratic governance.[23]

There is one available mechanism in the Canadian Constitution that has obvious importance and effect in bringing about a sea change in the democratic stand-ing of organised governmental arrangements. Under s 33 of the Constitution Act 1982, a provincial or federal legislature can by a simple majority declare any legislation within its jurisdiction exempt from Charter and, therefore, judi-cial scrutiny. Presently relied on perversely by the Supreme Court to justify a more active and dominant role for itself (as legislatures can end-run it in the final analysis), this override power has enormous potential to counter-balance the constitutional authority of the Supreme Court. Although its use is viewed by many judges and jurists to be somehow inappropriate, its exercise has been sporadic and selective: it is argued that it offends the democratic spirit of the whole governmental and constitutional division of powers. This response seems wrong-headed because, as much as the critics would wish otherwise, use of the override is not a flouting of the Constitution or the Rule of Law. The override is as much a part of the Canadian Constitution as the s 15 equality guarantee or s 2's freedom of expression. Furthermore, as history attests, there would have been no Charter introduced without s 33's override provision; it was a condition prec-edent by some provinces.[24]

Nevertheless, the existence of such a provision opens up significant possibilities for recalibrating the authoritative centrality of Supreme Courts in constitutional law. Although it offers a zero-sum solution (ie, either the courts or the legislators have final say, but no one else), it does introduce a modicum of accountability even if it fails to disperse or filter down decision-making to the citizenry more generally.

[23] See, eg, US Constitution 1787, art III, s 2 and the Federal Courts Improvement Act (US) 1988. See also Robert Bauer et al, 'Final Report' (Presidential Commission on the Supreme Court of the United States, 2021).

[24] For a more extensive account of the history and contemporary practice of the Canadian override provision, see Hutchinson, *Democracy and Constitutions*, above n 6 at 77–79.

However, again mindful of Ely's caution that although 'we may grant until we're blue in the face that legislatures aren't wholly democratic, but that isn't going to make courts more democratic than legislatures',[25] this leaves the final say with a more democratic body; there is no judicial review (as yet) of a legislature's exercise of the override power. Furthermore, this constitutional state of affairs might at least require both institutions to take a more interactive and less dogmatic attitude to their respective responsibilities under the Constitution; each might be willing to seek to uphold their respective roles in a way that is more attuned to political sensibilities and popular views. At the very least, if used sensibly and regularly, it should re-centre some of the presently Court-dominated constitutional landscape.

None of these manoeuvres will cause a major transformation in the overall democratic status of existing governmental structures and workings. However, taken together, they might begin to adjust the democratic balance of power by redistributing and diffusing the interpretation and exercise of constitutional authority. If the courts are put more on the democratic defensive on a regular basis, they might be willing to relinquish some of their self-proclaimed constitutional supremacy. Importantly, there is nothing to be lost by making such efforts; there is no obvious downside even if they fail. But, if they succeed, that will be both government and society's own democratic reward. Supreme Courts that are less supreme will have less impact, have less control, and defer more often to other branches of government: they will more live up to the promise of democratic governance. Moreover, once it is recognised and acted upon that Supreme Courts are inescapably political in fulfilling their constitutional duties, this shift in the checks and balances that can be introduced and acted upon will confer greater legitimacy on Supreme Courts. It will not be a perfect outcome, far from it, but it will be better and more compatible with the rhetoric and practice of democratic governance than present arrangements are.

Making Progress

If law is inherently political, then the political and democratic branches of government can take up and share the institutional slack of constitutional decision-making.[26] By so acting, the whole of government might galvanise citizens' authority and primacy in establishing and developing the terms and conditions for the attainment of democratic ends. But that will not be sufficient. It will be essential that all branches of government commit themselves to such a democratic mission. As regards Supreme Courts, this means that the phony war over whether constitutional law can and should be treated as something separate and different from politics could be abandoned. Rather than be a bogus trade in so-called

---

[25] John Ely, above n 9.
[26] See, eg, Mark Tushnet, *Power to the People*, above n 15.

'constitutional truths' or 'neutral principles', the worth of constitutional law would be measured in terms of its capacity to protect and enhance democracy. In this way, it might become possible to combine the institutional form and the ideological substance of constitutional law – what are the most democratic locations and methods to engage in political debate about those values and commitments that can best advance a democratic society?

In asserting this, I am firmly insisting that constitutional law-making will not, in Wechsler's words, be reducible to 'the *ad hoc* in politics' in which unprincipled, transient and self-serving ideological allegiances are the order of the day.[27] In contrast, I am recommending that judicial adjudication can occur in a law-infused, principled, reasoned and good faith way. Indeed, the compelling issues of constitutional law are not about identifying and applying abstract or neutral jurisprudential theories, but about the substance of law's politics that is achieved. Accordingly, while constitutional law can and should be about reasoned justice, there is no one overarching or available standard that will decisively or authoritatively determine whether any particular outcome represents constitutional correctness. As forums of politics, Supreme Courts will be governmental locations that recognise, not reject, the idea that constitutional lawyering cannot be done without contestation and difference of opinion. But, in a very significant way, this is no different than what occurs today, albeit in denial and disguise.

The major and telling difference is, of course, that this fact about constitutional law's politicalness will and must be accepted and embraced, not denied and worked around. This will have both a professional and popular dimension. As regards citizens, they will have to be open to this understanding of constitutional law being thoroughly political. In many ways, this will be less of a stretch than many professionals think or protest. The public already place great weight on the political substance of decisions in its evaluation of Supreme Court's claims to legitimacy. Even if temporary and sporadic, approval of the Courts' work depends as much on whether decisions made or directions followed align with a citizen's political leaning as much as anything else, including the general constitutional methodology adopted by judges or courts generally.[28] This is particularly the situation in Canada where judges are considered to be acting more legitimately than their American colleagues and are more deserving of approval than politicians. Consequently, although the shift towards a more nakedly political Supreme Court will not be without issue or contestation, it will not be as seismic as many judges and jurists pretend.

As regards the professional response, it is important that both the arguments presented to the courts and the judgments rendered by the courts will be transparent and even candid in their understanding of constitutional law as a mode of

---

[27] Herbert Wechsler, 'Toward Neutral Principles of Constitutional Law' (1959) 73 *Harvard Law Review* 1, 19. See also Cass Sunstein, *Constitutional Personae* (New York, Oxford University Press, 2015).

[28] See chs 2 and 7.

political decision-making. This will require both judges and jurists to stop hiding behind jurisprudential and interpretive theories as though these accounts can relieve them of their responsibility for decisions reached and their commitment to the political character and content of any reasoning relied upon. Within a democratically transformed system (even if only marginally so), constitutional law will become a significant resource and occasion through which society can make and re-make itself in a way that is better responsive to the needs and demands of its citizens. In this way, constitutional law can more openly fulfil its acclaimed objective to be both a source and a reflection of democratic justice in contemporary society: judges will not be working against democratic politics, but will be more fully and genuinely part of it.

A necessary corollary of this critical understanding is that constitutional law has to be thought of as being neither fixed nor stable. Indeed, the traditional approach offends the idea and practice of democracy as something that belongs to today's citizens, not those of yesteryear. Instead, a critical model recognises that existing values and settled interests have no necessary democratic valence on their own. While critics and activists must work with the justificatory tools of their society, they are not condemned to work within its past decisions or remain beholden to its present orientations. The past consensus is only a starting point, and the present accord is only a temporary respite from continuing debate and engagement. As such, extant democratic arrangements must themselves not only allow, but also facilitate critical engagement. Justificatory standards endure only as long as they retain the confidence and support of the community as the best and most useful benchmarks available; they thrive and wither in the good faith debate between intelligent interlocutors about what counts as 'working best'.

As regards constitutional law-making, this strongly endorses the notion that it is a living practice that evolves and changes. However, this must not be appreciated in the way that it has traditionally been championed. Canadian constitutional law relies on the idea that the Constitution is 'a living tree capable of growth and expansion within its natural limits'.[29] Although this is suggestive of what I am proposing, it does not go at all far enough. Indeed, it perpetuates the idea that constitutional law has a natural life that is somehow independent of the judicial arborists who tend and observe it. While it allows for change and development, it gives the impression that this occurs as something apart from the work and values of the judges who comprise the Supreme Court at any particular time. In contrast, I want to abandon all naturalistic trappings and insist that the constitutional tree is a projection of the judges' own individual and collective sense of what the constitution is and should be. As such, under my democratic and pragmatic account, the Constitution and its development is a truly living and fully human enterprise. It is not about imaginary trees or other natural entities, but about creating new and

---

[29] *Edwards v Canada (AG)* [1930] AC 124. See also *Reference re Same-Sex Marriage* (2004) 2004 SCC 79 and *Canada (AG) v Bedford* (2013) 2013 SCC 7.

vibrant practices of people's own through law-making. In a manner of speaking, we (especially including lawyers and judges) are our own forest of trees and its living occupants.

Neither originalists nor organicists have been strong or open in sketching out a political interpretation of the Constitution. They both try to hide behind their theories of constitutional interpretation. Mindful that originalist 'judges are not conservatives because they are originalists; they are originalists because [originalism] is conservative',[30] originalists hide behind the façade of the presumed meaning of textual terms at end of eighteenth century. In a similar vein, organicists have spent enormous time and energy putting out originalist fires. In doing so, they have claimed to be reading the Constitution in line with the contemporary *volkgeist*: they recognise that social values change and that it is a Constitution for today as much as yesterday. Like the originalists, organicist judges and jurists are not non-conservatives because they are non-originalists; they are non-originalists because this better enables them to advance a non-conservative or more progressively liberal politics. So, both originalists and organicists make the same jurisprudential moves – they both insist theirs is the real or true meaning of the constitutional law and that the resulting law is not reducible to their own political values and commitments.[31]

Under a more democratic and pragmatic view of constitutional law, both organicists and originalists will have to argue frankly and vigorously for their preferred view of constitutional politics. Accepting that there is no one true and exclusive meaning to the Constitution, they will have to persuade others that their chosen political approach offers a set of values and outcomes that will contribute to a better and more compelling vision and practice of modern democratic politics. This will not be a straightforward or easy task. Most importantly, I do not suggest that this will increase the likelihood of an elusive consensus or even temporary agreement among decision-makers. However, it will oblige judges and jurists to come clean on the primary motivating factors and forces that energise and make persuasive their political take on constitutional law. It will bring judges out into the open and require them to take a stand. When they do so, their judicial work can be directly evaluated by its political results and reasoning, not only by its pseudo-legal and jurisprudential persuasiveness and correctness.

Judges and jurists will need to develop a fuller vision of substantive politics than has presently been offered. While conservatives have an account of what kind of political community the Constitution instantiates (ie, individualistic, property-based, freedom-loving, minimalist government, and traditional values), progressives do not; they are often too content to be viewed as simply not being conservative. It will be imperative, therefore, for them to assemble and promote a progressive politics of constitutionalism that can challenge the conservative

---

[30] Michael Waldman, 'The Supermajority: How the Supreme Court Divided America' (New York, Simon & Schuster, 2023) 257.

[31] See ch 4.

account in its substantive content and appeal (ie, a social welfare state, civil rights for demographic minorities, protections for workers and labour unions, and environmentalism, among others).[32] This is an urgent task that cannot be delayed. As things stand, a vision of constitutional law as being distinct and separate from politics is inherently destructive to a more progressive politics as it de-levels the playing field to a marked extent; it cuts the Constitution loose from any kind of political community or vision that might animate and sustain it. Rather than think of the Constitution being a source of political community, it is viewed as a limitation on what a political community can be and do. This must change.

As the *Dobbs* saga so vividly reveals, it will not be enough for progressives to bemoan the flawed interpretive methods of the present conservative majority. As unconvincing as originalism is, it will not be displaced by one more defence of the preferred superior appeal of organicism. Fighting political fire with fire, progressive lawyers must offer a substantive vision of political community that can flesh out, not merely hint at, what a progressive society can be. So, for instance, while decriminalising abortion is important, it is also insufficient to ground a woman's right to choose. It must be augmented by a fuller and more positive account of society and its informing institutional structures in which women's reproductive freedom and equality can be fully appreciated and substantively realised. Moreover, there must be a shift away from the underlying and animating idea that people's rights are only negative in kind and cut. A constitutional law that puts substantive equality, democratic process and individual empowerment to the fore will provide a strong, but by no means decisive, challenge to a conservative account.[33]

Conclusion

Thinking about constitutional law and judicial decision-making in a more directly political and democratic way will serve to bring Supreme Courts more in line with the realities of government power and organisation. Moving beyond the cramped logic of the counter-majoritarian dilemma, Supreme Courts that look towards alleviating the existing limitations of popular participation in governmental

---

[32] What counts as 'progressive' is, of course, a matter of stern debate. In constitutional law, a progressive approach has a number of powerful advocates. See Robin West, *Progressive Constitutionalism: Reconstructing the Fourteenth Amendment* (Durham, Duke University Press, 1994); Andrew Petter, *The Politics of the Charter: The Illusive Promise of Constitutional Rights* (Toronto, University of Toronto Press, 2010); Mark Tushnet, 'Progressive Constitutionalism: What Is "It"?' (2011) 72 *Ohio State Law Journal* 1073; Erwin Chemerinsky, *We the People: A Progressive Reading of the Constitution for the Twenty-First Century* (New York, Picador, 2018); and Joseph Fishkin and William Forbath, *The Anti-Oligarchy Constitution: Reconstructing the Economic Foundations of American Democracy* (Cambridge, Harvard University Press, 2022).

[33] For a compelling and progressive judicial account of what this might entail for constitutional law in regard to welfare claims, see *Gosselin v Quebec (AG)* (2002) 2002 SCC 84 (Arbour J). This approach stands in strong contrast to a half-hearted American recognition of a procedural protection in welfare benefit cases, see *Goldberg v Kelly* (1970) 397 US 254.

decisions can help to undercut, not reinforce, some of the elitism that pervades politics today. In measuring the work and contribution of Supreme Courts on such a metric, the question ought not to be how far Supreme Courts fall short of a perfectly participatory scheme of governance (and it clearly still would), but how far transformed Supreme Courts might be able to do a better job than at present. I maintain that, although there is still a very long democratic road to travel that will take much more radical changes, the proposals that I have put forward and defended will bring about a significant improvement in the terms and substance of constitutional justice in societies that aspire to be more, not less, democratic.

11

The Justices' New Clothes:
A Cautionary Tale

The City had originally been a swampy stretch of land. Reclaimed over the decades and now home to grand buildings and varied residences, it had changed entirely. Growing in size and importance, it had become a thriving and sprawling metropolis that encompassed all that was good and bad about societies generally. It was at the hub of the country's social, political and cultural life: little happened that could not be attributed to the efforts and ideas of the City's denizens and officials.

At the heart of the City and, therefore, the country was the imposing edifice that housed the Governing Council. It comprised nine members who were held in high esteem for their wisdom, experience and acumen. This was an elite body that held enormous power and authority over society at large. Membership was reserved for senior and proven supporters of the existing regime of governance. The Council issued 'resolutions' about issues that vexed society and around which no general social consensus had emerged.

The members of the Governing Council had originally been titled 'councillors'. But this was thought by earlier members as too prosaic to represent the important functions that were performed by them; it smacked too much of them being policy wonks who simply calculated the technical costs and benefits of various options and then operationalised those outcomes. Instead, they wanted a title more fitting to their prestige and responsibilities. They had settled upon 'Justices'. This would not only lend them some of the cache that other societies used for the honorific of 'judge', but it would also elevate them into being seen as more high-minded thinkers who were devoted to improving the quality of social life. So, the members became known as the chosen group who, not being distracted by the insinuations of petty politics or bureaucratic fiddling, defined and dispensed what was right and good to all and for all.

One of the things that brought together the Justices was their disdain for those they termed 'political hacks'; these were pundits and self-appointed analysts who lacked integrity and simply sailed in the political direction of any prevailing winds. Mud-slinging and febrile polemics were their standard fare; this was considered to have no connection or comparison to the more rarefied and elevated work of the Justices. Indeed, few things rankled the Justices more than being treated as if they were in a similar game to such persons. But, with long-suffering restraint, the Justices accepted the institutional burden of being both misunderstood and unappreciated.

The Council had originally been the preserve of older white men, but it had recently begun to bring in less homogenous appointments. The actual workings of the Council were never very transparent or open. Indeed, there was a tendency to encourage the mystery and mystique that swirled around the Council and its operations. Nevertheless, notwithstanding the increasing diversity of the Council in both composition and viewpoint, its members seemed to agree that how they appeared to the public was almost as important as what they decided: presentation and perception were understood to be potent factors in maintaining the legitimacy and status of the Governing Council. Behind closed doors and in their lighter moments, the members had begun to subscribe to the idea that 'if trends come and go, style remains eternal.'

In recent years, the popularity of the Council and its edicts became more fragile than had historically been the case. Some of its decisions had not been well received. This was nothing new; it could not be a reasonable expectation that everyone would like or approve of their decisions. More disturbingly for the Council, though, people began to agitate more openly and express doubts about the judges' fabled wisdom. Some of the Council's members were minded to ignore this simmering discontent; they thought it would soon pass and a normal measure of deference would be restored. Other Council members were not so sure and took the unprecedented step of defending the Council and its work; they insisted that not only were such critics mistaken and being hurtful to the judges personally, but that they were being disloyal to society generally and should stop such subversive criticism.

Because criticism continued unabated, the Council members decided that enough was enough. Something needed to be done. And preferably it should be done collectively by the judges themselves; they decided to demonstrate that the Council and its members were worthy of continued support and deserving of respect. As they all agreed, it was a demanding job and was becoming more so. By doing something striking and together, they might be able to turn the tide of public opinion and return to 'business as usual'.

After several impromptu meetings and informal conversations, the Council unanimously settled on a course of action. The standard garb for members of Council was business attire, although, in some circumstances, they donned simple black gowns to add a little formality to their proceedings. The judges had long cast an envious eye on the leaders of other pivotal institutions, like churches and universities, who had a range of fine vestments to use on ceremonial occasions and, at times, for more mundane events – 'we should also have a kind of splendid finery so that we can lend a deserved majesty to our positions and our callings.' In particular, many of the judges coveted the garments that others wore – the sumptuous brocade, the exquisite embroidery, the sparkling trim, the sophisticated patterns and, most of all, the vivid colours.

Of course, the judges did not all share the same sense of fashion or agree what the new apparel should look like. Much time and effort were spent on trying to reach some basic agreement, but to no avail; the justices coveted their individual independence. So, although the judges had a shared sense that new outfits were required, they agreed to disagree about what each of them would wear. There would a general format and design, but each judge could accessorise as they saw fit. It was a sensible compromise that evidenced an increasingly rare united front among the nonet of judges – 'let's spruce things up. But let's do so in a way that is unique to each individual judge; a personal sense of style should be tolerated in small ways, if not demanded' was the common refrain among them.

Some took the stance that any official attire should be decidedly traditional in cut and line. For them, old was new; a retro-look was the fashion to go for. They insisted that it was only by dressing modern Council members in the established elegance of yesteryear (when the Council first came to governmental prominence) that they could recapture the seriousness and standards that would reinforce their work as being detached from the passing fads of contemporary political service. As such, a tailored look that evoked the halcyon days of the original Council would be the *de rigueur* mode of justicial gravitas.

Another set of justices wanted something that was a little more understated and, in their view, of ageless grace. Although they went along with the general ambition of crafting a new set of garments, they would have preferred a more modest set of working clothes that did not remind the public of quasi-religious vestures for the daily doings of the Council. Grandeur was fine, but it had its limits. For them, it was becoming enough of a challenge to show that the Council was not a body that had some divine claim to people's obeisance: the adoption of a lavish and showy set of robes would not help. Accordingly, a straightforward and unobtrusive outfit was the desired way to go.

Finally, a couple of Justices were firmly of the opinion that, if there was to be a change in sartorial habits, something new and contemporary was the sensible option. There was no need to be too *au courant*, but it was important for the Council to be viewed, at least superficially, as part of, not apart from, the general sensibilities of the day. For them, this might suggest a look that drew upon the many different traditions and styles of the country's people; it was no longer acceptable or even prudent for the Council's members to present themselves as fuddy-duddies who were out of touch with the more modern vibes of society. Perhaps a more up-to-date and even *avant garde* initiative would shake things up and actually work to enhance the Council's bruised reputation.

These differences of opinion ran deep and divisive. Squabbling became a feature of the Justices' interactions. Rather than bring the Justices together, this bickering only seemed to drive them further apart and reinforce the vying cliques with the Council. Although most of this acrimony occurred behind closed doors, occasional leaks would occur. Moreover, some of the Justices even went so far as to make veiled comments by way of lectures, interviews or opinion pieces in favoured media outlets. It was not an edifying or appeasing turn of events.

Of course, once news got out that the Council's Justices were planning on a new wardrobe, there was excited and agitated discussion over what that new look should be. Indeed, everyone seemed to become overnight a *fashionista*; even the most dowdy and dreary had a view on what was best and most fitting. The media ran competitions and assembled panels of experts on what should happen. The basic disagreements among the Justices were replicated among the public – some maintained that the retro-look was more becoming; some said go bold or go home; and others opted for a more modest and unassuming ensemble.

Nevertheless, although surprised by the intensity and depth of the public furore, the Council proceeded with its planned make-over – 'we need to stick to our guns; public opinion is fickle and we must not be distracted from our time-honoured responsibilities,' said the most intransigent among them. Like most things at the Council, because that Justice and the Chief Justice were in the Council's majority, their views prevailed.

Notwithstanding the deeply held reservations of their colleagues, the 'old guard' pushed ahead. It was a numbers game – those who could put together a coalition of five got their way and those who could not lost. Of course, much was heard about how principle and reason supported this decision, but the reality was that the majority had the final and, therefore, day-carrying word. For those in the majority, reason and good sense had prevailed; for those in the minority, reason and good sense had given way to power and preference.

So, detailed plans began to be made about who would be selected to produce the Justices' new clothes. Having decided against a formal tendering process, unofficial soundings were made. After considerable debate and as a concession to the minority, a newly founded fashion house was chosen; it was being celebrated for its ability to produce new fabric in stunning patterns. Although the majority had their doubts, a contract was signed that gave considerable artistic freedom to this fledgling company to choose the fabrics, designs and colours that would be used.

The fashion house had assembled an enviable team of creative designers, innovative weavers and consummate tailors that drew upon and combined the artisanship of reputed old-hands and up-and-coming young talents. It promised to be an exciting commission that would put the clothiers' house on the map and set them up for future greatness in the fashion industry. So, with real purpose and a genuine will to please, everyone began work with special intent and enthusiasm.

The project took a few months of demanding creativity and exhausting labour to take shape. In particular, one of the weavers developed a tantalising new textile that was a mix of natural fibres, synthetic materials and high-tech wizardry. Kept under secret wraps, the revolutionary fabric had a diaphanous and gossamer quality that, depending on who viewed it and where they viewed it, was opaque to some, but entirely transparent to others. This state-of-the-art cloth possessed the subtle power to expose disbelievers and sceptics. True devotees in the style and majesty of the wearer would see the clothes and recognise their splendour. But other of a more distrustful mien would see right through them and their vanity;

they would make out the shared and revealing humanity of the wearers in all their truthful nakedness.

As the undertaking was coming to completion, the Justices sent some of their trusted staff and clerks to inspect the clothes. At first, they hesitated; they were unsure what to make of it all. But, with the reassurance of the designers, they soon began to believe that the finery was a work of genius and a stunning success. After their extended visit, they made their way back to the Council and enthusiastically reported that the produced garments were unsurpassed in their quality and refinedness – 'What patterns! What colours! What quality! What perfection!'

When it was time for the Justices themselves to view the final outfits, there was a certain trepidation among all concerned. Would they like them? Would they appreciate the craft and skill involved? Would they experience the necessary sense of grandeur that the robes were supposed to project? In a private showing, the Justices, like the clerks earlier, were initially unsure how to react. In a certain light, the outfits seemed truly perfect; they were a wonderful blend of the bright and the serious, the polished and the playful, and the stylish and the sensible. But, in a different light, they were seen and believed to be entirely see-through; the naked bodies of the wearers could be glimpsed in all their failings and flaws.

However, after the initial indecision and with encouragement of the outfitters, the Justices were persuaded that all was well. Indeed, like the clerks, they were reluctant to be viewed as doubters or sceptics. So, buoyed by the verve and vivacity of their new uniforms, they praised the garments and waxed rhapsodic about them. In particular, they gushed about the gold and purple motifs – 'What unparalleled construction! What marvellous value! What unique styling! What dazzling colours!' At the end of the day, all the judges agreed that the clothes had an almost magical quality that made the wearers seem special; it added to their sense of majesty and importance.

Still a couple of weeks away, the Justices decided that there would be a ceremonial unveiling of the new clothes at the Annual Procession; this was a gala event at which all the members of the Government's different branches walked through the streets of the City and mingled among the public. When the day arrived, the Justices donned their new liveries and stepped out to join the historic walk-about that welcomed a new session of the Council's deliberations. Although they could not shake off entirely the foreboding sense that they were being scrutinised more closely than they would have liked in their new clothes, they had a fresh spring in their steps and a new confidence in their demeanours.

The crowds greeted the Justices with gasps and applause. Everyone clearly recognised that the new finery was startlingly original and simply startling. No one seemed to dissent from the general opinion that the Justices would not be viewed in the same light ever again. Of course, whatever they really thought, few who had taken the time and trouble to attend the Procession felt able to admit that the new clothes were as transparent as they were stunning. The Justices could be seen in all their nakedness and humanity – some were tall; some were short; some were weighty; and some were slender. For the crowd to concede anything other than the magnificence of the new clothes would be tantamount to confessing that they did not believe in the power and professionalism of the Council. Because they did.

But there were a handful who were less willing to believe and who were more able to see through both the clothes and the processual pretence. For them, it was a matter of civic pride that the Justices should be called out for their hubris and their readiness to pull the techno-wool over people's eyes. These protesters held up placards – 'Clothes Do Not Justices Make' and 'Style Is Not Substance.' As well, this small group chanted constantly – 'We can see you! We can see you!' Most of the crowd failed to take the protesters seriously and simply saw them as spoiling the celebratory mood of the day.

But the Justices were not at all impressed by the protesters' placards and chants; they were disruptive and uncalled-for. In short order, they instructed the police to remove the demonstrators from around the procession. With fitting restraint, the official forces were directed to relocate the protesters towards more remote locales and inconsequential side-streets. With that being done, the Procession continued. The Justices walked even more proudly and magisterially.

The Justices supposed that, in a vibrant society, there would always be some misguided and unappreciative souls who did not grasp or recognise that 'ruling' was an arduous responsibility. For them, it was matter of principle that, if stylish outfits do not entirely make the office holder, suitable appearance was a pre-requisite to ensuring proper substance was achieved. Candour and complete clarity were not always possible or desirable in fulfilling the responsibilities of governing. If there was any threat to society, the Justices maintained that it came from the protesters, certainly not from the Justices themselves or other high-status officials.

The coverage in the media was mixed. For the most mainstream news sources, the Procession and the Justices' new clothes were cause for praise and approval. The Council was congratulated on its sartorial efforts to improve the perception of its image and ideals in the public's opinion. At their most pragmatic, some commentators conceded that, if the Council was to retain its authority and legitimacy, the occasional noble lie was required, albeit reluctantly and rarely.

But there were others in the media who were slightly disillusioned by the recent resolutions of the Council and the overall performance of the Justices. But, for them, it was not so much that they saw straight through the new clothes, but that they maintained that, with some adjustments and reworking, their new wardrobe could still cover the nakedness of the Justices. Half-believers, they saw that such a refurbishment would require both Justices and citizens to redouble their efforts to live up to the promise that the new garments offered. So, viewed in the right or, at least, appropriate light, all could be redeemed; society could go back to the ways things were and should be – *plus ça change, plus c'est la même chose.*

However, there was a handful of less conventional and bolder journalists and bloggers who were more sanguine; they appreciated the candour of the judges. Viewed in their full and direct glory as unvarnished politicians, it was thought that, whatever the Justices lost in ostentation and preening grandeur (and that was not much), they more than made up for with their new artlessness and lack of pretention. For these onlookers, something approaching *realpolitik* was much preferable to and more acceptable than the dazzling, if empty, flourishes and embellishments that had been a large part of their councillary reputation and standing. It was less the look and more the actuality that counted.

After the Procession was over and throughout the Council's new session, life went on much as before. Draped in their new robes, the Justices continued to bicker among themselves and handed down decisions that curried favour and disfavour in almost equal measure. The fashion-house that had produced the new clothes became an overnight sensation; their services were in high demand throughout the society. But they were most revered and sought after by the rest of the governing elite who wanted to follow in the *haute couture* steps of their justicial colleagues. Golden and purple became the new black.

However, some people did lose faith in the Council as an institution of governance. Having identified the Justices' new clothes as a charade, they could not return to business as usual. Although they were portrayed as being disloyal and, by some, as even traitorous, these protestors knew that, in the republic of the half-blind, it was the clear-eyed who could best achieve justice – they had seen what they had seen and there was no un-seeing. So long as the Council's resolutions were favourable, all would be well. But, once they were not, all bets were off.

As for the ordinary people, they were somewhat indifferent. Of course, there was disagreement and division. As months turned into years, people went about their daily routines, much as before. Other pressing matters of social and political challenge caught their attention. It was action and change that people wanted; the appearance of justice was not enough. An influential body of opinion committed itself to helping others see what they had seen. It was no longer the case of 'seeing is believing'; it was now much more about 'believing is seeing'.

As with most fashions, the Justices' new clothes would soon become passé. But, more tellingly, people would slowly and surely begin to accept that the authority and legitimacy of the Council ran no deeper (and perhaps no shallower) than the cut and colour of their new and diaphanous clothes. If the Council's role was not abandoned, at least there would have to be a re-think of the nature of its role, its authority, and its legitimacy. Both people and populisers did what they could to move on. The Council no longer seemed so central to the City's sense of itself nor to its overall well-being. Some even dared to suggest that it was what people wanted and did that counted, not the way that the Council and its members looked and performed, that was the measure of the good society.

INDEX

abortion, 1, 4, 13, 23, 52, 54, 59–60, 66–67
  politicised constitutional law and
    adjudication, 125–27
  politicised constitutional reasoning, 76–81
  *see also Dobbs v Jackson Women's Health
    Organization; Roe v Wade*
accountability, 11, 42, 45, 112–13, 121,
    148–49, 154
  checks and balances, 160–62
  dialogists, 47
  federalism, 92–93
  law-is-politics approach, 115, 128
  political accountability, 17, 20, 25
affirmative action, 15–16, 26, 53, 54
Alito, Samuel A.:
  Dobbs case, 66–67
  Roe case, 72, 79–81
appointment of judges, 4–5, 15, 20, 23,
    60, 66, 74, 76, 152
  Dobbs case, 78–81
  democratic accountability, 160, 162
assent, 14, 15–16
  legitimacy of courts, 21, 37
  political legitimacy, 16–21
autonomy of constitutional law, 102,
    104–5

bad faith, 52, 61, 84, 121
  Dobbs case, 65, 76
  GGPPA case, 93, 99
balance:
  democracy and judicial review, 149–50
  federalism and the constitutional division
    of powers, 94–95, 97
  freedom and equality, 37, 140–42
  see also checks and balances
Bentham, Jeremy, 136
bias of judiciary, *see* impartiality and
    independence of the judiciary;
    neutral principles
Bickel, Alexander, 27, 35–38, 42, 45
  Bickel-Wechsler-Dworkin project, 58, 62
  Dworkin, relationship with, 38–40

Biden, Joe, 79, 150
Breyer, Stephen, 59–60
Brown, Russel S., 95
Brown v Board of Education, 3, 22, 29, 30,
    33–34, 65–66, 68, 73, 104, 127,
    143

Canada, 2, 27–28
  balancing freedom and equality, 142
  criminalisation of the wilful promotion
    of hatred, 140
  growth and prosperity, 27–28
  legitimacy threatened, 4–5
  regulation of greenhouse gas emissions,
    91–99
  student protests, 134–35
  *see also References re Greenhouse Gas
    Pollution Pricing Act;* Trudeau,
    Justin; *and individual justices*
candour of judges, 109–12
Carter v Canada, 143
checks and balances, 5
  democracy and judicial review,
    149–50
  democratic accountability, 160–64
  federalism and the constitutional division
    of powers, 94–95, 97
  freedom and equality, 37, 140–42
Chemerinsky, Erwin, 60–61
  candour of judges, 109–12
  traditionalism, 111
citizen participation, *see* participatory
    deficit
compliance failures, 149
  democratic accountability, 162
composition of courts, 10, 60
  democratic accountability, 162
conformity/compliance, 14–16
consent, 14, 15–16
  legitimacy of courts, 21, 37
  political legitimacy, 16–21
constitutional adjudication, 45–46, 48,
    52–55, 60–61

constitutional authority, 75, 91, 93–94,
    105–9, 111, 155, 163–64
constitutional democracy, 5, 9, 12–13, 19,
    40–41, 148–49
  see also democracy
constitutional interpretation, 4–5, 49–52,
    55–56, 57–58, 58, 61–62, 64,
    65–66, 69, 112, 156, 167
constitutional law, 9, 26–27
  autonomy of constitutional law, 104–5
  judicial decision-making, 106–7
  politicalness of constitutional law, 164–68
constitutional scholarship, 44–46
  deep moralists, 46
  democratists, 47–48
  dialogists, 47
  organicists, 46–47
  originalists, 46
  pragmatists, 47
constitutional truths, 41, 75, 108, 117,
    120–22, 124, 143, 151–52,
    158–60, 164–65
  pseudo-constitutional truths, 117
  see also neutral principles
Côté, Suzanne, 95
courts as political institutions:
  benefits, 101, 114–15, 122, 137–38, 154–55
    Dobbs case, 126
    GGPPA case, 126, 129
  expressive conduct, 139, 143–46
courts of last resort, 20, 107–8, 157–58,
    163–64
critical theory, 82, 87–88, 100–1
curial legitimacy, 21
  substantive matters, 21
  procedural matters, 22
  trade offs, 22–23

de Tocqueville, Alexis, 44, 153
deep moralists, 46
deliberative democracy, 148
  see also democracy
democracy:
  concentrations of power, 156
  law-is-politics approach, 147–48
  minorities and majorities, 148–52
  non-democratic public institutions, 20–21
  participatory deficit, 150–52
  political legitimacy, 17–18
    constitutional constraints, 18–19
    popular participation, 19–20
    see also political legitimacy

role and centrality of courts, 156–60
  types of democracy, 148–49
democratic socialism, 148
  see also democracy
democratism, 47–48, 51, 63, 155–56
dialogisms, 47, 51, 63
direct democracy, 148
  see also democracy
discrimination, 15–16, 28, 33, 53–54, 90,
    141–42
  see also freedom and equality
division of powers, 90–91, 91, 94–95, 96,
    128, 163
*Dobbs v Jackson Women's Health
    Organization,* 8, 10, 23, 60,
    64–65
  aftermath, 68–72
  good/bad faith in reasoning, 76–81
  majority opinion, 73
  minority opinion, 73–74
  organicism, 71, 73–75
  originalism, 73
  politics and judicial decision-making,
    75–76
  principled reasoning, 72
  Roe v Wade, 65–66
    dissenting opinions, 67–68
    leading opinion, 67
    overruling of, 66–67
  rule of law, 72
due process, 64, 80
Durkheim, Emile, 136
Dworkin, Ronald, 27, 31, 34, 38–42, 45,
    50, 70, 82, 108, 125, 130
  Bickel-Wechsler-Dworkin project, 58, 62
  courts as forum of principle, 88, 90, 92

enforcement failures:
  democratic accountability, 162
entrench opinions, 122–23
Epps, Daniel, 60
euthanasia, 20, 26, 53
expectations, 14–16
  curial legitimacy, 21
  political legitimacy, 17

Fallon, Richard, 59–60, 62
federalism, 91, 92–93
  cooperative federalism, 94–95, 96
    exclusive dualism compared, 96–97
  federalism spectrum, 97
  modern approach, 97–98

Franks, Mary Ann, 61, 121–22
freedom and equality, 140–42
freedom of speech:
   criminalisation of the wilful promotion
      of hatred, 140
   hate speech as protected speech, 140
   student protests, 138–40
Fuller, Lon, 2–3, 39, 88

good faith, 18, 43–44, 47, 61, 85–86, 90,
      119–20, 121, 128, 130, 133, 140,
      158, 165–66
   Dobbs case, 76–81
Gorsuch, Neil M., 80
greenhouse gas emissions, 91–93
   federalism, 91, 92–93
      cooperative federalism, 94–95, 96
      exclusive dualism, 96–97
   federalism spectrum, 97
   majority opinions, 93–95
   minority opinions, 95–96
   modern approach, 97–98
   politicised constitutional law and
      adjudication, 127–30
   see also References re Greenhouse Gas
      Pollution Pricing Act (2021)
Greenhouse Gas Pollution Pricing
     Act (GGPPA) 2018, 91–92
   see also References re Greenhouse Gas
      Pollution Pricing Act (2021)
Grotius, Hugo, 136
gun control, 4, 23, 59–60, 150
   Bruen case, 60, 77

Habermas, Jürgen, 17
Hart, H.L.A., 31, 39, 50, 82
   see also positivism
Hegel, George W.F., 136
Hobbes, Thomas, 136
homophobia, 54–55
Hume, David, 136

impartiality and independence of judiciary,
      20, 45, 54, 79, 90, 92–93, 113,
      119–20, 146, 156, 157–59
independence, *see* **impartiality and**
     independence of judiciary

judges' role, 6–8, 119–20
   impartiality and independence, 20, 45,
      54, 79, 90, 92–93, 113, 119–20,
      146, 156, 157–59

   politicised constitutional law and
      adjudication, 123–25
   political pragmatism, 123–24
   transparency, 120–23
judicial appointments, 4–5, 15, 20, 23, 60,
      66, 74, 76, 152
   Dobbs case, 78–81
   democratic accountability, 160, 162
   political appointments, 78–81
judicial decision-making, 7–8, 9, 26–27,
      39, 42, 68, 75, 76–77, 106–7,
      159–60, 168–69
   law's politics, 83–87, 89–90, 112–13
   principled reasoning, 43–44, 49–50, 52–53
   transparency, 120–21
judicial review, 21, 26–27, 75, 101–2, 119, 164
   Bickel, 35–36
   Chemerinsky, 60
   democratic governance, relationship
      with, 149–50, 159–60
   dialogists, 47
   Dworkin, 40, 41–42
   originalism, 46
   Wechsler, 31–32, 33–34
jurisdiction, 155–56
   democratic accountability, 163
   Parliamentary jurisdiction, 91, 97
   federal versus provincial/state law, 92,
      94–95, 128–29, 157, 163
jurisprudence, 6–7, 117–18
   candour of judges, 109–12
   constitutional authority, 105–9
   critical theorists, 100–1
   politics of law's politics, 101–5
   rethinking legitimacy, 112–17
   traditional theorists, 100–1

Kagan, Elena, 10–11
Kant, Immanuel, 136
Kavanaugh, Brett M., 67, 72
   Dobbs case, 76–77, 80–81

law/politics debate, 6–9
   law-is-politics approach, 10, 58, 83, 101, 120,
      130, 132–33, 143–44, 147–48
   judges, *see* judges' role
   jurisprudence, *see* jurisprudence
   law's politics, 83–87
   politics of law's politics, 101–5, 114,
      115–16, 117–18
   politics, *see* political legitimacy
   principled reasoning, 87–91

legal process trend, 29–30, 31, 39
legal reasoning, 8, 39, 52–53, 72, 73–76,
        84–87, 89, 109–10, 113, 115–16,
        133–34
    see also judicial decision-making; principled
        reasoning
legislative pushback:
    democratic accountability, 162
legitimacy concept, 13–16
legitimacy threatened, 1, 2–5, 22–23, 60,
        112, 147
Locke, John, 136

Machiavelli, Niccolo, 6, 7
Marbury v Madison, 3, 157
Medicare, 23
moralism, 54–55
    deep moralism, 46, 47, 51, 63

natural justice, 82, 110–11, 166–67
    see also Dworkin, Ronald
neutral principles, 31–34, 36, 53–55, 107,
        117, 122, 164–65
    see also constitutional truths
neutrality of judges, *see* **impartiality and
        independence of judiciary**
*New York State Rifle & Pistol Association Inc v
        Bruen,* 60, 77

openness to political debate, 120–21
organicism, 46–47, 51, 63, 65–66, 67, 71,
        73–75, 108, 112, 167–68
originalism, 46, 55–58, 63, 65–66, 67, 71,
        73–74, 108, 110–12, 125, 167
ownership:
    use of private property, 136–37

participatory deficits, 150–52, 153–54
Peretti, Terri, 114–15
polarisation, 4, 91, 112, 122–23
**politicised constitutional law and
        adjudication,** 123–25
    abortion law, 125–27
    greenhouse gas emissions, 127–30
political legitimacy, 16–21, 131–32
political protests on university campuses,
        132–34
    constitutional law, 134–38
        freedom of speech/expression,
            138–42
        law-is-politics approach, 143–46
popular sovereignty, 150–51

positivism, 38–39, 82
pragmatism, 47, 51, 63, 107, 152–53
    Fallon and Breyer, 59–60
    political pragmatism, 123–24, 145–46
presumption of legitimacy, 15–16
principled appraisal, 8, 50–51, 114–17, 119
principled reasoning, 27, 43–44, 48, 64, 90,
        146
    adjudicative purposes, 50–51
    application of generalised norms, 50
    Bickel, 35–38
    constitutional adjudication, 52
    constitutional interpretation, 49–52
    Dobbs case, 72, 73, 78–79
    fragility, 48–49
    law-is-politics approach, 87–91
    nature of, 50–52
    operation of, 50–52
    role, 49
    Weschler, 31–34
    see also legal reasoning
private property:
    constitutional rights, relationship with, 132,
        134–38
    student protests, 136–37
public support for courts, 26, 75–76, 119–20
    Canada, 2, 24
    United States, 2, 3–4, 22, 23–24
Pufendorf, Samual von, 136

racism and race issues, 27–29, 33, 53–55,
        108–9, 141
Rawls, John, 61–62
*References re Greenhouse Gas Pollution
        Pricing Act* **(2021),** 92–93, 94–95,
        99, 127–29
    cooperative federalism versus exclusive
        dualism, 96–99, 126
religious tolerance, 54–55, 86–87
    Catholicism and *Dobbs,* 78
representative democracy, 17–18, 37, 148
    see also democracy
Roberts, John G., 67
Roe v Wade, 22–23, 65–68, 143–44
    backlash, 68–70
    politicization of the courts, 79–81
    substantive due process, 65, 127
    *see also Dobbs v Jackson Women's Health
        Organization*
Rorty, Richard, 105–6
Rowe, Malcolm, 95–96
rule of law, 72, 123, 163

same-sex marriage, 52, 54–55
separate, but equal, 28
separation of powers, 90–91, 91, 94–95, 96,
　　　128, 163
sexism, 54–55, 141
Sitaraman, Ganesh, 60
Smith, Adam, 136
Sotomayor, Sonia, 1–2, 10
student protests, 132–34
　　constitutionalism, 134–38
Sunstein, Cass, 61–62

Thomas, Clarence, 72, 79–81
traditional theorists, 82, 88–89, 100–1,
　　　101–2, 147
　　Chemerinsky, 111
　　democracy, 147, 149–50, 154
　　equality and freedom, 141
　　judicial review, 119–20, 130
　　law/politics debate, 143
　　principled appraisal, 116–17
transparency, 101, 109, 115, 120–21, 154,
　　　165–66
　　appointments, 162

Trudeau, Justin, 92, 150–51
Trump, Donald, 60, 78–80, 150–51

United States, 1, 28–29
　　growth and prosperity, 27–28
　　hate speech as protected speech, 140
　　legitimacy threatened, 2–5
　　loss of support, 23–24
　　racism, 27–29
　　student protests, 134–35
　　see also Biden, Joe; *Dobbs v Jackson Women's*
　　　　　Health Organization; Roe v Wade;
　　　　　Trump, Donald; *and individual justices*

Wagner, Richard, 92, 94–95
Warren Court, 29–30, 37–38, 39, 41, 57, 69–70
Weber, Max, 136
Wechsler, Herbert, 7–8, 27, 31–34, 42, 165
　　Bickel-Wechsler-Dworkin project, 58, 62
　　Bickel compared, 35–38
　　Dworkin compared, 39–40
　　law/politics debate, 88–89
　　principled appraisal, 50–51, 52
Wendell Holmes, Oliver, 87

www.ingramcontent.com/pod-product-compliance
Ingram Content Group UK Ltd.
Pitfield, Milton Keynes, MK11 3LW, UK
UKHW020650011125
464520UK00007B/198

9 781509 985326